first

fta

Third Edition

Flexographic
Image Reproduction
Specifications & Tolerances

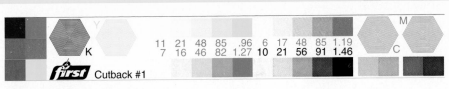

Narrow Web–Flexo Label Sheet Printed By:
Dunwoody College of Technology
818 Dunwoody Blvd
Minneapolis, MN 55403

Why FIRST?

The intention of FIRST is to provide all participants in the flexographic reproduction process with a common set of guidelines, tutorials and data that can be used as communication and production tools.

Prior to FIRST, many of our customers, out of frustration, were creating specifications for the reproduction of their packaging. While these individual attempts at creating specifications helped improve their process, there were problems with this approach. It was felt that the generation of too many individualized specifications would become overwhelming to the industry with the end result being mass confusion and the specifications would no longer be of value. At this point, the FTA membership reached out to our customers', the consumer product companies, and asked them for their help.

The aim of FIRST is to create a common set of specifications and communication protocols for the industry. This platform should establish common communication and identify the responsibility of the provider(s). The FIRST Committee and the FTA Consumer Advisory Council together have dedicated themselves and agreed to the following creed:

Mission

To understand our customers' graphic requirements for reproduction and translate their aesthetic requirements into specifications for each facet of the flexographic printing processes.

Objective

- Identify key basic flexographic procedures and guidelines to be used from beginning of the process to the end; including designers, consumer product companies, prepress providers, raw material and equipment suppliers and printers.
- Improve quality and consistency through improved communications and measurement procedures.
- Reduce cycle time and minimize rework.
- Control production costs.
- Enable consumer product companies to obtain true flexographic capabilities, which are equal to or exceed offset lithography and gravure printing.

FIRST is a set of specifications, not standards. When adhered to, the specifications are meant to produce a predictable consistent result. It is the responsibility of our customers to determine where, when and how these specifications are to be implemented. This does not imply that a printer's capabilities cannot exceed FIRST, or that the printer is limited to these specifications as a maximum quality level. The processes and specifications outlined in FIRST are intended to improve quality, develop better raw materials and grow the overall flexographic industry.

Published by the Foundation of Flexographic Technical Association, Inc.

Printed in the United States of America.

Inquires should be addressed to:
FFTA
900 Marconi Ave.
Ronkonkoma, NY 11779-7212
www.flexography.org / www.ftastore.com

International Standard Book Number (ISBN): 0-9720474-4-1

Content Notes:

1. This reference guide is designed and formatted to facilitate ease of use. As such, pertinent information–to include text, charts and graphics–is repeated in the Design, Prepress and Print sections.

2. Registered trademarks—e.g. 3M Imation®, Adobe Acrobat®, Adobe Illustrator®, Adobe InDesign®, Adobe PageMaker®, Adobe PhotoShop®, Aladdin Systems Stufflt®, Corel Draw® DuPont Cromallin®, DuPont Dylux®, Fractal Design Painter®, MacBeth®, Macromedia FreeHand®, Pantone Matching System®, Pantone®, QuarkXpress®, and X-Rite QA Master Software®—are identified on this note page. These products are identified for information purposes only. All other products mentioned in this book are trademarks of their respective owner. The author and publisher assume no responsibility for the efficacy or performance. While every attempt has been made to insure that details described in this book are accurate, the author and publisher assume no responsibility for any errors which may exist, or for any loss of data which may occur as a result of such errors.

Table of Contents

List of Tables

The Flexographic Technical Association would like to recognize the contributions and dedicated efforts of those involved in the development, editing and evaluation of FIRST, Third Edition. These individuals exhibited tireless enthusiasm in spearheading the continuous advancement of the flexographic printing process.

FIRST Committee

TOM THACKERAY | **Chairperson, Preprint**
Weyerhaeuser, 380 Shorland Drive, Richwoods, KY 41094
tthackeray@wii.com

RICK MIX | **FTA Staff Vice Chairperson**
Flexographic Technical Association, 900 Marconi Avenue, Ronkonkoma, NY 11779
rmix@flexography.org

JEFFREY RANDAZZO | **FIRST Chairperson Emeritus, Prepress**
OEC Graphics, 555 West Waukau Avenue, Oshkosh, WI 54902
flexojar@aol.com

JEAN JACKSON | **Flexo Quality Consortium**
Allison Systems Corp., P.O. Box 275, Western Springs, IL 60558
jean.m.jackson@att.net

JOE AKER | **Multiwall Bag**
Hood Packaging, Inc., 1400 Sentinel Drive, Anniston, AL 36207
jaker@hoodpackaging.com

TOM COOPER | **Corrugated**
Alliance Group, A Rock-Tenn Company
5900A Grassy Creek Boulveard, Winston-Salem, NC 27105
tcooper@rocktenn.com

SCOTT GILBERT | **Folding Carton**
Smurfit-Stone Board Sales Division, 19th & Main Streets, West Point, VA 23185
sgilbert@smurfit.com

RAY PITSCH | **Consumer Products Companies**
Kimberly-Clark Corporation, 401 North Lake Street, Neenah, WI 54957-0349
rpitsch@kcc.com

BLAKE SCHLAEPPI | **Wide Web Flexible Packaging**
Curwood, Inc., A Bemis Company, P.O. Box 2968, Oshkosh, WI 54903
brschlaeppi@bemis.com

LUCINDA COLE SEMANS | **Teaching**
Packaging Corporation of America, 1900 W. Field Court, Lake Forest, IL 60045
Lsemans@packagingcorp.com

DEAN A. STRAUSS | **NARROW WEB**
Belmark Inc., 600 Heritage Road, De Pere, WI 54115
deans@belmark.Com

DONALD R. VOAS | **Print Specialist**
International Paper Company, 6283 Tri-Ridge Boulevard, Loveland, OH 45140-8318
don.voas@ipaper.com

FIRST Subcommittees and Contributing Resources

CONSUMER ADVISORY COUNCIL AND CERTIFICATION
SUBCOMMITTEE CHAIR: **John Fulcoly**, Frito-Lay, Inc.; **Ray Pitsch**, Kimberly-Clark
SUBCOMMITTEE MEMBERS: **Sherri Dutter**, Sargento Foods, Inc.; **Jamie Grayson**, Labatt Brewing Company; **Elizabeth Johnson**, Western Family; **Gennifer Levey**, The Sunflower Group; **Bill Lunderman**, Campbell; **Edwina Walker**, Schawk, Inc.

ANILOX ROLLERS AND DOCTOR BLADES
SUBCOMMITTEE CHAIR: **Jean Jackson**, Allison Systems Inc.
SUBCOMMITTEE MEMBERS: **Joe Aker**, Graphic Mpressions; **Lloyd Field**, BTG Americas Inc.; **Pete Hartman**, Harper Corporation of America
CONTRIBUTING RESOURCES: **Marty Cansler**, Max Daetwyler Corporation; **Tony Donato**, Benton Graphics, Inc.

COLOR MANAGEMENT
SUBCOMMITTEE CHAIR: **Mark Mazur**, Dupont Imaging Technologies
SUBCOMMITTEE MEMBERS: **Kevin Chop**, Matthews International; **Larry Wm. Evans**, Printing Services Inc., **Dr. Sam Ingram**, Clemson University; **Mike Miejeski**, AGFA Corporation; **Jeffrey Randazzo**, OEC Graphics; **Mark Samworth**, Artwork Systems; **Steve Smiley**, Vertis Inc.
CONTRIBUTING RESOURCES: **Al Bowers**, Banta Digital Group; **Dave McDowell**, NPES

COMMUNICATION & IMPLEMENTATION
SUBCOMMITTEE CHAIR: **Steve Smiley**, Vertis Inc.
SUBCOMMITTEE MEMBERS: **Cindy Cole Semans**, Packaging Corporation of America; **Kevin Chop**, Matthews International Corporation; **Neil Harrelson**, Schawk, Inc.; **Roger Siljander**, Computer Integrated Color Control

DESIGN
SUBCOMMITTEE CHAIR: **Dave Olberding**, Phototype
SUBCOMMITTEE MEMBERS: **Dan Vosel**, Phototype; **Terri McConnell**, TMcConnell Communications
CONTRIBUTING RESOURCES: **Design Dept.**, Vertis Design Studio

DIGITAL PLATE
SUBCOMMITTEE CHAIR: **James Kulhanek**, DuPont Imaging Technologies
SUBCOMMITTEE MEMBERS: **Al Bowers**, Banta Digital Group; **Ray Bodwell**, DuPont Imaging Technologies; **Bob Dalton**, Creo, Inc.; **Michael Daum**, Inland Paperboard and Packaging (Graphics Resource Center); **Mike Heckaman**, Heckaman and Associates; **Ian Hole**, ESKO Graphics; **Bill Hounshell**, Phototype Engraving Company; **Scott Laurin**, Midwest Imaging & Roller Services, Inc.; **Pat O'Connor**, Cage Graphic Arts, Inc. (A Southern Graphic Systems Company); **Jeffrey Randazzo**, OEC Graphics; **Jeff Rechner**, Banta Digital; **Dan Rosen**, MacDermid Printing Solutions; **Greg Wishon**, Inland Paperboard and Packaging (Graphics Resource Center)

EXPANDED GAMUT
SUBCOMMITTEE CHAIR: **H. Conaty**, Coates Inks/
CO-CHAIR: **Dr. Penny Osmond**, California Polytechnic State University
SUBCOMMITTEE MEMBERS: **Mike Buystedt**, Akzo Nobel Inks; **Gary Hilliard**, Hood Flexible Packaging; **Mike Impastato**, Flint Ink; **Mike McGinnis**, Banta Corp.
CONTRIBUTING RESOURCES: Special attention to the following for their time and material donations to the project: **Yates Downes**, Spectrum Label Corporation; **Brian P. Lawler**, Graphic Arts Consultant; **Mark Massey**, Spectrum Label Corporation; **Arleen Neustein**, The Excelsior Packaging Group

INK
SUBCOMMITTEE CHAIR: **Sam Gilbert**, Sun Chemical Corp.
SUBCOMMITTEE MEMBERS: **David Argent**, Flint Ink; **Stanley Field**, Flint Ink; **Danny C. Rich**, Sun Chemical Corp.; **Kent Shah**, Color Converting Industries Company

PRINT ON SPECIALTY SUBSTRATES
SUBCOMMITTEE CHAIR: **Blake Schlaeppi**, Curwood, Inc., A Bemis Company
SUBCOMMITTEE MEMBERS: Lamination Color Shift; **Jeff West**, Color Converting Industries; **Larry Davis**, Pechiney Plastics Packaging

SLEEVES
SUBCOMMITTEE CHAIR: **Scott Laurin**, Midwest Imaging & Roller Services, Inc.
SUBCOMMITTEE MEMBERS: **Bob Booker**, Rogers Corporation; **Dan Dietrich**, Schawk Inc.; **David Frank**, Rossini North America; **Dana Green**, Carolina Sleeve Technology; **Mike Heckaman**, Heckaman and Associates; **Karen Mattson**, New Hudson Corporation; **Rick Munns**, Milprint Inc.; **Dean Re**, MECA & Technology Machine, Inc.; **Brett Schermann**, Rotec North America; **Ron Schroder**, Williamson Printing Materials; **Tina Schuelke**, Bemis Company, Inc.; **Mark Siegel**, Georgia-Pacific; **Paul Stepflug**, Stork Rotaform

SUBSTRATE
SUBCOMMITTEE CHAIR: **Dean A. Strauss**, Belmark Inc.
SUBCOMMITTEE MEMBERS: **Don Armel**, Georgia Southern University; **Patti Bartlett**, DuPont Imaging Technologies; **Donald Voas**, International Paper; **Jack Fulton**, Printron Engravers; **Dennis Ray**, Evansville Courier & Press; **Mike Schliesmann**, Kell Specialty Products; **Ken Shanton**, Jefferson Smurfit Stone; **Mark Siegel**, Georgia Pacific Corporation

FIRST Content Contributors and Resources

Dr. John Anderson, FCA Associates; **Kern Cox**, Clemson University, Graphic Communications Department; **Larry Wm. Evans**, Clemson University, Graphic Communications Department; **Megan Garner**, Dunwoody College of Technology, Graphics & Printing Technology Department; **Dr. Sam Ingram**, Clemson University, Graphic Communications Department; **Dr. Malcolm Keif**, California Polytechnic State University, Graphic Communications Department; **Mark Keller**, Fox Valley Technical College; **Dan Muthig**, Fox Valley Technical College; **Arleen Neustein**, The Excelsior Packaging Group; **Liam O'Hara**, Clemson University, Graphic Communications Department; **Dr. Penny Osmond**, California Polytechnic State University, Graphic Communications Department; **Tim Reece**, All Printing Resources; **Pete Rivard**, Dunwoody College of Technology, Graphics & Printing Technology Department; **Dr. Mark Snyder**, Clemson University, Graphic Communications Department; **Joe Tuccitto**, Dunwoody College of Technology, Graphics & Printing Technology Department; **Steve Utschig**, Fox Valley Technical College

Consumer Product Company Members

Coca-Cola USA; Dr Pepper/Seven Up, Inc.; General Mills, Inc.; Health Care, Logistics, Inc.; Kimberly-Clark Corporation; Labatt Brewing Company; Loblaw Brands Limited; M&M/Mars, Inc.; Owens Corning; Pac National; Potlatch Corporation; Procter & Gamble; R. R. Donnelley; Roman Meal Company; Sargento Foods, Inc.; Scotts Company; Tyson Foods, Inc.

Contributing Technical Associations

ANSI, American National Standards Institute, Inc. PH2.30-1989

CGATS, Committee for Graphic Arts Technologies Standards

ISO, International Standards Organization

Flexo Print Specifications for Newspapers

NPES, The Association for Suppliers of Printing and Publishing Converting Technologies

SGAUA. Production Ready Electronic

SNAP, Specifications for Newsprint Advertising Production

SWOP, Specifications for Web/Wet Offset Printing

UCC, Uniform Code Council, Inc.

Packaging Contributors of FIRST

The challenge to the flexographic industry is to further integrate the FIRST process with innovative and creative approaches, collaborative efforts and disciplined implementation. FIRST provides an extraordinary opportunity for flexographic package development and execution excellence.

The design and execution of the packaging, book covers and page components were designed to fully capture the flexographic print capabilities with a focus on creativity and innovation. This attractive and effective packaging artwork was created using the technical and procedural recommendations in FIRST.

We wish to thank the following companies for their contributions and efforts in producing the FIRST packaging. Their commitment and excitement exhibits the true spirit and principals of the FIRST process.

DESIGN AND PRODUCTION ART   Project Leader: Megan Garner, Dunwoody College of Technology

CONTIBUTORS TO COVER DESIGN
Katrina Spivey, ZOOM180, Atlanta, GA
Jason Drury, Universal Creation, Dayton, OH
Kristen Osborne, Clemson University, Clemson, SC
Alexander James, Harper Corporation, Charlotte, NC
Sonja Huie, H+A Productions, Wantagh, NY

PROJECT MANAGEMENT   Robert Moran, Rick Mix; FTA, Ronkonkoma, NY 11779

SEPARATIONS   Jon Schloesser and Jeffrey Randazzo, OEC Graphics, Oshkosh, WI 54902

PRINTED PRODUCTION PIECES LISTED IN ORDER OF APPEARANCE
CARTON BOARD COVER – FLEXO PAPERBOARD, Cascades Boxboards, Cobourg, ON Canada

FLEXIBLE PACKAGING INSERT – POLYETHELYENE SHEET, Banner Packaging, Oshkosh, WI

CORRUGATED INSIDE COVER – FLEXO/N-FLUTE, Packaging Corporation of America, Burlington, WI

NEWSPRINT INSERT – FLEXO NEWSPRINT, Chattanooga Times Free Press, Chattanooga, TN

NARROW WEB INSERT – FLEXO LABEL SHEET, Dunwoody College of Technology, Minneapolis, MN

ENVELOPE INSERT – FLEXO ENVELOPE, Mail-Well Envelope, Chicago, IL

CARTON BOARD BACK COVER – LITHO/PAPERBOARD, International Paper, Loveland, OH

FIRST EDITOR:
Michelle Beuscher, 16 Beechwood Drive, Landenberg, PA 19350
mbeuscher@juno.com

DESIGN/LAYOUT:
Sonja Huie, H+A Productions, POB 970, Wantagh, NY 11793
hnaproductions@mindspring.com

ILLUSTRATIONS:
Shane Kelley, Kelley Graphics, 3417 University Blvd., Kensington, MD 20895

1.0 Communication and Implementation

The role of the customer is crucial to the communication and implementation of specifications for the production of flexographic materials. The customer (consumer product company) determines their requirements, which sets the objectives for each particular job. The printers and suppliers help the customer realize quality standards based on material and job specifications. It is the responsibility of the suppliers to be the driving force for process control.

The suppliers and customer should have a detailed workflow diagram. This helps all involved understand what the workflow is, when and what they are responsible for, and the path to follow if something does not pass quality standards at a certain stage. Refer to the Packaging Workflow Process (see page 2 and 3). This chart provides an overview and highlights the role of each segment within the production flow. Implementation of specifications must be undertaken by each group within the workflow to ensure that the resulting print is compliant.

Additionally, the Committee for Graphic Arts Technologies Standards (*CGATS TR-011 2002 Graphic Technology—Package Development Workflow – Design Concept Through Approved Production File*) describes a model workflow for the package development process from the identification of a project through preparation of an approved production file. It is intended for use as a reference in the creation of workflow procedures for specific organizations or products. *CGATS TR-012 (2003 Graphic Technology Color Reproduction and Process Control for Package Printing)* outlines the steps necessary to understand and objectively define the color and tone reproduction capabilities of a printing process. The steps identified in *CGATS TR-012* provide information required in the package development workflow (*CGATS TR-011*). *CGATS TR-011* and *CGATS TR-012* can be purchased from NPES. See the appendix section for contact information.

1.1 | Definition and Overview

FIRST outlines and describes a controlled process as well as a set of technical specifications for use from design concept to print. The customer, sales personnel, suppliers and printers adhere to a controlled production process as well as use specifications and standards. Resulting in cost control, production efficiencies, improved yield, consistent and predictable outcome and achieved quality standards. The specific suppliers best understand each stage of the process; as a result all must drive and guide the process.

1.2 | Terminology

In this document the interaction of the four following groups are addressed:

- **Consumer Product Company:** Customer
- **Graphic Designers:** creators of the original file.
- **Prepress Providers:** color correct and apply characterization data to art file, provide contract proofs and make plates, cylinders or other image transfer device.
- **Printers:** produce the final printed piece.

Digital design files represent the visual "look and feel" of a particular package but are not "production ready."

Digital mechanical files will not necessarily "look right", but will go through

1.2 Terminology Low resolution "For Position Only" images will be replaced in production with a high-resolution image. FPOs sometimes are used by designers to keep their design files small and easy to transfer by disk or modem.

Packaging Workflow Process

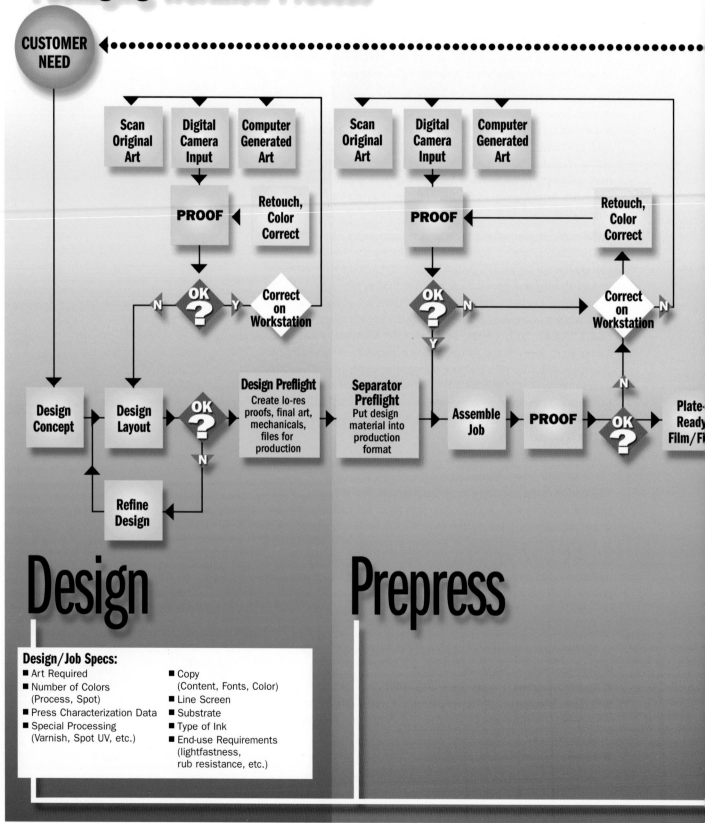

CUSTOMER NEED

Scan Original Art

Digital Camera Input

Computer Generated Art

PROOF

Retouch, Color Correct

OK? N Y

Correct on Workstation

Design Concept

Design Layout

OK? N

Refine Design

Design Preflight
Create lo-res proofs, final art, mechanicals, files for production

Design

Scan Original Art

Digital Camera Input

Computer Generated Art

PROOF

Retouch, Color Correct

OK? N Y

Correct on Workstation N

N

Separator Preflight
Put design material into production format

Assemble Job

PROOF

OK?

Plate-Ready Film/F

Prepress

Design/Job Specs:
- Art Required
- Number of Colors (Process, Spot)
- Press Characterization Data
- Special Processing (Varnish, Spot UV, etc.)
- Copy (Content, Fonts, Color)
- Line Screen
- Substrate
- Type of Ink
- End-use Requirements (lightfastness, rub resistance, etc.)

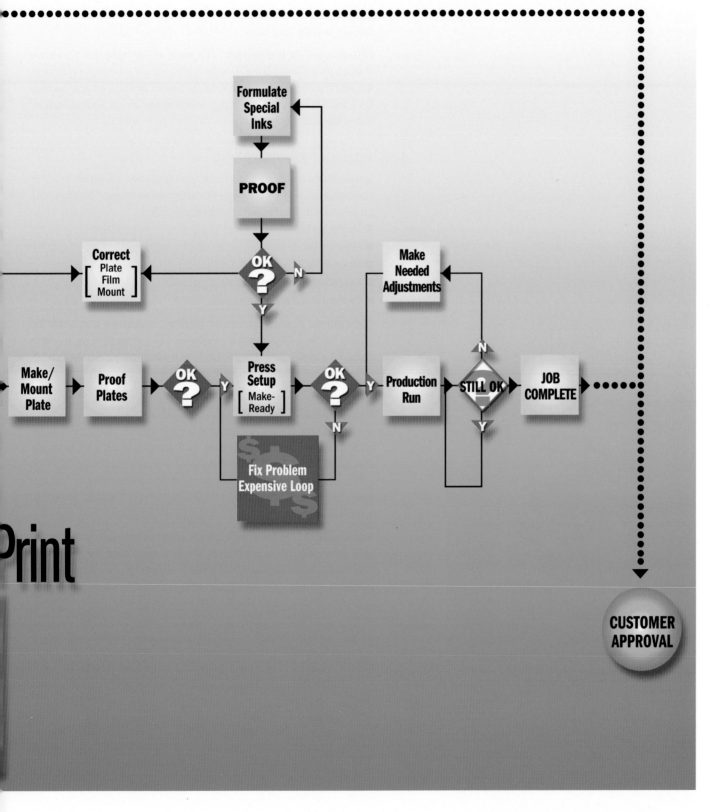

Print

the production process smoothly and are the "production-ready" files. Production ready files have been color corrected and compensated according to the press characterization data.

"Desktop publishing", "electronic publishing," "digital publishing," "digital" and **"electronic mechanical"** may be used interchangeably.

LIVE indicates a scan or illustration in an electronic document that is ready for production of the final image.

FPO indicates "For Position Only." This image will be replaced in production with a high-resolution image. Designers often use low-resolution FPO images to keep their design files small and easy to transfer by CD or modem. For both LIVE and FPO files, these markings should appear on the annotation layer and/or the hard copy proof.

1.3 | Values of Specifications

Specifications are intended to increase communication among all groups in developing design, final art, prepress and printed packaging. This open communication can result in packaging produced with:

■ Shorter lead-times.
■ Lower costs.
■ Less rework.
■ Understood and achieved quality standards.
■ Predictable and better print results.

Specifications are a quality tool for suppliers. Compliance means that the process has been adopted and implemented. This process is advantageous to consumer product companies and can be recognized in the company's presentations, design work and in production processes.

1.4 | Adopting and Implementing Specifications

The utilization of specifications and process control systems cannot be achieved without the full cooperation, understanding of the value and adherence by the customer and graphic designers. The printer and material suppliers are experts in print production and may need to provide verification and data indicating how the specifications bring value and predictability to the customer's end product.

Suppliers need to support specifications inside their company and outside with their customers and suppliers. The objectives of the project must be understood and the supplier's help is needed to engineer the communications process.

1.4 Adopting and Implementing FIRST Consumer product company buyers and design managers must adopt FIRST company-wide and provide consistent support to the process.

1.5 | Project Team

The project team is composed of, but not limited to, the following groups of people:

CONSUMER PRODUCT COMPANY:

- **Direct Responsibility:** Packaging Director/Manager
- **Indirect Responsibility:** Design Managers, Purchasing
- **Key Responsibilities:**
  - ☐ Design Brief
  - ☐ Package Structure (primary and secondary)
  - ☐ Consumer Research Strategy
  - ☐ Promotion Strategy
  - ☐ Legal Copy
  - ☐ Product Development
  - ☐ Package Design and Implementation

DESIGN FIRM:

- **Direct Responsibility:** Account Manager
- **Indirect Responsibility:** Designer, Production Staff
- **Key Responsibilities:**
  - ☐ Design Strategy
  - ☐ Final Digital Production Art
  - ☐ QC

PREPRESS PROVIDERS:

- **Direct Responsibility:** Account Manager
- **Indirect Responsibility:** Customer Service, Technical Representative
- **Key Responsibilities:**
  - ☐ Color Separations
  - ☐ Film Assembly
  - ☐ Contract/Color Proofing
  - ☐ QC all deliverables
  - ☐ Platemaking

PRINTER:

- **Direct Responsibility:** Account Manager
- **Indirect Responsibility:**
  - ☐ Design Manager/Art Director,
  - ☐ Print Production Staff, Platemaker,
  - ☐ Ink Company Representative
- **Key Responsibilities:**
  - ☐ Plate Making
  - ☐ Maintain Process Control – as defined in *CGATS TR-012*
  - ☐ Press Optimization
  - ☐ Print Optimization
  - ☐ Press Characterization
  - ☐ Package Production to specifications

It is important to bring the project team together as early in the design process as possible. It is advisable to meet after the stage 1 design has been reviewed. Although the designs are not final, the group can begin to understand the overall project objectives and provide initial feedback on the designs. The communication in the group must focus on how the designs can be reproduced instead of how the designs cannot be reproduced within the specifications. Often alterations to design elements are required, this can be done while maintaining the intended graphic look and style

FIRST Packaging Timetable

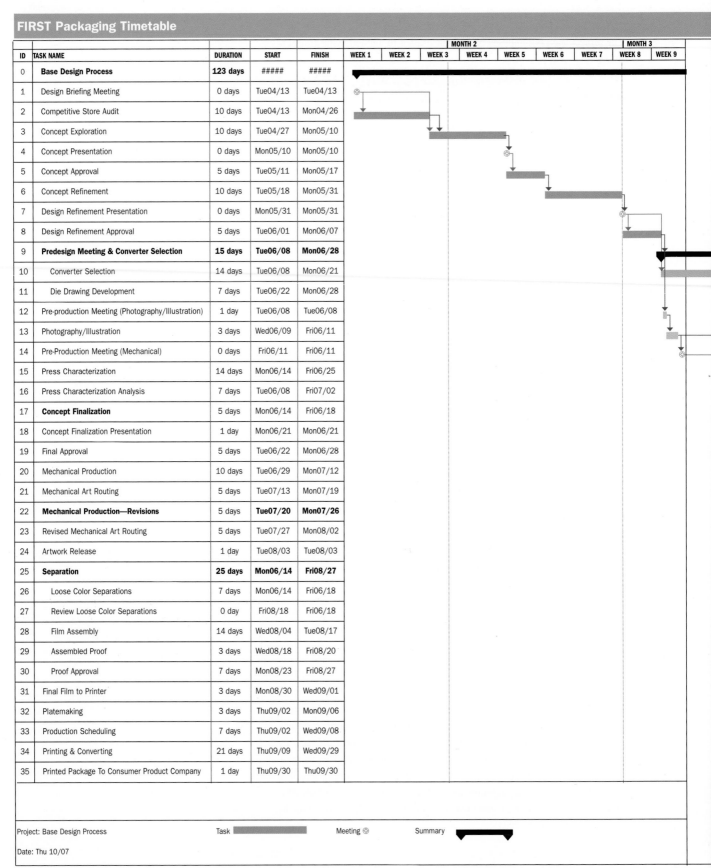

ID	TASK NAME	DURATION	START	FINISH
0	**Base Design Process**	**123 days**	#####	#####
1	Design Briefing Meeting	0 days	Tue04/13	Tue04/13
2	Competitive Store Audit	10 days	Tue04/13	Mon04/26
3	Concept Exploration	10 days	Tue04/27	Mon05/10
4	Concept Presentation	0 days	Mon05/10	Mon05/10
5	Concept Approval	5 days	Tue05/11	Mon05/17
6	Concept Refinement	10 days	Tue05/18	Mon05/31
7	Design Refinement Presentation	0 days	Mon05/31	Mon05/31
8	Design Refinement Approval	5 days	Tue06/01	Mon06/07
9	**Predesign Meeting & Converter Selection**	**15 days**	**Tue06/08**	**Mon06/28**
10	Converter Selection	14 days	Tue06/08	Mon06/21
11	Die Drawing Development	7 days	Tue06/22	Mon06/28
12	Pre-production Meeting (Photography/Illustration)	1 day	Tue06/08	Tue06/08
13	Photography/Illustration	3 days	Wed06/09	Fri06/11
14	Pre-Production Meeting (Mechanical)	0 days	Fri06/11	Fri06/11
15	Press Characterization	14 days	Mon06/14	Fri06/25
16	Press Characterization Analysis	7 days	Tue06/08	Fri07/02
17	**Concept Finalization**	5 days	Mon06/14	Fri06/18
18	Concept Finalization Presentation	1 day	Mon06/21	Mon06/21
19	Final Approval	5 days	Tue06/22	Mon06/28
20	Mechanical Production	10 days	Tue06/29	Mon07/12
21	Mechanical Art Routing	5 days	Tue07/13	Mon07/19
22	**Mechanical Production—Revisions**	**5 days**	**Tue07/20**	**Mon07/26**
23	Revised Mechanical Art Routing	5 days	Tue07/27	Mon08/02
24	Artwork Release	1 day	Tue08/03	Tue08/03
25	**Separation**	**25 days**	**Mon06/14**	**Fri08/27**
26	Loose Color Separations	7 days	Mon06/14	Fri06/18
27	Review Loose Color Separations	0 day	Fri08/18	Fri06/18
28	Film Assembly	14 days	Wed08/04	Tue08/17
29	Assembled Proof	3 days	Wed08/18	Fri08/20
30	Proof Approval	7 days	Mon08/23	Fri08/27
31	Final Film to Printer	3 days	Mon08/30	Wed09/01
32	Platemaking	3 days	Thu09/02	Mon09/06
33	Production Scheduling	7 days	Thu09/02	Wed09/08
34	Printing & Converting	21 days	Thu09/09	Wed09/29
35	Printed Package To Consumer Product Company	1 day	Thu09/30	Thu09/30

Project: Base Design Process   Task �▓▓▓▓▓   Meeting ⊗   Summary ▼▼▼

Date: Thu 10/07

1.7 Project Timetable The FIRST Packaging Timetable is a general timetable and task list for packaging development. The timeframes in each of these steps or tasks are only general guidelines, which will change based on the individual company requirements and project scope. The tasks listed here can be used as a starting point.

FIRST Packaging Timetable

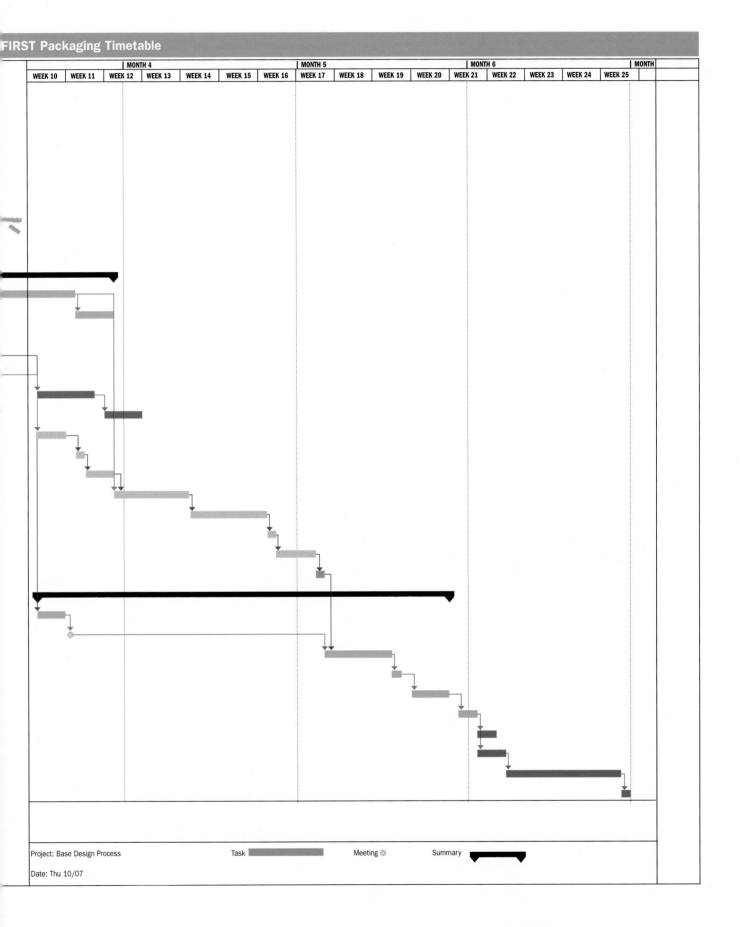

	MONTH 4						MONTH 5				MONTH 6				MONTH
WEEK 10	WEEK 11	WEEK 12	WEEK 13	WEEK 14	WEEK 15	WEEK 16	WEEK 17	WEEK 18	WEEK 19	WEEK 20	WEEK 21	WEEK 22	WEEK 23	WEEK 24	WEEK 25

Project: Base Design Process

Date: Thu 10/07

Task   Meeting ⊚   Summary

PREPRODUCTION MEETING

☑ PACKAGE DESIGN OBJECTIVES _____
☑ DESIGN REVIEW _____
☑ SPECIFICATIONS _____
☐ NUMBER OF COLORS _____
☑ ELECTRONIC ASSEMBLY _____
☑ TRAPPING _____
☑ PRINT CONTROL TARGETS _____
☐ PACKAGE SIZES _____
☑ CONTRACT PROOF REQUIREMENTS _____
☐ TIMETABLE _____
☐ ON-PRESS APPROVALS _____
☐ IMAGE CARRIER/PLATES _____

1.6 Pre-design/Pre-production Meetings The consumer product company representative usually calls these meetings but the design firm, prepress provider(s) or the printer(s) can also initiate them. The meeting agenda should include the above items for discussion.

DESIGN BRIEF MEETING

☑ PROJECT DESCRIPTION _____
☑ BACKGROUND _____
☑ PRODUCT DESCRIPTION _____
☐ PRODUCT POSITIONING _____
☑ PROJECT TIMING _____
☐ TARGET CONSUMER _____
☑ COMPETITION _____
☑ PACKAGE MESSAGES _____
☐ LEGAL COPY _____
☑ COMMUNICATION PRIORITIES _____
☐ PROJECT SPECS/FIRST COMPLIANCY _____

1.8 Design Briefing Meeting The purpose of this meeting is to review all aspects of the packaging design objectives and strategies and to exchange ideas on anticipated design directions that should be pursued. All information that is relevant to the above listed items must be supplied.

1.6 | Pre-design/Pre-production Meetings

The consumer product company representative usually initiates these meetings but the design firm, prepress provider(s) or the printer(s) can also initiate them. The meeting agenda should include these items for discussion:

- Package Design Objectives.
- Design Review.
- Specifications with Regard to the Design.
- Number of Colors Needed.
- New Characterization Needed.
- Electronic Assembly.
- Color-to-Color Trapping.
- Print Control Targets.
- Package Sizes; Similarities and Differences.
- Contract Proofing Requirements.
- Timetable.
- On-Press Approvals.
- Image Carrier/Plates.

Many of the topics reviewed at this meeting come from the printers' press characterization data. It is important that the printer fully understand and control the press characterization process so their data is reliable and repeatable during production. *CGATS TR-012* outlines the steps necessary to understand and objectively define the color and tone reproduction capabilities of a printing process. The steps identified in *CGATS TR-012* provide information required in the package development workflow (*CGATS TR-011*).

1.7 | Project Timetables

The project timing is directed by the consumer product company and usually coincides with product introduction dates, factory changes or government regulation changes. The project team can work together to refine the steps to accommodate the timeframes (*see enclosed CD*).

The FIRST Packaging Timetable, as shown on pages 6–7, exhibits a general timetable and task list for packaging development. The timeframes in each of these steps or tasks are only general guidelines, which will change based on the individual company requirements and project scope. The tasks listed here can be used as a starting point.

1.8 | Design Briefing Meeting

The purpose of this meeting is to review all aspects of the packaging design objectives and strategies and to exchange ideas on anticipated design directions that should be pursued. Preliminary budget requirements and timing are also to be discussed. All information that is relevant to the following items must be supplied:

- Project Description.
- Background (needed especially in the case of redesigns or sub-brands).
- Product Description.
- Product Positioning.
- Project Timing.
- Target Consumer.
- Competition.

- Package Messages.
- Legal Copy.
- Communication Priorities.
- Project Specifications/FIRST Compliancy.

Decisions need to be made at this time regarding the timetable, project and design expectations.

The following information and materials are to be available for the meeting:
- Product Name.
- Packaging Design Objectives and Strategies.
- Relevant Research (quantitative and qualitative).
- Print Specifications (number of colors, die line, print process, printing substrate).
- Supplier Names and Contacts (prepress provider, printers, etc.).
- Research Strategy (if applicable).
- Promotional Strategy (if applicable).

1.9 | Competitive Store Audit

The purpose of the competitive store audit is to evaluate the competitive material and environment in order to understand:
- Product Category.
- Packaging Forms.
- Color and Category Positioning Norms.
- Product Merchandising.

The outcome of the audit will provide the designers with a frame of reference and guide them to concentrate on design solutions that will enable the package to visually compete within the specific store environment.

1.10 | Concept Exploration

The purpose of concept exploration is to review the initial thought process and design development for the project assignment, eliminate any directions that do not have merit and further provide direction to include new areas of development if necessary. The outcome of the exploration should be several concept alternatives that are to be presented to the consumer product company or client for review and approval.

1.11 | Concept Refinement

The purpose of this step is to review the design exploration and refine the concept(s) selected by the consumer product company or client for further development. Additionally, the concept will address all panels and show the graphic placement of all the copy that is required on the package. Additional refinement phases may be necessary to address issues such as side panel design or promotions efforts.

1.10 Concept Exploration The purpose of this step is to review the design exploration and refine the concept(s) selected by the consumer product company or client for further development. Additional refinement phases may be necessary to address issues such as side panel design or promotion efforts.

1.12 | Pre-Production Meeting (Mechanical)

The purpose of this meeting is to review all information relating to the digital art production of the package prior to the execution of any mechanical production.

Decisions needed at this time include the number of colors on the job and the method of printing and designation of the printing substrate. Topics for discussion at this meeting should include:

● Separation—Printer Concerns.
● Specific Trapping/Film Assembly Issues.
● Process Control Targets (placement of run and control targets).
● Press Characterization Requirements and Layout (if necessary).
● Timetable.
● Photo Retouching (if necessary, who will execute, who will direct).

At this meeting, a final approved layout of the package and photography needs to be available for evaluation. The number of printers involved with the print production must be determined.

1.13 | Concept Finalization

The purpose of this step is to review the design refinement, the information discussed during the mechanical pre-production meeting and to finalize the concept selected by consumer product company or the client.

1.14 | Mechanical Art Production

The purpose of the mechanical production step is to create the digital art files required for the printed package. The digital art mechanical will adhere to the print requirements set forth during the mechanical pre-production meeting.

It is determined at this step if the construction of the digital art files adheres to the prepress provider's electronic requirements. All materials, including photography, illustrations, and finalized information must be addressed.

1.14 Mechanical Art Production It is determined at this step if the construction of the digital art files adheres to the prepress provider's electronic requirements. All materials, including photography, illustrations, and finalized information must be addressed.

1.15 | Applying Specifications to Art Through Print

At each stage, the receiving company must check all materials (art, plates, proofs, etc.) to verify they are within specifications and tolerances. Establishing a process of checking and rejecting materials by all parties (including the consumer product company, designer, prepress provider and printer) is critical. Many times materials are not rejected (when they should be) because the company that has to reject the materials is still held accountable for deadlines. Deadlines may need to be adjusted when materials are rejected.

Documentation is crucial; the specific reason for a rejection must be documented and communicated so it may be used in the future to improve the process and to avoid rejections. This process should include all stages from design concept to final print approval.

2.0 Introduction

2.1 | Overview

This section is intended to:

- Provide the graphic designer with an understanding of the flexographic reproduction process, prior to concept design.
- Aid in the production of better quality graphic files, faster turn-around and the consumer product companies' overall fulfillment.

The underlying tone throughout this document is to develop an awareness of how to build an electronic document so it has a positive impact on the quality, cost and speed of manufacturing. This must be balanced with the fact that designers want and need to maintain creative control over their projects. It is in everyone's best interest to understand the requirements of flexographically printed products and address them during the design and layout stages. In addition, end users must take a lead role in facilitating communication between the design firm, the prepress provider and the printer.

Depending on the methods and practices of the companies involved, and the complexity and frequency of the work between them, it is worthwhile to spend time establishing ground rules and procedures for package designs before actual production begins. This is a necessary step when providing services to the packaging industry because of the complexity of the graphics, print issues and packaging equipment considerations. Someone in the production loop (designer, consumer products company/end user, prepress provider or printer) should initiate dialogue regarding design and production issues. This document provides guidelines that will help projects flow more smoothly through the process.

A designer requires a great deal of information before the actual design work begins. The accuracy of the answers provided will affect the efficiency and speed of the project. It is extremely important that the parties involved organize their systems to be able to give accurate, timely information.

2.2 | Responsibility

As desktop systems have become more powerful, the process of creating a package is being performed electronically by many sources. These specifications and guidelines have been developed to help in the production of a quality product. Assignment of responsibilities in a workflow requires planning and collaboration among all suppliers and is necessary to assure optimal results of final printed packages.

2.3 | Assumptions

Certain assumptions have been made while building these guidelines in order to keep the content focused and pertinent. They are as follows:

- The immediate audience consists of professional users who are working with current, mainstream versions of software and hardware.
- Although certain programs and computer manufacturers are mentioned, FIRST recognizes these are not the only viable solutions.
- The audience is familiar with electronic design terminology and workflow in a digital environment.

2.2 Responsibility As desktop systems have become more powerful, the process of creating a package is being performed electronically by many sources. These specifications and guidelines have been developed to help in the production of a quality product.

■ The technology used is changing rapidly. It is not possible to keep this document up-to-date related to electronic hardware or software. This means that some recommendations made here may become obsolete

3.0 The Process Flow

3.1 Flexographic Printing Process Attributes Before Beginning

There are differences between flexography and the other printing processes. The use of spot colors, true metallic inks and fluorescent inks are some of the ink choices available with flexography in addition to a wide variety of substrates. Designers must be informed about the advantages of the flexographic printing process in order to make use of them during the design process. It is recommended the designer contact the project's printer to review that particular print segment's capabilities, which could enhance the final package's shelf appeal.

3.2 Materials and Information Needed to Begin

■ Template: When a die drawing or template is supplied by a client/supplier, it must include bleeds, glue area and live areas. There is pertinent information on the template, (e.g., die number, size, count number, etc.) that the designer must document on the digital file.

■ Other production information gathered by the design team such as the substrate, number of ink colors, ink sequence, and printing process should also be documented on the digital file.

■ Client or customer specifications.

■ Design brief.

■ Brand and corporate art guidelines.

■ Legal and government regulations.

3.3 Responsibilities of the Designer

■ A basic color sequence scheme and color palette should be established before layouts are constructed.

■ All type and copy must be kerned and spell-checked.

■ Common elements/logos must be treated consistently in the layout(s) even though these elements may not yet be considered final.

■ Elements that are approved should be archived as master images to be re-used at a later date.

■ All copy and vector based elements should be built within the tolerances and specifications of the printer that will be producing the final product.

3.4 Designer Responsibilities: Final File

■ Complete a file release form. If the form is digital, include a copy on the disk with artwork file(s).

■ Unlock "all" and show all multiple layers/flavors in one file.

■ All nonessential elements, points, blends and colors must be deleted from the file(s).

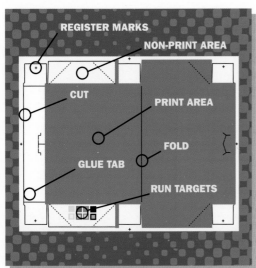

3.2 Materials and Information Needed to Begin When a die drawing or template is supplied by a client/supplier, it must include bleeds, glue area and live areas. There is pertinent information on the template, (e.g., die number, size, count number, etc.) that the designer must document on the digital file

■ Establish and use a checklist to verify the file is complete and correct. See Design Section 9.12 for checklist.

■ All graphics held away from cuts and scores should be verified to be within print tolerances.

■ Verify that necessary bleeds are correct for single knife/double knife applications (cartons and corrugated).

■ See Design Section 9.0 for specifics about content of complete design.

3.5 | Understanding Color Management from A Designer's Point of View

The number of colors the average human eye can perceive is much larger than the number of colors that can be reproduced on workstation monitors, proofing devices, and printing presses. Each color output method has limitations based on the type and number of pigments, the imaging engine, pigment delivery technology, and the substrates being used. The more a designer understands these limitations, the better the graphic intent of the design is managed.

Key to understanding color management is to have a familiarity with the concept of color space. Digital cameras and scanners record images in the RGB color space, while proofing devices and film/platesetters output images in other color spaces: CMYK, CMYKOG, CCMMYK, etc.

Although digital tools can make the process seem as simple as a click of a mouse, converting from one color space to another is the first place where detail, color fidelity and contrast can be significantly compromised. Once information is lost in the conversion process it cannot be restored.

Even when saving an image in RGB and sending it to a digital proofing device, there is an automatic conversion. The proof is actually a CMYK rendering that was run through a default lookup table unless a more specific lookup table has been generated and applied.

A more comprehensive explanation of CIELab color management is described in Prepress Section 13.0. In the event that a known output source (a specific printing press) is identified prior to the creative stage, the photographer/designer may contact the prepress provider and request a color profile for that press. This is often referred to as an ICC (International Color Consortium) profile. With this profile, a spectrophotometer, and a color management program, the designer can control the conversion process precisely and manipulate the proofing device to simulate the expected results from the printing press.

3.5 Understanding Color Management from a Designer's Point of View Understanding RGB and CMYK color space is paramount in maximizing the results achieved. Although it may appear that the conversion process of RGB to CMYK is as simple as a click of a mouse, it is the first place where detail, color fidelity and contrast can be significantly compromised.

3.6 | Color Proofing

Every party involved with the project must agree upon the process and terminology that all will use to evaluate and communicate color. Specifically, every proof examined throughout the project cycle should be clearly labeled as to:

■ Its purpose.

■ The system or device on which it was created.

■ Whether and to what output it was profiled.

■ Its suitability for judging color.

Following are some different types of proofs and typical designations:

■ **Concept Proof:** common in the early creative stages of the project, it is typically not color profiled. Not used for matching color.

■ **Color Target:** this proof is not profiled using the output source profile;

however, it does represent the customer's color expectations for the final printed product and copy content.

- **Contract Analog Proof:** this proof uses film separations as an intermediate media to create an image. It is made to manufacturer's recommendations for exposing and processing by (brand name of analog proofing system) and has been made according to FIRST specifications, and must accurately represent the customer's color and content expectations.

- **Contract Digital Proof:** this proof uses electronic files processed by a color imaging device. It is profiled to a (brand name of digital proofing system) and has been made according to FIRST specifications, and must accurately represent the customer's color and content expectations.

- **Profiled Contract Proof:** this proof represents the customer's complete content and color expectations for the final printed product and is the basis for negotiations on project performance. This proof is profiled using a color management system (CMS) and is prepared based upon profiles provided by a specific printer or prepress provider. It has been made according to FIRST specifications.

In addition to carrying identification data agreed upon by all parties, contract proofs must contain a control target that is processed and imaged as part of the proof. This control target contains screen values of 3%, 10%, 30%, 70%, and 100%—in each of the four process colors. These tonal scales will be used to verify the accuracy and consistency of the final contract proof. Although most digital proofing devices may not reproduce a conventional dot pattern the tonal scales should still be read using a densitometer in the dot area function. Each one of the tonal scales must equal the weight (dot area) as identified by the press profile. For the specification of solid ink density for a print segment, refer to Prepress Section 15.3.1.3. For a more detailed description of CIELab color management see Prepress Section 13.0.

3.7 | File Naming Conventions

Alternate versions of an electronic file should have separate and distinct names from the original version. File naming conventions for live, high-resolution images should be in accordance with the criteria of the collaborating parties. For example, workflow may dictate files reflect or reference an existing convention such as SKUs for product, pertinent job/docket or task numbers, UPC references. An 8.3 naming convention (88888888.333) is desirable to support users of earlier Unix, and various pre-Windows 95 PC platforms.

Suffixes should be used to identify/distinguish formats and variations of working files. Examples of this are as follows:

12345678.**tif**   12345678.**eps**   12345678.**jpg**

or

abcdefgh.**raw**   abcdefgh.**rgb**   abcdefgh.**cmy**

Special characters such as "**!**", "**@**", "**#**", "**$**", "**%**" and "*****" should never be used.

4.0 Type and Design Elements

4.1 | Typography: Know the Print Process Capabilities

Each print segment determines the minimum weight of thin rules and the minimum point size for type. If type is stroked, swelled or framed to increase its thickness, the "counters" (holes in letters such as a, d, o, e and R) may close up. The best solution is to use a "bold," "heavy," or "black" version of the font. Many serif fonts, such as Garamond, have very thin strokes, even in bold versions. If at all possible, do not stroke serif fonts. Check the text because when a font version is changed, type will re-flow. Fine type will print well in a solid color, but detail reversed out of a solid may become plugged.

Thin keylines around a tint should be in the same ink color as the tint.

Print-to-print and print-to-cut production tolerances may vary depending on several factors, from press width to press type (i.e., central impression, stack, in-line). Important elements should be kept away from cuts and scores. Die position tolerance is typically ±0.030" (±0.8 mm) for thin board stock, and more for thicker stock. Consult the printer for specifics of each print type.

4.1.1 | Registration Tolerance

When one word is printed in one color and another word next to it is printed in a second color, register shifts can cause these two words to overlap or misalign. Due to this register shift, different color text should be more than twice the image trap dimension away from each other. See prepress section for specific register tolerance for print to print and print to cut.

4.1.2 | Process Color Type

All type must use the fewest possible colors when printed in process color. In no case should type be made up of more than three colors. The combined use of solid type and graphics on screen decks requires consultation with the printer regarding feasibility.

4.1.3 | Process Reverse/Knockout

A holding line should be used when type is reversed out of more than one color.

If a holding line is not used, the darkest or predominant color should be made at full size and the remaining color must be choked back the width of one row of dots as determined by the screen ruling. If possible the background color should be limited to one color.

The holding line should be a single color (dark) to hide any slight misregistration that is likely to occur during the printing process. The weight of the holding line should be twice the registration tolerance for the print segment.

FOUNDATION 5

SMALL TYPE CLOSING IN

900 Marconi Avenue
Ronkonkoma, NY 11779-7212
Phone (631) 737-6020
Fax (631) 737-6813
www.flexography.org

SERIFS POOR TYPE CHOICE FOR REVERSE

4.1 Typography: Know the Print Process Capabilities
Many serif fonts have very thin strokes, even in bold versions. If type is stroked, swelled or framed to increase its thickness, the "counters" (holes in letters such as a, d, o, e and R) may close up. If at all possible, do not stroke serif fonts.

IMAGE TRAP TOLERANCE

WIDE WEB		PROCESS TO TO PROCESS	LINE TO LINE TO PROCESS	LINE TO LINE TO LINE
PREPRINT LINERBOARD	SBS Board	±0.0035" ±0.089 mm	±0.01" ±0.254 mm	±0.01" ±0.254 mm
COMBINED CORRUGATED	Bleached White	±0.03" ±0.762 mm	±0.03" ±0.762 mm	±0.03" ±0.762 mm
	Coated Paper	±0.015" ±0.381mm	±0.015" ±0.381 mm	±0.015" ±0.381 mm
FOLDING CARTON	SBS Board	±0.003" ±0.076 mm	±0.003" ±0.076 mm	±0.0075" ±0.1905 mm
	CRB Board	±0.003" ±0.076 mm	±0.0045" ±0.114 mm	±0.0055" ±0.14 mm
MULTIWALL BAG	Coated Paper	±0.0075" ±0.1905 mm	±0.0175" ±0.444 mm	±0.0175 ±0.444 mm
	Uncoated Paper	±0.0075" ±0.1905 mm	±0.015" ±0.381 mm	±0.03" ±0.762 mm
FILM PRODUCTS	All	±0.0075" ±0.1905 mm	±0.0075" ±0.1905 mm	±0.0075" ±0.1905 mm

NARROW WEB		PROCESS TO PROCESS	LINE TO PROCESS	LINE TO LINE
PAPER PRODUCTS	All	±0.0045" ±0.0114 mm	±0.005" ±0.13 mm	±0.005" ±0.013 mm
FILM PRODUCTS	All	±0.0045" ±0.114 mm	±0.005" ±0.13 mm	±0.005" ±0.13 mm

4.1.4 | Line Reverse/Knockout

Reverse copy printed on a line deck must be limited to one color.

4.1.5 | Drop Shadow

Be sure to move the drop shadow by more than twice the specified image trap for the appropriate print segment. If the drop shadow is abutting another color, it will need to trap.

It is best to use drop shadows only for larger type, unless the color selected for the type is darker than the color it is abutting (remember these abutting colors will be required to overprint each other to form the image trap).

4.1.6 | Spaces and Tabs

Always use tabs rather than multiple spaces to position text. It is far easier to adjust a tab, and if a font change is required, the spaces will change size. Tabs will not change.

4.1.7 | Text Wrap

Most programs will wrap text around imported images. If an image is replaced in production, text will reflow if automatic text wrapping features were used to define the text wrap area. Use the polygon tool or other shape to define the text wrap or run-around instead of letting the text automatically wrap around the image. When the high-resolution image is placed into the file, the program may see its edges differently and rewrap the type. The prepress service provider will have to rebuild the desired wrap to get the text to reflow the same way.

4.1.8 | Outlining Text

An option for handling type in a drawing program is to convert it from a text element to an outlined or vector element. This makes text no longer editable, but it will display the final appearance of the type. A vector element will not rewrap or carry font compatibility issues.

4.1.5 Drop Shadow It is best to use drop shadows only for larger type, unless the color selected for the type is darker than the color it is abutting (remember these abutting colors will be required to overprint each other to form the image trap).

4.1.9 | Fonts

4.1.9.1 | Type 1 Fonts that are encoded in the Adobe Type 1 standard. Not all Type 1 fonts are created equal; some are auto traced. Refer to Design Section 7.4 on Auto-traced Re-vectorized Images.

4.1.9.2 | True Type Avoid True Type fonts. There are still some conflicts between True Type fonts and Type 1 fonts. Some imagesetters do not deal with True Type correctly. Some Apple system installers put True Type fonts into the system (some with the same name as PostScript Type 1 fonts). A result can be that a designer may use a True Type font unknowingly or may send the wrong version of the font. In either case, this will cause text to reflow, changing it from the designer's original text flow.

4.1.9.3 | OpenType Fonts OpenType Fonts are intended to combine the strengths of both Type 1 and TrueType font formats, while addressing three issues regarding font management; cross platform incompatibility, intermittent failure of TrueType Fonts at the RIP and separation of screen and printer fonts during file submission. OpenType is also designed to give typesetters more precise control over type positioning and alignment, special characters and non-English language support. Currently, only Adobe InDesign and Photoshop provide native support for all OpenType features; therefore, users should test OpenType usage carefully before implementing.

4.1.9.4 | Manufacturers Sometimes companies working on a design file may not have easy access to fonts used. If so, convert these fonts to outlines or paths. Indicate where the font may be purchased.

4.1.9.5 | Styles of Fonts In some applications, there is a style menu with type attributes such as bold, italic, outline, shadow, small caps and all caps. Do not use this feature. Use only the actual font, such as Times Bold, rather than Times with the bold attribute. When using attributes, results vary depending on the RIP, printer drivers and application being used. Selecting style attributes usually creates a pseudo version of the typeface, which is degradation from the original font design. Many newer RIPs, printer drivers and applications ignore pseudo commands, and simply use the plain printer font. Example: the italic command from a style menu is selected for Humanist 541 Condensed Bold (which has a corresponding printer font). On screen, the font will display as a condensed bold italic; however, when printed the condensed bold version will most likely print out not in italics.

4.1.9.6 | Outline Effect To use an outline only, use a vector program and give the type a stroke in the desired color and a fill of none or white. To stroke only the outside, use a copy of the type, with no stroke and a white fill, exactly on top of the stroked copy. Be sure the stroke is at least twice the specified image trap for the print segment to be used.

4.1.9.7 | Foreign Fonts Fonts are available for many languages such as Lithuanian, Hebrew, Kanji or Vietnamese, and usually require a keyboard layout file to work correctly If this file is not installed correctly, characters may appear correctly on screen but may fail to print. Send the keyboard layout file along with the font to the prepress provider, or convert the fonts to outlines.

4.1.9.8 | Proprietary Fonts Fonts can be created by font software. The proprietary font must be sent each time the design file is sent out. Indicate where the font may be bought if you did not create it. If the font license permits, send the fonts (both printer and screen) with the design files.

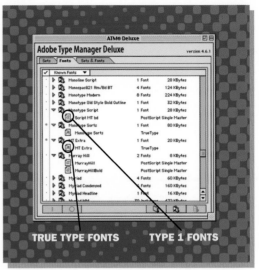

4.1.9 Fonts Type 1 fonts, also known as Adobe fonts, are actually fonts by any manufacturer that are encoded in the Adobe Type 1 standard. Not all Type 1 fonts are created equal; some are auto traced.

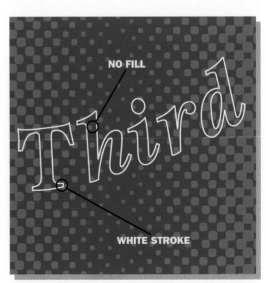

4.1.9.6 Outline Effect To use an outline only, use a vector program, and give the type a stroke in the desired color, and a fill of none or white. Be sure the stroke is at least twice the specified image trap for the print segment to be used.

4.1.9.9 | **Other Font Architectures** Multiple Master, True Type GX and other new font architectures must first be tested with the output service provider. Confirm that the service provider has and can work with these fonts.

4.1.9.10 | **Poorly Written Fonts** Poorly written fonts may be node heavy (built with too many points), have bad kerning pairs or incomplete character sets. They should be avoided. If there is a typeface that absolutely must be used, test it first through an imagesetter. If using a font that is not available from the output supplier, convert it to outline. If the font is public domain, send it with the files.

4.1.9.11 | **Specially Kerned Fonts** Any modified kerning, tracking tables or suitcases containing specially kerned fonts must go to the output service provider along with the project. Modifications like this must be documented. In the case of a suitcase, the fonts can be renamed to identify them, and they will still connect with the same printer fonts. Be conservative with the renaming. Example: "MyHelvetica."

4.1.9.12 | **Using a Suitcase** Create a suitcase for every customer product line. Place only the exact font approved for this product line by the consumer product company in this suitcase. From this point on, use only the suitcase for that customer's product line.

4.1.9.13 | **Supplying Type Fonts** It is strongly recommended that, in addition to the original design type fonts, both screen and printer, Type A suitcase is provided to the prepress provider, along with the digital file. To avoid copyright infringements or unauthorized use of type fonts, the licensing responsibility resides with both the creator of the file and the company outputting the file. The creator must check with the supplier of the fonts required to make sure that the license held for the use of these fonts allows for the use not only by the creator but also the output supplier. In most cases, this is the general practice used.

4.1.10 | **Converting Type to Outline or Paths**

■ This feature in drawing programs is appropriate for small amounts of large sized text, as in headlines or logos. By converting to paths or outlines, a font call is eliminated, and many of the font problems can be avoided.

■ If an EPS file containing text is to be placed in another document, convert all text to outlines or paths. Fonts in placed images often are not reported as missing until the file is RIPped.

■ With poorly written fonts, text should be converted to outlines. By doing so, any corrupt fonts will be identified by the "This font may not convert—font outline is missing" message.

■ Once type is converted to outline, the text is no longer editable, which effectively locks the text. Unless the font specifications were documented, it could be difficult to recreate the exact font look for future text revisions. For this reason, it is advisable keep a copy of the original file prior to converting the type.

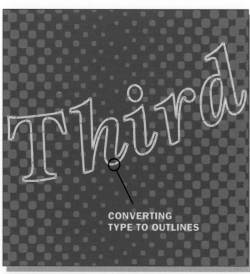

4.1.10 Converting Type to Outline or Paths This feature in drawing programs is appropriate for small amounts of large sized text, as in headlines or logos. By converting to paths or outlines, a font call is eliminated, and many of the font problems can be avoided.

4.2 | Custom and Special Colors

The "custom colors" defined in a file should represent only the actual inks, or tints of inks, that will be printed, with the following exceptions:

Use special colors for special treatments if it is necessary to have white copy reversed out of more than one color. It is common for the prepress provider to create a stay-back of one or more of the printing colors to keep the copy from looking blurry when slightly misregistered.

4.3 | Handling and Labeling of Special Colors

4.3.1 | Custom Colors

A designer should know, specify or confirm the actual colors that will be used on press. Most packages are printed with colors other than CMYK. Correct usage of "custom colors" can expedite the production process. A file containing 15 or 20 custom or spot colors leaves the printer or prepress provider with great uncertainty when attempting to interpret the intentions of the designer.

In some programs, the designer can specify whether a custom color is meant to be created using a CMYK mix, or a single custom color ink. The designer must be sure the color make-up is clearly indicated. On the annotation layer, it must be specified how each color is to output. It is not uncommon for special colors to be used in process illustration, either as touch plates or even as a replacement for one of the traditional process colors. In these cases, special separation and proofing techniques are required.

CMYK equivalents of custom colors do not always match. If the custom color is to be made out of process, the prepress provider must know if they are expected to use exact percentages, or if they are responsible for verifying that the necessary tints are used to match as close as possible to the custom color callouts.

Using industry standard ink color designations can enhance color communication.

4.3.2 | Reverse Out or White Ink

If a custom color named "White Reverse" (with CMYK values of 0,0,0,0 and 100% white ink) is created, it can be easier to differentiate this white from the ink color white as well as other non-printing areas.

If white is to be an ink, a custom color is created and used to specify which areas print white, as opposed to reversed out of another color, or not printed. This white ink could be set up with a slight tint (5% black) for clarity. This color should be named "white ink" for better clarification.

4.3.3 | Color Proof Files vs. Production Files

If a file includes custom colors that overlap to create a third "color," it is necessary to produce two final files: a file for color comps, and a file for production with two separate layers. Mark up a proof with instructions for how the color is to be created. Example: "100% yellow overprinting 40% navy." There is no easy way to create one file that shows this effect and also prints the correct tints. Consult the printer for the resulting third "color". One other solution is to substitute process colors for custom colors (i.e., magenta channel might print as red, the cyan as reflex blue, the yellow as gold, and the black as green). Be sure to specify the colors on the annotation layer in the file.

4.4 | Design Considerations for Bar Codes

4.4.1 | Bar Code Specifications

Bar code print specifications are produced by combining three types of related specifications:

■ Application Standards are published by accredited standards organizations. Before explaining what application standards specify, it might be useful to know more about what they are. Simply put, bar codes are used in many different ways or "applications". For example, one bar code application is bar coding products for retail checkout lanes and

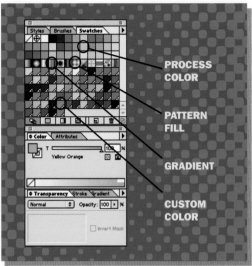

4.3.1 Custom Colors A designer should know, specify or confirm the actual colors that will be used on press. Most packages are printed with colors other than CMYK. Correct usage of "custom colors" can expedite the production process.

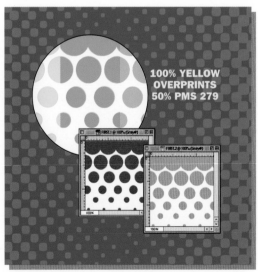

4.3.3 Color Proof vs Production Files If a file includes custom colors that overlap to create a "third" color, it is necessary to produce two final files: a file for color comps, and a file for production with two separate layers.

another application is bar coding shipments for conveyor lane routing in distribution centers. The specifications for the bar codes in these two application areas are different because the conditions for scanning the bar codes are very different. Accredited standards organizations (see Appendix) provide specifications in the form of guidelines and standards to assist in answering:

- What bar code type should be used?
- How to structure the data inside the bar code?
- How to print human-readable information that is inside the bar code?
- What bar code size ranges are acceptable?
- Where the bar code should be placed on the package or container?
- What are the minimum print quality requirements?
- Print Specifications prescribe a minimal level of capability for all printers. All specifications will fall within the acceptable specification limits of the appropriate application standard for the bar code being printed.
- Job Specifications should be published within the job specification for film or plate output. This type of specification should answer:
  - What output resolution was selected for film or plate production?
  - What bar-width reduction (BWR) was used in film or plate production?

The second type of specification is published within FIRST to prescribe a minimal level of capability for all compliant printers. All specifications will fall within the acceptable limits of the appropriate Application Standard for the bar code being printed. Specifications will assist in answering:

- What is the minimum size for a bar code depending on selected printing press type and substrate?
- How should the bar code be oriented given the direction the web will travel?

The third type of specification should be published within the job specification for film or plate output. This type of specification should answer:

- What output resolution was selected for film or plate production?
- What bar width reduction (BWR) was used in film or plate production?

It is important to know that the level of bar code information covered in this section is limited to creating a FPO (for position only) symbol. Anyone involved in the actual creation of the production ready symbols should also see Section 2, the Prepress Section. Designers play a critical role in communicating bar code specifications. In creating a FPO symbol, the designer should communicate the symbol type, the color(s) used to print it, the area where the symbol will be located, the direction the symbol will be oriented in, and the size symbol required. This section takes designers through the process of creating a FPO symbol for their design.

4.4.2 | Bar Code Type

The type of bar code depends on many factors including where it will be scanned and how it will be printed. Designers should rely on the print buyer for the specification of which bar code type to use.

4.4.3 | Bar Code Substrate and Color Considerations

Because designers are often involved in the substrate and color selection process, they should be aware of the design implications on bar code performance. They should determine if the current design specifications could create scannability problems. Common design revisions requested based on the selected substrate or color might include larger symbols, a different symbol orientation, an extra layer of background ink, or a dedicated bar code print station.

4.4.3.1 | Substrate Considerations

Bars and spaces are most accurately produced on smooth substrates with high ink holdout. The rougher, more textured and more porous a substrate, the greater the potential for printing bars with voids and/or printing specks in the spaces, either of which can reduce scanning rates. Textured and more porous stocks also tend to increase bar edge roughness, bar growth and bleeding. Any of these substrate characteristics can negatively affect scanning rates.

4.4.3.2 | Color Considerations

The optimum bar code color combination is opaque black ink for the bars and opaque white substrate or ink for the background. Bars printed in opaque black, dark blue, or dark green and backgrounds (spaces and quiet zones) printed on an opaque white material or on a white, red, orange, pink, peach, or yellow ink generally scan successfully. It is important to remember that colors with acceptable ANSI Symbol Contrast on an opaque substrate may be completely unacceptable on an opaque substrate of another color or on a translucent or transparent substrate. When printing on a transparent substrate or colored substrate, a solid, light-colored (white is optimum) background, with maximum reflectance, is recommended in the area where the bar code is to be located. It is recommended that bar code symbols should not be placed on a plate used to provide a large solid coverage of ink. This is because these plates may have requirements for extra impression and a higher volume of ink. Ink color specifications should be evaluated individually for different substrates.

Bar codes require bars with sharp edges in order for the scanner to perform successfully. The bars comprising a bar code must be printed in one color, using a solid line image, on a single print station, because scanning accuracy is reduced when variation in register occurs.

4.4.4 | Bar Code Placement

Bar codes are placed in different locations based on the shape of the product and where the product will be scanned. The designer should check with the product manufacturer for placement specifications based on these factors or refer to the Appendix. The designer should also consult with the package engineer to ensure the symbol will not be creased, scored, sealed, or folded. Placement of the codes in these areas may cause the ink to crack, producing voids in the bars or spots in the symbol background. A poor placement may also have the bar code being folded, which will result in the symbol being wrapped around adjacent print or package panels.

4.4.2 Bar Code Type The type of bar code depends on many factors including where it will be scanned and how it will be printed. Designers should rely on the print buyer for the specification of which bar code type to use.

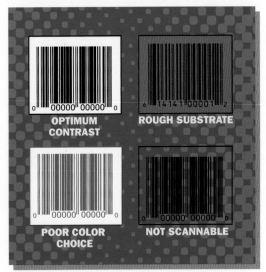

4.4.3.2 Color Considerations The optimum bar code color combination is opaque black ink for the bars and opaque white substrate or ink for the background.

PICKET FENCE

LADDER

4.4.5 Bar Codes Bar code orientation is critical. The top figure illustrates the bars on the UPC symbol traveling in the machine direction, while the bottom figure, illustrates the bars running across the press direction. If print slur occurs with the symbol in the picket fence orientation, the bars grow in length only and are still scannable; however the symbol printed in the cross web direction will cause the bars to grow in width, likely causing the code on the printed package to fail minimum grade specifications.

4.4.5 | Bar Code Orientation

It is strongly recommended that the bars in a bar code be printed parallel to the direction the web is moving through the press to avoid slurring. It is not recommended, but under certain situations the bars in a bar code must be placed in the transverse (across the web) direction. In these cases, the printer should be consulted. Using a larger symbol may be required to meet the minimum print quality requirements specified by the appropriate application standard.

4.4.6 | Bar Code Size

The area reserved for a bar code depends on several inter-related specifications. First, it is important to know what symbol type is specified based on where the package will be scanned. For example, if the package will be scanned at the retail POS (point of sale), an EAN/UPC symbol is specified. After the symbol type is known, it is important to know the allowable range of dimensions (height and width) for the symbol including the human-readable text associated with it. It is important to note that certain symbols have a fixed relationship between their height and width, while others have minimum heights specified. Bar code truncation is a reduction of a symbol's height below the application standard or symbol specification and is not recommended.

All compliant printers will be able to meet the minimum bar code sizes outlined in Prepress Section 11.5.5. However, the smaller the symbol's size, the tighter the tolerance on bar width growth; therefore larger symbols are better. Printing a bar code below the minimum size specified by the bar code application standards is not acceptable.

4.4.7 | Quiet Zones

The quiet zone is the area free of printing, that precedes the left bar and follows the right bar in a bar code symbol. The quiet zones allow scanners to detect when a bar code starts and stops. Quiet zones are based on multiples of the symbol's narrowest element width (X-dimension). Minimum quiet zone specifications depend on the symbol specified. For example, the UPC-A symbol requires a quiet zone of 9X on each side, while an ITF-14 symbol (Interleaved 2-of-5 symbol specified by the UCC) requires a 10X quiet zone on each side. Bar code specifications where the quiet zone is omitted, obstructed or too small are not supported by FIRST.

4.5 | Die-Cut Specifications

4.5.1 | Die Drawing or Electronic Drawing

When there is a die cut, a final die drawing or electronic file must be provided with the art before any final assembly is started. All supplied die drawings must indicate cuts, folds and scores as well as non-print areas. The design firm, in conjunction with the packaging buyer, should indicate areas in which the control target may be placed Refer to Prepress Sections 12.5 and 12.6 for print process measurement and control.

4.5.2 | Using the Template Layout
| (Key Line, Die Drawing, Full Scale Drawing)

It is the responsibility of the printer and the consumer product company to provide the design firm with the appropriate electronic file and template including layout dimensions and other vital information prior to the conceptual design phase.

This template should include non-image area, non-print area, print direction, varnish area, seal area and "inside view" identification.

It is the responsibility of the design firm to take these non-print areas into consideration during the design process.

The final template or die drawing in an electronic file must be provided to the prepress facility to assure that all job elements are correctly positioned as required for the package assembly.

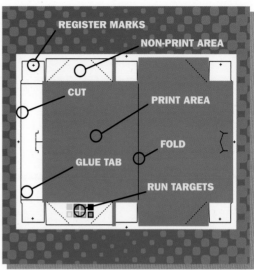

4.5.2 Using the Template Layout This template should include non-image area, non-print area, print direction, varnish area, seal area and "inside view" identification. It is the responsibility of the design firm to take these non-print areas into consideration during the design process.

4.5.3 | Die Origin

Dies are typically built (for die-cut labels, fiberboard and corrugated cartons) for the final package using a computerized CAD system. Files generated from the majority of these systems can be translated into a format compatible with programs used to create graphics. Incorporation into dies, bleeds, or press-marks (internal and external), can be determined on a case-by-case basis. Early communication about who will build a die line and how it will be used is essential.

4.5.4 | Printing Form Layout Considerations

Printing form layout indicates the way in which individual die cut units are arranged on a sheet. This may affect control target placement and create additional design considerations. If certain knives are common, or shared, between individual units, the design may be affected at the perimeter of the unit. This information can only be obtained through contact with the printer. Designers should be able to work through their consumer products company and the printer to receive this vital information.

4.5.5 | Electronic Format

It is important that the designer work with an accurate representation of the unit form to avoid later adjustments to the design. Sometimes the die is modified to match graphic elements (windows, cut-outs or coupons). Most translation programs provide a link from the more common package design programs to CAD formats (i.e., DXF, DDES2, IGES); the structural designer should indicate what formats can be produced.

4.5.6 | Measurement of Die Drawings

Measurements should be indicated on the die drawing file with all dimensions and marks as close as possible to the live print area to keep the material size required to a minimum.

4.6 | Screen Rulings

Screen rulings vary based on imaging method, plate material, and print conditions (such as press width, anilox configuration and substrate). For laser engraved rubber plates the maximum screen ruling is limited to 120 line screen because the material currently cannot hold dots smaller than 5% at 120 lpi. Technology is being developed to expand the process capability of laser engraved rubber but this is the current process limitation (Fall 2003). The screen ruling for digital photopolymer is restricted by the printing process not the imaging process or plate material. The lower range of line screens for photopolymer plates, both conventionally and digitally imaged, is determined by print and substrate constraints. The screen ruling should be specified by the printer and taken into account by the designer. The graphics and process images to be used should be selected carefully because some print conditions require low screen rulings (45 lpi, 55 lpi, 65 lpi).

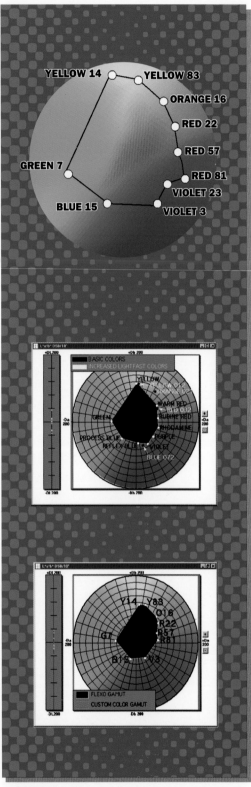

4.8 FIRST Ink Pigments The gamut shown in the top illustration is created by plotting FIRST recommended line pigments. The middle graph illustrates the change in the color gamut created by adding additional pigments. The bottom graph compares the color gamut created with FIRST line pigments to the gamut created with Pantone® bases (lithographic). All pigments were proofed in a water-based ink formula on Leneta stock for demonstration purposes only.

LINE SCREEN/RULING (LPI)

WIDE WEB		CONVENTIONAL PLATES	DIGITALLY IMAGED PHOTOPOLYMER	LASER ENGRAVED RUBBER/ CURED POLYMER
PREPRINT LINERBOARD	SBS Board	110–133 lpi 43–52 lpcm	110–175 lpi 43–69 lpcm	110–120 lpi 43–47 lpcm
	Uncoated	100–133 lpi 39–52 lpcm	100–133 lpi 39–52 lpcm	100–120 lpi 39–47 lpcm
COMBINED CORRUGATED	Bleached White	55–100 lpi 22–39 lpcm	55–100 lpi 22–39 lpcm	55–100 lpi 22–39 lpcm
	Coated	55–110 lpi 22–43 lpcm	55–110 lpi 22–43 lpcm	85–110 lpi 33–43 lpcm
FOLDING CARTON	SBS Board	120–150 lpi 47–59 lpcm	120–175 lpi 47–69 lpcm	110–120 lpi 43–47 lpcm
	CRB Board	110–133 lpi 43–52 lpcm	110–133 lpi 43–52 lpcm	110–120 lpi 43–47 lpcm
MULTIWALL BAG	Coated Paper	75–120 lpi 30–47 lpcm	75–120 lpi 30–47 lpcm	75–110 lpi 30–43 lpcm
	Uncoated Paper	65–85 lpi 26–33 lpcm	65–100 lpi 26–39 lpcm	65–100 lpi 26–39 lpcm
FILM PRODUCTS	All	110–133 lpi 43–52 lpcm	110–150 lpi 43–59 lpcm	85–120 lpi 33–47 lpcm

NARROW WEB		CONVENTIONAL PLATES	DIGITALLY IMAGED PHOTOPOLYMER	LASER ENGRAVED RUBBER/ CURED POLYMER
PAPER PRODUCTS	Coated Paper	133–175 lpi 52–69 lpcm	133–175 lpi 52–69 lpcm	110–120 lpi 43–47 lpcm
	Uncoated Paper	110–133 lpi 43–52 lpcm	110–133 lpi 43–52 lpcm	100–120 lpi 39–47 lpcm
FILM PRODUCTS	All	110–133 lpi 43–52 lpcm	110–150 lpi 43–59 lpcm	85–120 lpi 33–47 lpcm

4.7 | Tints

When tints are used, the values are adjusted during output using a print curve to compensate for the dot gain experienced in the printing process. A 2% minimum dot can print as high as an 8% to 15%, while a tint value of 75% may print as 100%. Extensive use of tints to manufacture special colors should be minimized. Try to restrict tints to two colors.

4.8 | Ink Colors Used

A designer should collaborate with the printer and consumer product company as to how many colors are available for a product line. Many packages are printed with additional colors other than CMYK; always note the print sequence. At times, transparent and/or opaque inks may be used and must be identified prior to prepress by the printer. The characteristics and print sequence of the inks used may require special considerations during the prepress phase.

In an effort to improve color matching across the product line, twelve ink pigments are identified by color index name and number and recommended by FIRST. These twelve pigments are combined to create custom line colors (e.g., PMS 186 or "Shelly's Soda" Red). These pigments are recommended because they provide the largest color gamut with reasonable fade resistance required by most packaging applications. Standardizing ink pigments improves the consistency of the color match between pressruns and between printers while minimizing metamerism. This results in a more cohesive package appearance on the store shelf. Any combination of ink pigments, delivery systems and substrates result in color matching limitations. The designer needs to be aware of the potential color match limitations with the inks, ink delivery system, and substrate specified for the project.

When these twelve pigments are plotted to create a color gamut, colors within the gamut can be reasonably matched. When a designer or consumer product company selects a color that falls outside of the gamut, the printer will not be able to achieve an accurate color match using FIRST pigments. In such cases, the printer may opt to include additional pigments that expand the color gamut in order to achieve the desired color. Sometimes, due to limitations in pigments available for a given ink chemistry, it is not possible to match a color precisely.

In figure 4.8, the FIRST recommended pigments for line inks have been proofed on Leneta stock and plotted to create a color gamut (top illustration). The middle graph illustrates how substituting yellow 12, orange 21, red 32 and blue 72 to increase fade resistance also alters the color gamut. Printers should proof FIRST pigments on their print stock/s and plot using a spectrophotometer to create the color gamut which will best predict their ability to match color on press. All colors are dependent on the substrate being printed upon. The designer and consumer product company should see drawdowns of the specified color match on the intended substrate before any job is approved for prepress. Substrate substitution in this approval process is not recommended

Refer to Print Sections 19.3.2.2 for FIRST recommended process ink pigments and 19.3.3.1 for FIRST recommended line ink pigments.

4.9 | Print Substrate

A sample of the substrate should accompany the project as soon as available. The whiteness, color, and texture of the substrate should be considered—printing on foil or a colored paper or printing white behind the graphics can vary the printed color gamut. Often the colors on the printed product will deviate from the approved contract proof if the proof is not made to reflect the printed white ink on some packaging, but this white is much darker (dirtier) and typically less opaque than white paper or film.

When printed, various packaging substrates exhibit different color properties. For example, some stocks will inconsistently absorb ink, resulting in darker areas of the images that look muddy.

4.10 | Production Run Targets

The run targets must contain the minimum dot percent and maximum shadow tone as specified for the print segment in which the package is to be printed (i.e., wide web polypropylene). Run targets must be placed in the live print area of the package. The printer uses these targets to measure dot gain and solid ink density during the production run. They are not removed and therefore must be considered and properly placed when creating the design.

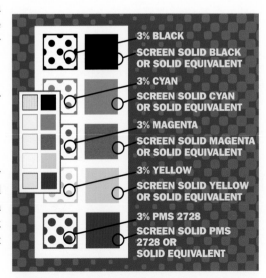

3% BLACK
SCREEN SOLID BLACK OR SOLID EQUIVALENT
3% CYAN
SCREEN SOLID CYAN OR SOLID EQUIVALENT
3% MAGENTA
SCREEN SOLID MAGENTA OR SOLID EQUIVALENT
3% YELLOW
SCREEN SOLID YELLOW OR SOLID EQUIVALENT
3% PMS 2728
SCREEN SOLID PMS 2728 OR SOLID EQUIVALENT

4.10 Production Run Target Run targets must be placed in the live print area of the package and must contain the minimum dot percent and maximum shadow tone as specified for the print segment in which the package is intended to be printed (i.e., wide web polypropylene).

TRANSPARENCY

COLOR PROOF

DIGITAL PHOTO

5.1 Digital vs Conventional An RGB image must be converted to CMYK in order to provide a color proof. Variability is introduced with the RGB to CMYK conversion and could be significantly different when performed by two different people using two different look-up tables.

5.0 Digital Photography

5.1 | Digital vs. Conventional

In this section, workflows and points of measurement are identified to ensure that the creative mood of the photographer's digitally captured image is maintained and the responsibilities for handling, processing and repurposing are clearly identified and communicated, regardless of who works with the digital file.

The detail and vibrancy of an RGB captured image is greater than a converted CMYK image due to the differences in their respective color gamuts. The photographer will generally review a digitally captured image on a computer monitor in RGB; however color proofing is accomplished in CMYK – which has a much smaller color gamut. Variability is introduced with the conversion from RGB to CMYK and could be significantly different when performed by two different people using two different look-up tables.

When a photo is conventionally captured in the form of a transparency, the tonal range is approximately 2.90 transmission density points while the tonal range of a printed sheet is approximately 1.80 reflection density points. The traditional role of the separator is to move from the dynamic range of a transparency while maintaining the same color, contrast and intensity when flexographically printed in a smaller color space. This conversion is crucial to printed results and can yield less than desirable results if not properly performed.

Refer to Design section 5.3 for specifications that relate to camera set-up and responsibilities for the capture and communication of digital photos provided in RGB or CMYK color space. They are intended to capture the full range of the item being shot and do not take into consideration special effects and mood shots that may be desirable and intended but cannot be achieved with strict adherence to the highlight, shadow setting and gray scale aim point. In this instance, special comments should be added to the file stating that a creative license has purposely been taken. Accompanying color proof(s) should be identified according to the recommendations described in Design Section 3.6.

5.2 | Digital Proofs for Digital Photography

The digital proof generated from the digital shot in many cases is the approved color target. If the color management integrity of the proof is not present then the expectations of digital photography may be compromised. For print applications, the digital contract proof of choice should take into account the following aspects of the actual printing segment to be used. This includes but is not limited to:

■ Line Screen.
■ Substrate.
■ Ink Densities.
■ Ink Hue.
■ Color Rotation.
■ Special Color Simulation.
■ Dot Structure.
■ Screen Angles.

The contract proof must contain the FIRST control target (Prepress Section 12.5), which includes color patches of all inks to be used exhibiting 3%, 10%, 30%, 70%, and solid ink density. Also incorporated in the control target is a highlight and shadow gray patch to assist in the evaluation of color balance. The contract proof must be calibrated to the profile of the printing process in which it is going to be reproduced. When a profiled contract proof is required, it is the responsibility of the supplier to contact the printer and/or prepress provider to obtain the press profile and any other specific requirements.

5.3 | Camera Set-Up Ranges

5.3.1 | Black Settings

In the RGB color space, a highlight setting that can still produce a dot structure should be used and fall between 236 and 240.

5.3.2 | White Settings

In the RGB color space, a shadow setting that will still hold the detail without filling up should be used and fall between 18 and 22.

5.4 | Gray Scale in Photo Shot

It is imperative to use a standard photographer's gray scale for setting up any digital shot. The gray scale should be in all shots and positioned in order to best capture the scale within the outline of the shot. If there are several dropout shots and the scale cannot be placed in the shot, then start with shooting the scale in test shots to obtain correct gray scale settings.

It is recommended that a photo scale be placed in all digital photography shots. When creating mood images or images where the light is filtered for an effect, photograph the gray scale with and without the filter on the light. Then supply both shots to the prepress provider noting the difference between the two for the color reproduction.

The MacBeth 200 and Kodak Q12/Q60 are examples of special color and gray scales that should be used as gray scale targets for digital photography to measure density and color. Place this gray scale in the main light source of the image. If a full gray scale cannot be used, use patches of white, black and a mid-tone neutral gray.

5.5 | Gray Scale Aim Point

The aim point of the shot should be the 40% neutral gray swatch or the number 3 or 4 block on the photographer's scale.

5.6 | File Format

All shots should be RGB.TIFF format when they are going to the prepress provider for conversion. If the photographer creates the color-converted (color separation) file, the file format to the prepress provider should be "CMYK TIFF".

5.7 | RGB Conversion

Though many off-the-shelf programs are capable of converting from RGB to CMYK color space, there are many factors to consider, including ink pigments, printing substrate, screen ruling, etc. It is critical to identify which party is best

5.4 Grayscale Aim Point The aim point of the shot should be the 40% neutral gray swatch or the number 3 or 4 block on the photographer's scale.

5.8 Unsharp Masking Unsharp masking is a technique, which produces the appearance of sharpness to detail within an image, accentuating edges where different densities and contrasting colors meet.

equipped and responsible for making color conversions and for documenting the color status of any digital files and accompanying proofs. Traditionally, this is a core responsibility of the prepress provider because of his/her advanced knowledge of the many variables involved.

5.8 | Unsharp Masking

Unsharp masking is a technique, which produces the appearance of sharpness and detail within an image, accentuating edges where different densities and contrasting colors meet. The amount of masking applied is determined by factors such as image content, screen ruling enlargement, image grain and printing substrate. The prepress provider usually has the needed information to make the necessary unsharp masking determination. Applying this technique at the photographic stage will limit the sharpness detail irreversibly. The photographer for proofing purposes may apply unsharp masking, although the digital file sent to the prepress provider should be sent without the unsharp filter applied.

5.9 | Resolution

The number of pixels (picture elements) in a given area determines the resolution of an image (typically specified as # pixels per linear inch). 300 pixels per inch is the typical resolution for color images at 100% for 133 –150 line screen. The formula for calculating the optimum resolution is two times the output screen ruling (two rows of pixels for every row of halftone dots). Although this is the "rule of thumb", the amount of captured resolution is related to the final image quality and must take into consideration the enlargement of the image, the screen ruling it will be printed at and the image content, (particularly detailed content).

SCREEN RULING/ RESOLUTION	
SCREEN RULING (LPI/LPCM)	RESOLUTION (PPI/PPCM)
55 / 22	110 / 43
65 / 28	130 / 51
85 / 33	170 / 67
100 / 39	200 / 79
110 / 43	220 / 87
120 / 47	240 / 94
133 / 52	266 / 105
150 / 59	300 / 118
175 / 69	350 / 138
200 / 79	400 / 157

LPI = Lines per Inch
LPCM = Lines per Centimeter
PPI = Pixels per Inch
PPCM = Pixels per Centimeter

To convert from English measurement (LPI or PPI) to metric measurement (LPCM or PPCM), divide the number of lines (pixels) per inch by 2.54.

Example: Original resolution (1,240) ppi divided by enlargement (350%) equals (354) lines of resolution at the reproduction size (pixels per inch) divided by screen ruling (175 lpi) = (2.02). There should be no noticeable loss in detail as long as the answer is over 2.

5.10 | Recommendations for File Transfers

The receiver of any digital file should be contacted for the recommended transfer media and method agreed to be used. The following is a partial list of viable sources of electronic transfer of digital data:

- ISDN lines.
- T-1 lines.
- E-mail.
- FTP.
- PDN.
- Disk.
- Commercially available proprietary solutions.

It is required that a hard copy proof accompany every digital file, even if the file is delivered the following day.

Regardless of the file transfer method, all jobs processed should be accompanied by:

- A list of file names relevant to the job.
- Organized by directories/folders.
- All high-resolution images embedded or linked in the job.
- All supporting profile files (source and destination).
- Hard copy reflecting files on disk.
- Screen and printer fonts (when applicable).

6.0 Programs and Applications

6.1 | Applications

Applications used in package design are divided into three categories:

- **Drawing (Vector Creation) Programs**: Adobe Illustrator, Macromedia FreeHand, Corel Draw, etc.
- **Photo Editing**: Adobe Photoshop, Live Picture, Fractal Design Painter, etc.
- **Page Layout**: QuarkXPress, Adobe PageMaker, Adobe InDesign, etc.

6.1.1 | Drawing Programs

A line is merely the coordinate of two points and the instructions to connect them with a line of particular weight and color. Shapes have more points and indicate a fill color. There is no resolution to these graphics, thereby allowing an element to be scaled up or down with no loss of detail. Furthermore, they are inherently accurate and are best for graphics with a fixed set of colors (line copy). Most drawing programs also include the ability to create gradients, vignettes, and blends. Drawing programs create files that contain objects therefore are referred to as "object-oriented" files.

When composing a job in a drawing program, always include the die drawing or template information on a separate layer or use a unique spot color such as "die line" so it can be isolated at output. It is recommended that die-cut jobs (labels, cartons, corrugated) be produced entirely within a drawing program.

6.1.2 Raster Images are photographic images or art that may contain thousands of shades of color. Graphics are made of many rows of pixels and each pixel can have its own shade. These files have a fixed resolution when created or scanned and cannot be enlarged without losing sharpness. There is a limited amount of data in those pixels.

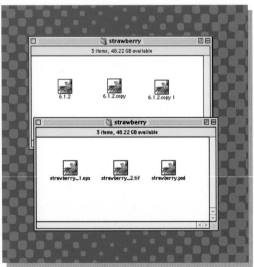

7.1.1 File Names File names should be short but descriptive. In some instances, file names may be truncated down to the first eight characters when RIPped.

6.1.2 | Photo Editing Programs

Photographic images or art created in photo editing programs may contain thousands of shades of color. The graphics are made of many rows of pixels and each pixel can have its own shade. These files have a fixed resolution when created or scanned and cannot be enlarged without losing sharpness. When enlarging a previously captured image, check with the prepress provider for input on maximum enlargement without significant loss of quality (image detail).

6.1.3 | Page Layout Programs

Page layout programs provide an assembly environment where all kinds of elements can be combined. These programs, such as QuarkXPress and PageMaker, generally are superior for dealing with many scanned images and volumes of text in multi-page documents but are less adept at accurate placement of elements relative to a template. Therefore, FIRST does not recommend using page layout programs for package design.

6.2 | PC vs. Mac

The packaging industry commonly uses the Macintosh platform for graphics production, though there are PC/Windows versions of many popular applications available. It should be determined and documented to what level of cross-platform compatibility the electronic file will be made.

7.0 Document Structure

7.1 | Naming Conventions

When the design process is in the early stage, identifying a common naming convention is in the best interest of all parties and is vital in assuring smooth production. Many times the package being developed is part of a larger project or product line. Before the design and production files are created, check with the consumer product company to identify if they have already developed a common naming convention to be used by all suppliers.

7.1.1 | File Names

File names should be short but descriptive, containing no more than eight characters. On some systems, file names may be truncated down to the first eight characters when RIPped. Some systems cannot handle characters such as asterisks, spaces or punctuation, so never use these characters when naming files and/or document elements.

7.1.2 | Naming for Image Replacement

In some production environments, low-resolution versions of images (FPOs) are used through various stages of concept, design, and approval. These low-resolution images are smaller in size and faster to process then the actual high-resolution version. With the correct and agreed upon naming convention, the FPO can be linked to the high-resolution files and replaced automatically during the output stage. Determine with the separation, film, or plate provider if image replacement procedures will be used, and what naming procedures are to be followed.

7.2 | Document Size

Designs must be built to actual size. If the art is too big to proof in one piece, it will be necessary to tile the proof. All proofs should be made to the final package size (100%).

7.3 | Working in Layers

These specifications support the use of layers to organize a file. Put the template on one layer, marks on another and each separate color on different layers. Use layers for variations in designs, such as special price banners, line extensions, etc. This assures that the underlying graphics are identical in content, placement and prepress execution. This can also be helpful in jobs with common colors (cylinders or plates shared between two similar designs).

Give the layers meaningful names, which is part of documenting the file. Put notes, instructions, color mixes and other documentation on a layer, or include them on a separate annotation layer with the art. This assures these important instructions will not get lost along the production chain.

Some separators and/or RIPs require that colors be pre-separated; layers are an ideal way to organize these separations.

7.3 Working in Layers Use layers for variations in designs, such as special price banners, line extensions, etc. This assures that the underlying graphics are identical in content, placement and prepress execution. This can also be helpful in jobs with common colors (cylinders or plates shared between two similar designs).

7.4 | Auto-traced or Re-vectorized Art

Much of the fine-tuning of designs to achieve printability, die matching and cross matching may be done during the prepress stage of production. To eliminate doing these changes to each new revision of a base design, it is necessary to get all changes back to the designer and/or consumer product company or end user if any changes are made by prepress.

Many high-end systems can now convert completed files back to Mac format as Illustrator or FreeHand. Such files should be used with extreme caution. Auto tracing features ask a program to make decisions about placing nodes or points. These automatic choices are not the most efficient choices, and produce complex files with too many nodes that can slow or stop file processing. In addition, the files are so large they require large amounts of RAM to open them.

7.4.1 | Re-vectorized Files

Files that were created on a Mac, converted to a high-end system and then converted back to a Mac are called "re-vectorized." If possible, these files should not be used. If these files are used, they should be simplified as much as possible. When a RIP converted the file to raster, the RIP decided which pixels to turn on, using the PostScript information sent by the application. Now another program has processed it, making more decisions about where to place nodes, making this a third generation image. Some change is inevitable; in the best case it maybe in the range of 0.001" (0.025 mm). For best results, use this image for position, and move or adjust the original art to fit. Recreate the art whenever possible; that is, redraw the elements in the program to create new elements that are native to the program. This solves the file size issue and produces elements that are easily incorporated into future designs and changes.

7.4 Auto Traced or Re-vectorized Art Auto tracing features ask a program to make decisions about placing nodes or points. These automatic choices are not the most efficient choices, and produce complex files with too many nodes that can slow or stop file processing.

7.5 | Blends, Vignettes, Gradations

Digital blends (sometimes referred to as degradés, gradations, gradients, fountains, vignettes or graduated tints) are subject to unpleasant banding or steps where tints do not blend smoothly. This can be minimized with a little planning in the design process. There are several approaches to building good-looking blends. Although applications have improved algorithms for blends, they are still not foolproof.

Blend terms:
- Length refers to the physical length of the blend.
- Range refers to the difference in color across or down the blend. (A blend of 30% to 50% has a range of 20%.).
  - The longer the blend, the more likely it is to show banding.
  - The shorter the range of the blend, the more likely it is to show banding.
  - The fewer steps used, the greater the potential for banding.
  - Banding is more visible with darker inks.
  - Lower screen rulings are less likely to show banding

There is a distinct relationship between length, range and the number of steps in a blend. Too few steps or short range on a long blend will show banding.

Higher output resolutions may also help reduce banding that may appear on some low-resolution printers and computer monitors. Professional film and direct-to-plate output devices usually run at a resolution of least at 1,200 dpi resolution, which also helps minimize banding. If objectionable banding is seen during the handling of the file, make a notation on the annotation layer of the file, placing the final inspection responsibility on the party outputting the file.

7.6 | Building a Blend

The minimum dot size of a blend in the highlight area of the plate making film should be no less than the minimum for the print section and no greater than the maximum allowed for the print section in the shadow area.

There are other problems in using blends, some concerning the way they print, others concerning the way they are specified in the program. While newer software versions have corrected many problems in building blends, they are made differently based on print applications and therefore are best created by the prepress provider. Some typical problems in creating blends are described in Design Sections 7.6.1 – 7.6.4.

7.6.1 | A Spot Color into Another Color

When blending one spot color into another spot color, two final files should be produced: a file for color comps and a file for production with two separate blends. In this scenario mark up a proof with instructions for how the blend is to be created in addition to including instructions on the annotation layer. Example: "100% to 20% yellow overprinting 40% to 80% navy." There is no easy way to create one file that shows this effect and prints the correct tints except in process colors. One other solution is to substitute process colors for custom colors (i.e., the magenta channel might print as red, the cyan as reflex blue, the yellow as gold and the black as green, etc.).

7.6.2 | A Spot Color into White

When creating a blend of a spot color to white, specify the minimum dot percentage of the spot color on the lighter end of the blend. In most applications, designating white makes the blend change to the process color model in mid-blend.

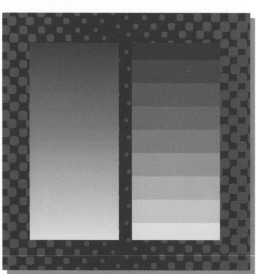

7.6 Building a Blend There are other problems in using blends, some concerning the way they print, others concerning the way they are specified in the program. Talk to the prepress provider or printer. Generally, the prepress provider is best suited to create the final blend.

7.6.3 | Trapping Blends

Blends are difficult to trap. The lighter color should trap into the darker color, but that relationship changes in a blend. When placing type or graphics over a blend, be aware that when the necessary trapping is applied, undesirable results may become an issue.

It is preferable that no color on a blend end before the edge of the panel in which the blend appears.

7.6.4 | RIPping Blends

Blends are complex operations for RIPs to execute. Illustrations using many blends will extend processing times. Consider using a raster program for the image. If there is a part of the art that is like a picture, it may be much easier to process as a raster file. Use vector art for type and other elements that need hard, clear edges, or very fine detail.

Some RIPs will RIP blends from drawing programs to a continuous tone and add noise to prevent banding. This lets the prepress provider separate the art, but it still takes more time to RIP.

Because of the intricacy of blends, communication with prepress is extremely important. Blends can look and print quite differently with different processes. Many times, blends will have to be rebuilt by the prepress provider.

7.7 | Nesting Files

Images placed into another document are nested. An image imported into another document is nested two layers deep. By importing the combined image into yet another document, nesting becomes three layers deep. During processing, the RIP will take time to follow the links to find each of these nested elements. Beyond two layers deep, the RIP may never find them. If the RIP cannot track down all elements, the graphic may have to be rebuilt without nesting (elements may have to be isolated and copied/pasted into a single document—eliminating nesting complications).

7.8 | Follow the Links

Most page layout programs treat imported images as electronic "pick-ups" and refer back (by following the link) to the image file at output. After placing an image, do not rename the files. File names are a critical reference link between the document and the image file. All images placed in the document must travel with the document for output. Always take care in assuring that all links are updated properly before sending files. If an imported image is modified, always update it in the final document to make sure that it hasn't shifted position.

In many programs, it is an option to save the placed image data with the EPS file. This is not adequate because some editing may be needed. Send the native application files so changes can be made.

Some current drawing programs can place graphics and incorporate them into the file, making the copying of multiple files unnecessary—but using this feature greatly increases the size of the document.

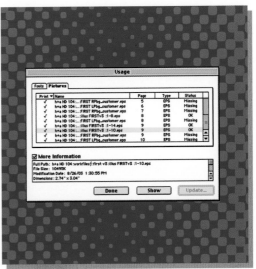

7.8 Follow the Links Most page layout programs treat imported images as electronic "pick-ups" and refer back (by following the link) to the image file at output. After placing an image, do not rename the files. File names are a critical reference link between the document and the image file.

7.9 | Electronic Whiteout

Do not cover up unwanted elements with a white box. The RIP will still process unwanted elements. Files that are designed in drawing programs can use masking. Example: FreeHand, "Paste Inside" command. This is useful for complex shapes but the hidden part of the image must still be processed. Thus, if it does not print, delete it.

7.10 | Image Capture Quality

7.10.1 | Scan Resolution

All scanners capture RGB data and either supply the file "as is" to the desktop system or use hardware and/or software to translate the scanned data to CMYK or in some cases L*a*b* data. Less expensive scanners generally are not adequate for production scans. Many have an optical resolution of only 300 to 600 dpi. They can enlarge as they scan, or produce files of up to 1,200 dpi, but they do so by interpolation and real detail cannot be interpolated.

7.10.2 | Image Sharpness/Resolution

The most important factor is image capture or optical resolution. A scan at 100% scale should have a minimum sampling of 1.5 to 2 times over the "final" sized image. Fine detail images may be sampled at up to 3 times the output line screen. For example, an image that will print with a 200-line screen may need a scan resolution of 300 to 600 pixels per inch, depending on the detail required in the image. If the image is enlarged, it will lower the effective resolution. The goal is scanning live images to capture enough data to achieve the desired detail and at the same time, keep the file size as small as possible.

7.10.3 | Image Enlargement

Be aware that increasing image resolution above what was provided in the original scan can be done only through interpolation. The software makes calculated guesses about what information to add. The results are never as good as when scanning at, or larger than, the desired size and resolution. Real detail cannot be synthesized. It is always recommended to rescan the original image to the desired resolution.

7.10.4 | Line Art

Theoretically, line art should be scanned at the same resolution as the output device. There is, however, little visible improvement on most line art subjects scanned above 1,000 pixels per inch. Scaling will degrade quality; the best solution is to redraw line art in an illustration program. This also makes the file size smaller.

7.10.5 | Desktop Scanners

Desktop scanners generally have less dynamic range (the range of light values they can see). Most flatbed desktop scanners cannot "see" into the shadows of a picture to pick up the shape there. The sensitivity of the CCD array in these scanners is not high enough to sense the slight variations of value in very light or dark tones. They cannot hold the detail in highlight areas and there is often electronic noise (synthetic grain) in the shadows of the scan.

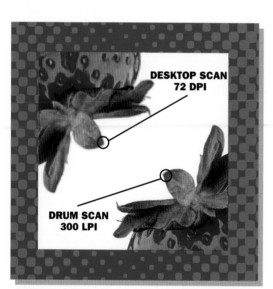

7.10.1 Scan Resolution All scanners capture RGB data and either supply the file "as is" to the desktop system or use hardware and/or software to translate the scanned data to CMYK or in some cases L*a*b* data. Many have an optical resolution of only 300 to 600 DPI and can enlarge as they scan, or produce files of up to 1,200 DPI, but do so by interpolation.

7.11 | Scaling and Rotating

7.11.1 | Rotating

When working with the high-resolution image in a layout or drawing program, rotating and scaling of placed raster files should be kept to a minimum, as the image quality will degrade when the files are eventually RIPped and output. The artist can import the image, scale, crop, and rotate to achieve the desired effect, and then measure the amount of each. This information can be given to prepress along with the original artwork, or the artist can modify the original live scan in the photo-editing program. A new file would be created at the final scale and angle, cropped to the final size and then placed into the design file at 100%. This produces better quality with less RIP time.

7.11.2 | Re-sizing and Scaling

Re-sizing and scaling of placed raster images should also be kept to a minimum. Scaling of live raster images should be done in a photo retouching program where re-sampling will produce a much better result. The general rule is not to enlarge an image more than 150%, but check with the company that scanned the image for input. Typically enlargements greater than 150% will be detrimental to the image sharpness and contrast.

7.12 | Color Space

Using color management software, it is possible to measure and synthesize the data representing any given color space. This information is called "characterization data," and describes, in spectrophotometric terms, the "color space." This information can then be used to alter dot percentages in the image and compensate the digital output to provide a balanced visual match to the contract proof. Only through the use of such data can compensation for ink trap, ink absorption, ink opacity and the differences in proofing colorants versus ink pigments be achieved. Refer to Prepress Section 13.0 for more detailed information on CIELab Color Management.

7.13 | Tone Scales

Tone scales used in the design for the printer can also be used to verify the color space and/or reproduction curve characteristics of the proof. Assuming that a digital file accompanies the proof (with the same scales in it), the prepress provider can evaluate the profile of the proof by measurement.

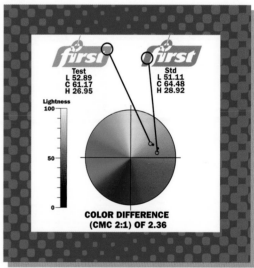

7.12 Color Management System Color Management Systems (CMS) translate from one gamut to another, which enable the proof to more accurately mimic the printing process.

8.0 File Formats

8.1 | Standard Formats

There are numerous types of electronic file formats that can be generated from drawing, photo editing, and page layout programs, such as:

- BMP
- PICT
- TIFF
- EPS
- DCS
- PDF
- JPEG
- JDF

In addition, many of the formats have derivatives (PDF/X-1a, PDF/X-3, etc.). Each type of file and each derivative have unique characteristics for rendering the image on screen and to an output device. Some formats are more "portable" and "universal" than others, meaning they will render the image predictably under a variety of conditions. Some are highly proprietary and can only be used by specific hardware and software systems. Some are editable; some are not. The specifications for file format, and the precise way in which a final file is saved to preserve its attributes are the subjects of ongoing debate throughout the printing industry.

It is possible to convert one file type to another, and most prepress providers have the equipment and knowledge to do so. However, in some cases critical image or job information can be "lost" in the translation, so it is imperative that all parties agree which file formats are to be created, exchanged, and archived throughout the project.

It is not the purpose of FIRST to dictate which formats are to be used in the creation of flexographically reproduced artwork; however, it is highly recommended that digital artists understand the significant differences between the formats. The prepress provider is in the best position to describe the advantages and disadvantages of each format for a specific purpose.

More information about the specifications and certification status of file formats approved for the printing industry can be found by contacting CGATS, the governing body responsible for reviewing and publishing standards for use and best business practices for these electronic file formats.

8.2 | Portable Document Formats (PDFs)

PDF is an imaging file format used to transport graphically rich content. It is especially used in computer-to-plate technologies. The "creator" of the file (designer, ad agency, prepress provider) must produce a file that meets the minimum imaging requirements of the "receiver" (prepress provider, printer). PDF/X is a PDF file with restrictions intended to facilitate the transfer of files from "creator" to "receiver" as outlined in ISO 15930-1:2001. Additional information can be obtained from the *Adobe PDF reference manual, version 1.3, second edition* and *Adobe Technical Note #5413.*

ISO 15930-1:2001 (Graphic Technology – Prepress Digital Data Exchange – Use of PDF Part 1: Complete exchange using CMYK data PDF/X-1 and PDF/X-1a) is both an application standard and a file format standard. It defines a set

8.2 Portable Document Format (PDF) PDF and PDF/X-1 are imaging file formats used to transport graphically rich content. They are especially used in computer-to-plate technologies.

of conditions to govern the creation, viewing and imaging of PDF/X-1 files. Content and structure of PDF/X-1 files are limited to ensure imaging integrity:

- **Required:** a PDF/X-1 file must contain this object or key.
- **Prohibited:** A PDF/X-1 file must not contain this object or key.
- **Restricted:** Certain values or combinations of objects and keys where contents are required or prohibited.
- **Recommended:** a PDF/X-1 file should contain this key.

The objective is to create a "blind exchange" of graphically rich content ready for imaging.

8.2.1 | Annotations

- Movies, Sounds & File Attachments are *prohibited* because they are not useful for digital imaging.
- Notes, Stamps & Acrobat Forms are *restricted*. They must be positioned outside of the bleed area and must not obscure any portion of the imageable area when displayed on screen.

8.2.2 | Key-Value Pairs

The "General Info" dictionary has nine default key-value pairs:

- Title, Subject, Author, Keyword, Creation Date and Mod Date are required.
- Creator and Producer are *recommended*.
- Trapped is *restricted*.
- "GTS_PDFX Version" and "GTS_PDFX Conformance" are two additional key-value pairs *required* by the PDF/X-1 standard.

The Trapped key-value pair in the "General Info" dictionary has a default setting of "unknown" which is *prohibited* for PDF/X-1 files. The setting must be changed to either "Yes" (files have been completely trapped) or "No" (file has not been trapped). Partially trapped files are *prohibited* in the PDF/X-1 standard.

8.2.3 | Arrays

An array is used to define literal names, integers and strings. It is often used to associate multiple values for a single variable. There are four arrays particularly important for PDF/X-1 files:

- **Media Box:** a *required* array in a PDF/X-1 file. It represents the physical size of the PDF page. It is derived during the PDF creation process from either:
  - PageSize Array (PostScript file).
  - BoundingBox Array (EPS file).
  - Default value determined by the normalizer (an application used to create a PDF file).
- **Trim Box:** a *restricted* array in a PDF/X-1 file. All PDF/X-1 files must contain either the TrimBox or the ArtBox array but not both. The TrimBox array defines the area of a PDF file that represents the final size of the page after printing and finishing. It uses crop marks and must not exceed the boundaries of the MediaBox. The PDF/X-1 file must be the complete page.
- **ArtBox:** a *restricted* array in a PDF/X-1 file. All PDF/X-1 files must contain either the TrimBox or the ArtBox array but not both. The ArtBox array defines the desired image area in a PDF/X-1 file where only a portion of the page is to be used for imaging. It functions as an electronic

"crop" without physically changing the dimension of the PDF/X-1 file. Its boundaries must not exceed those of the MediaBox.

- **BleedBox:** an *optional* array in a PDF/X-1 file. It defines the imaging area in excess of the trim. The boundaries must be within those of the MediaBox but not within those of either the TrimBox or ArtBox.

8.2.4 | Fonts

All fonts must be embedded in PDF/X-1 files (*required*). The creator of the PDF/X-1 file must ensure all fonts are used in compliance with licensing agreements.

8.2.5 | Compression

Compression of bitmapped images (ImageXObjects) is not required. If compression is desired, the PDF supported methods are *restricted* to include: Flate, RunLength, JPEG, and CCITT Fax.

8.2.6 | Color Space

Content of a PDF/X-1 file may be defined in "DeviceCMYK", "DeviceGray", "Separation", "DeviceN", "Indexed", or "Pattern" color spaces. All are *restricted*. Device dependent and device independent color spaces are *prohibited* ("DeviceRGB", "DefaultRGB", "CalGray", "CalRGB", and "CIELab").

Spot Colors must be defined as either "Separation" or "DeviceN". Black objects must be identified as either "DeviceGray" or "Separation – black".

Characterized Printing Condition:

- "OutputIntents" array must contain a single "OutputIntents" dictionary whose S key value must be expressed "/GTS_PDFX". This key value is called the "OutputIntent Object". It is *required*.
- The "OutputIntent Object" must have a corresponding "OutputConditionIdentifier" key value. Acceptable values for this key can be found in the ICC registry of characterized printing conditions. This key value is *restricted*.
- When the value of the "OutputConditionIdentifier" key matches a characterization found in the ICC registry, the "RegistryName" key value must be defined (http://www.color.org). This key value is *required*.
- If an "OutputConditionIdentifier" key value is used that is not in the ICC registry, a "DestOutputProfile" key must be present in the "OutputIntent Object". A string value describing the intended printing condition should accompany the "OutputConditionIdentifier" key value. An example of a string value could be: (This file was prepared in accordance with FIRST 3rd Edition).

PDF/X-3:2002 is a superset of PDF/X-1a:2001. It allows for color managed data to be included in color spaces (such as "CIELAb", "CalRGB", or using an embedded ICC profile) while other data can be in Black and/or CMYK. Solid black text will print in solid black without unexpected color shifts spreading the black data to all the process separations.

8.2.7 | Alternate Images

An alternate image is a secondary copy derived from a source Image XObject and is stored in the "Alternate" array. Use of alternate images is *restricted* for PDF/X-1 files.

One application for alternate images is to create a highly compressed low-resolution (72 dpi) replica for each original high-resolution image. The JPEG compressed alternate image will facilitate on-screen viewing. Restrictions for using alternate images include:

■ Alternate Images in the "Alternate" array must have their "DefaultFor Printing" key set to "False".

■ The alternate image must represent the same area as its high-resolution original.

■ If the high-resolution original is edited, the alternate image must be immediately regenerated or destroyed.

8.2.8 | Conformance Levels

The Standard Encryption feature is the Adobe Acrobat method of securing or limiting access rights to a file. Use of the Standard Encryption feature is limited:

■ PDF/X-1: Use is *restricted*. Standard encryption can be used; however, viewing and printing can never be denied and the password must be an empty string.

■ PDF/X-1a:2001: Use of the Standard Encryption feature is *prohibited*.

8.2.9 | New Software Versions

Software updates are frequent. Before using a new version of software, check with all companies downstream that will have to open and work with the electronic file to ensure compatibility. In newer versions, it is possible to save documents in older formats.

8.3 | Clip Art

Just as traditional illustrators' skills vary, so do the levels of sophistication of electronic clip art. Clip art may come in the form of low resolution PICTs, better-performing TIFFs or as well built object-oriented EPS images. Be sure to ask about the file format of the clip art being used to insure the appropriate level of quality. If the images are scans, find out at what resolution they were scanned. If they were scanned at 72 pixels per inch, the clip art piece will be suitable only for display on a monitor and printing to a low-resolution printer.

The particular image needed may be one of several on a clip art page. Remember that masking out all the other images does not remove the images; they will all be processed. Save individual images under a new name and import the single image into the document.

8.4 | Photo CD Products

Some photo CD technology uses proprietary color models, such as the YCC color model. These images must be converted to a CMYK color space for print production. Some photo CD processors have the capability to do this conversion, but other processors may return the files to YCC or RGB color model. If this happens, the prepress provider must then convert the files to CMYK through Photoshop or a similar program. Translation engines vary greatly in quality and color correction. Do not assume that the image is usable. Photo CDs are returned from processing with several resolutions of each image on the disk. Be sure to use the resolution best for the project. Refer to Design Section 5.9 on Resolution.

LOW RESOLUTION PICT

VECTOR EPS

8.3 Clip Art Just as traditional illustrators' skills vary, so do the levels of sophistication of electronic clip art. Clip art may come in the form of low resolution PICTs, better-performing TIFFs or as well built object-oriented EPS images.

8.5 Creating and Identifying FPO Images The letters "FPO" must be placed into the live image area because these files will go through many channels before being output, and if not properly identified as "for position only" images, will not be replaced.

8.5 | Creating and Identifying FPO Images

Whenever possible, FPO images should be created from actual high resolution scanned data with correct cropping and rotation. Otherwise, high-resolution images will need to be scanned by the prepress provider and manually placed. The letters "FPO" must be placed into the live image area because these files will go through many channels before being output, and if not properly identified as "for position only" images, will not be replaced.

8.6 | Special Effects

When editing low-resolution raster files to produce special effects, document the steps used. The effects of most functions change with a resolution change. It would be difficult to reproduce the same result with the high-resolution scan without the documented information. Even with instructions, it is difficult to recreate several complicated special effects. The "Action" set within Photoshop allows the creator of the "low-resolution" file to record each edit step, in sequence, used to create the file. The "action" set can then be saved and shared with the Photoshop user that will be creating the high resolution original.

8.7 | Image Substitution

8.7.1 | Using Low Resolution Files For Automatic Image Replacement

A low-to-medium resolution file may be provided to the designer for automatic image replacement. These files contain links to full resolution files on the prepress provider's system. This method allows the designer to move, crop or resize (within limitations) the APR/OPI image as if it were the live high-resolution image. It places the control of exact positioning in the hands of the designer. Re-sizing of low-resolution images must be employed with extreme caution. The high-resolution file will be scaled by the same factor. Enlarging the file more than 150% will reduce its effective resolution significantly and reproduce an image that appears out of focus and off color. Scaling down or rotating destroys detail as well. Resizing or rotating a raster image in a design could require that the image be rescanned to maintain quality. Having the original image scanned at the proper size and rotation is the only way to ensure optimum quality.

Upon receiving a low-resolution image for automatic placement from a vendor, do not rename the file. The file name is the link back to the high-resolution image. Renaming the file will cause an operator to have to re-establish the link.

Specific recommendations on working with images for automatic placement may vary based on the workflow of the individual designer and service provider. Ask the prepress provider how to handle this process.

8.7.1.2 | Naming Convention With any live image, and particularly with image substitution workflow, agree on a naming convention with the prepress vendor before scanning.

8.8 | Flatness

Flatness, a PostScript term, controls how accurately the RIP draws the paths. Flatness is a number referring to output resolution although different programs vary in their definition of this term. As applied to Adobe Photoshop, the flatness setting describes the accuracy of a clipping path; a flatness of 2 – 3 is typical. It does not refer to the resolution of the raster Photoshop image, but to the higher resolution of the imagesetter. That is, a 300 dpi file with a clipping path set to a flatness of 2 and output at 2,540 dpi will have a clipping path with an effective resolution of 1,270 dpi. The same file output on a 300 dpi laserwriter would have a path with 150 dpi resolution. A lower flatness setting in Photoshop can greatly increase RIP time.

Adobe Illustrator describes flatness in a very different way. Rather than a factor of output resolution, Illustrator objects are given an absolute resolution for RIPping; 800 dpi is default. On a 2,540 dpi imagesetter this is roughly the same as a flatness of 3 the way Photoshop defines it. Different objects can have different flatness settings in Illustrator, depending on the detail required. It is strongly advised that any object with a gradation fill be assigned a flatness of 2,540 dpi or higher to reduce banding. This attribute also limits the number of gradation steps that can be produced.

8.9 | Copy and Paste

Using the "Place Art" feature of drawing programs to import an EPS file makes the file more difficult to RIP. If the EPS is from the same drawing program, there is a better way: Open the file to be used, select only the part of the image needed, copy it and paste it in position in the final file. This is a way to view the placed file as it will actually print, rather than as the low-resolution preview of an EPS.

8.10 | Editable Files

When using embedded or nested files, always send the original file along with the job in case editing is required later.

8.11 | Colors

The custom colors used in a placed image must have the same name as the corresponding custom colors in the final design file. This applies to images pasted in as well. Otherwise, the two colors will not output as one film. Many programs will now import colors from placed images into their palettes, but the artwork must then be edited in the file to use these same colors.

TIP—For the placed raster file to output with the line art in the composite file, custom colors must be edited to the corresponding CMYK inks.

8.11 Colors Custom colors used in a placed image must have the same name as the corresponding custom colors in the final design file. This applies to images pasted in as well. Otherwise, the two colors will not output as one film.

9.0 Content of Completed Design

9.1 | Comment Layers

To ensure that all documentation accompanies the file, use comment layers. When using the report generating features, send the file on the disk as well as a printout.

9.2 | Preflight the Work

9.2.1 | Preflight/Reflight

Preflight/reflight is required by FIRST to assure that everything is set up as intended, and that the files have been tested prior to release from a company for

9.2.1 Preflight/Reflight Preflight/reflight is required by FIRST to assure that everything is set up as intended, and that the files have been tested prior to release from your company for further production.

further production. The most reliable way to do this is to take the disks to another computer. At least, recopy the files from the shipping disks to a different directory on the computer to confirm any links. Turn off or remove all fonts other than the standard 35 (Helvetica, Courier, etc.) and then do what the prepress provider will do. This is known as a "preflight" or "reflight":

■ Open the key file. This will flag any renamed or missing placed images and will show what fonts are used.

■ Load the fonts and try again.

■ Then print the file on a laser printer, at 100%, and tile if necessary. This proof has limitations but is usually the best available at this stage.

■ Compare this carefully to the approved comps. Remember that the use of page layout programs can simplify the production of 100% proofs for large packages.

If an additional check is needed, make a postscript file of the document. This could flag any corrupted printer fonts (if they are being sent with the job).

9.3 | Revised Art

It is the responsibility of the consumer product company to arrange the exact flow artwork revisions must follow and the timeliness in which they are communicated.

Revised files should be renamed with a revision number or date. Do not rely on the operating system modified date because each time the file is opened the date changes. Keep the old file name the same except for the revision number or date.

9.4 | Media

Make sure the disk media chosen is usable by everyone who will receive the disk. Many different media options are acceptable.

9.5 | Maintenance

Disks should be initialized before use and large media should be tested. If the media are more than a few years old, it is wise to reformat with a recent version of the drive's formatting program. Drive vendors will usually update the program for free or for a nominal fee. This maintenance assures compatibility with other computers. Verify that:

■ The disk contains key files.

■ The disk places each design in its own directory, with associated files.

■ The disk places art files.

■ If placed image files are shared by several designs, they can be in a placed image directory.

■ Editable original files are sent if EPS files are not editable.

9.6 | Kerned Suitcase

Screen fonts that are kerned should be included. Font licenses usually allow for this because the printer font is the actual software.

9.9 Documented Reports Send any document reports that have been produced. Remember that these can miss nested files beyond the first level. Include the sources for any fonts from less common vendors.

9.7 | Proprietary Fonts

Send any custom-made fonts, such as logo fonts from the end user (consumer product company).

9.8 | The Template

If it is not stated elsewhere, give the file name, date and source of the template file used to build the design. Send the file itself so that the printer can compare to the template.

9.9 | Document Reports

Send any document reports that have been produced. Remember that these can miss nested files beyond the first level. Include the sources for any fonts from less common vendors.

9.10 | Data Compression Information

To assure compatibility, create compressed files, generally .sea (self-extracting archive) or .zip files, that can be "self-extracting" or "unzipped" by anyone. Do not assume everyone uses the same utility. It is possible to use a program such as StuffIt Deluxe from Aladdin Systems Inc. to segment the files into pieces that will fit on the intended choice of media. The file does not have to be stuffed to use this feature. Be sure to to check with the prepress vendor to determine a compatible compression format.

9-10 Data Compression Information To assure compatibility, create .sea files (Self Extracting Archives).

9.11 | Documenting the Design

The final design may seem very simple to the designer, but it can be difficult to decipher when someone else in the production process starts to work with it. To make the design flow smoothly through production, details must be provided on how it was developed. Most programs, including Illustrator and FreeHand, have report features to list many details about a file. These can provide much of the documentation on a file; although, they often do not report internal information about the contents of placed images. This would require a separate report.

9.12 | Checklist

- List and include key files, FPO files placed in key file.
- List font(s) used (include if necessary).
- List correct names of fonts.
- List software names and versions.
- List final file that prepress is to open, all other support files listed.
- When including more than one design, put one design file and all support files in one folder.
- Annotate any layers that are common.
- List layers to be used with base design.
- Include hard copy of disk directory.
- Include hard copy of final art files, same size or 100%.
- List all file names.
- List all colors—process, special.
- Include instructions for blends.

■ Include instructions for special effects.
■ List of all FPOs.
■ List of all items provided (transparency, disk, color proof, etc.).

9.13 | Materials To Be Sent With the Job:

■ Documentation described in Design Section 9.12.
■ Printouts of document reports.
■ Printout of the disk directory, or the directory of the archive file on the disk.
■ The prepress provider is required to verify in a timely manner that all the parts arrived. This verification also helps the supplier to see how the project is set up, and what designs are included.

9.13.1 | Hard Copy of Electronic File:

The files must be printed to a PostScript level 2 proofing device in an effort to identify potential problems before forwarding for prepress production. The RIPped file should be forwarded along with the non-PostScript version of the same. (Every RIP is a little different, but this step will identify many problems.) Send 100% size (tiled if necessary) marked with the following:

■ File names.
■ The name of the file that printed the proof, and of the placed images.
■ Color Information.
■ Identify which colors are process, which are spot, and which are mixtures.
■ An instruction for blends and note if a blend is in several spot colors.
■ Do all images, illustrations and imported graphics indicate LIVE or FPO?
■ Clearly mark and indicate what art is to be used to create the actual LIVE image.
■ Start and stop points, percentages, colors.
■ FPO Images.

10.0 Electronic/Digital Files

These specifications support the work presently underway within the Committee for Graphic Arts Technology Standards (CGATS) and the International Standards Organization (ISO) Technical Committee for Graphics Technology (TC 130). Both groups are working to develop a standard format for digital data exchange. CGATS is the accredited standards development committee within the American National Standards Institute (ANSI); ISO TC-130 has a similar function in the area of international standards development.

Additional information on the exchange of digital data is available in the Design Section 8.0 of this publication. There are several principles that must be followed when dealing with digital data files to ensure a successful exchange.

10.1 | File Format

Digital files that are exchanged between the originator and the prepress provider must be in a format that can be written, read and manipulated easily by the prepress provider using those files. Digital files must contain data that will ultimately produce film, color proofs and plates that meet specifications.

10.1 File Format Digital files that are exchanged between the originator and the prepress provider must be in a format that can be written, read and manipulated easily by the prepress provider using those files.

10.1.1 | TIFF/IT Files

Prepress files can be exchanged as CMYK raster files using the P1 compliance level of the TIFF/IT file format as defined in *ISO 12639*. Typically, final packages (FP), continuous tone (CT) and line work (LW) files will be required. Incorporate all of the logical parameters for final graphic file output (UCR/GCR, gray balance, register marks, etc.). It is preferred that original Photoshop files of unflattened images be submitted to the prepress provider.

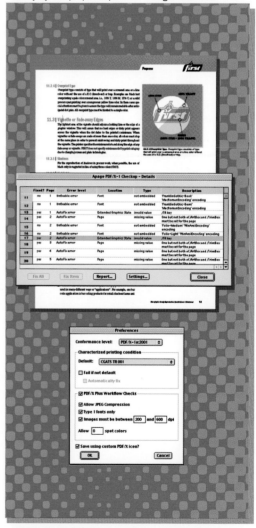

10.1.2 | Portable Document Format (PDF)

PDF is an imaging file format used to transport graphically rich content. It is especially used in computer-to-plate technologies. The "creator" of the file (designer, ad agency, prepress provider) must produce a file that meets the minimum imaging requirements of the "receiver" (prepress provider, printer). PDF/X is a PDF file with restrictions intended to facilitate the transfer of files from "creator" to "receiver" as outlined in *ISO 15930-1:2001*. Additional information can be obtained from the *Adobe PDF reference manual, version 1.3, second edition* and *Adobe Technical Note #5413*. Refer to Design section 8.2 for additional information.

ISO 15930-1:2001 (Graphic Technology – Prepress Digital Data Exchange – Use of PDF Part 1: Complete exchange using CMYK data PDF/X-1 and PDF/X-1a) is both an application standard and a file format standard. It defines a set of conditions to govern the creation, viewing and imaging of PDF/X-1 files. Content and structure of PDF/X-1 files are limited to ensure imaging integrity:

- **Required:** a PDF/X-1 file must contain this object or key.
- **Prohibited:** A PDF/X-1 file must not contain this object or key.
- **Restricted:** Certain values or combinations of objects and keys where contents are required or prohibited.
- **Recommended:** a PDF/X-1 file should contain this key.

The objective is to create a "blind exchange" of graphically rich content ready for imaging.

10.1.2 Portable Document Format (PDF) PDF and PDF/X-1 are imaging file fromats used to transport graphically rich content. It is especially used in computer-to–plate technologies.

10.1.2.1 | Annotations

- Movies, Sounds & File Attachments are *prohibited* because they are not useful for digital imaging.
- Notes, Stamps & Acrobat Forms are *restricted*. They must be positioned outside of the bleed area and must not obscure any portion of the imageable area when displayed on screen.

10.1.2.2 | Key-Value Pairs   The "General Info" dictionary has nine default key-value pairs:

- Title, Subject, Author, Keyword, Creation Date and Mod Date are *required*.
- Creator and Producer are *recommended*.
- Trapped is *restricted*.
- "GTS_PDFX Version" and "GTS_PDFX Conformance" are two additional key-value pairs required by the PDF/X-1 standard.

The trapped key-value pair in the "General Info" dictionary has a default setting of "unknown" which is *prohibited* for PDF/X-1 files. The setting must be changed to either "Yes" (files have been completely trapped) or "No" (file has not been trapped). Partially trapped files are *prohibited* in the PDF/X-1 standard.

10.1.2.3 | Arrays   An array is used to define literal names, integers and strings. It is often used to associate multiple values for a single variable. There are four arrays particularly important for PDF/X-1 files:

- **Media Box**: a *required* array in a PDF/X-1 file. It represents the physical size of the PDF page. It is derived during the PDF creation process from either:
  - PageSize Array (PostScript file).
  - BoundingBox Array (EPS file).
  - Default value determined by the normalizer. (an application used to create a PDF file).
- **Trim Box**: a *restricted* array in a PDF/X-1 file. All PDF/X-1 files must contain either the TrimBox or the ArtBox array but not both. The TrimBox array defines the area of a PDF file that represents the final size of the page after printing and finishing. It uses crop marks and must not exceed the boundaries of the MediaBox. The PDF/X-1 file must be the complete page.
- **ArtBox**: a *restricted* array in a PDF/X-1 file. All PDF/X-1 files must contain either the TrimBox or the ArtBox array but not both. The ArtBox array defines the desired image area in a PDF/X-1 file where only a portion of the page is to be used for imaging. It functions as an electronic "crop" without physically changing the dimension of the PDF/X-1 file. Its boundaries must not exceed those of the MediaBox.
- **BleedBox**: an *optional* array in a PDF/X-1 file. It defines the imaging area in excess of the trim. The boundaries must be within those of the MediaBox but not within those of either the TrimBox or ArtBox.

10.1.2.4 | Fonts   All fonts must be embedded in PDF/X-1 files (*required*). The creator of the PDF/X-1 file must ensure all fonts are used in compliance with licensing agreements.

10.1.2.5 | Compression   Compression of bitmapped images (ImageXObjects) is not required. If compression is desired, the PDF supported methods are *restricted* to include: Flate, RunLength, JPEG, and CCITT Fax.

10.1.2.6 | **Color Space** Content of a PDF/X-1 file may be defined in "DeviceCMYK", "DeviceGray", "Separation", "DeviceN", "Indexed", or "Pattern" color spaces. All are *restricted*. Device dependent and device independent color spaces are *prohibited* ("DeviceRGB", "DefaultRGB", "CalGray", "CalRGB", and "CIELab").

Spot Colors must be defined as either "Separation" or "DeviceN". Black objects must be identified as either "DeviceGray" or "Separation – black".

Characterized Printing Condition:

■ "OutputIntents" array must contain a single "OutputIntents" dictionary whose S key value must be expressed "/GTS_PDFX". This key value is called the "OutputIntent Object". It is *required*.

■ The "OutputIntent Object" must have a corresponding "OutputConditionIdentifier" key value. Acceptable values for this key can be found in the ICC registry of characterized printing conditions. This key value is *restricted*.

■ When the value of the "OutputConditionIdentifier" key matches a characterization found in the ICC registry, the "RegistryName" key value must be defined (http://www.color.org). This key value is *required*.

■ If an "OutputConditionIdentifier" key value is used that is not in the ICC registry, a "DestOutputProfile" key must be present in the "OutputIntent Object". A string value describing the intended printing condition should accompany the "OutputConditionIdentifier" key value. An example of a string value could be: "*This file was prepared in accordance with FIRST 3rd Edition.*"

PDF/X-3:2002 is a superset of PDF/X-1a:2001. It allows for color managed data to be included in color spaces (such as "CIELAb", "CalRGB", or using an embedded ICC profile) while other data can be in Black and/or CMYK. Solid black text will print in solid black without unexpected color shifts spreading the black data to all the process separations.

10.1.2.7 | **Alternate Images** An alternate image is a secondary copy derived from a source Image XObject and is stored in the "Alternate" array. Use of alternate images is *restricted* for PDF/X-1 files.

One application for alternate images is to create a highly compressed low-resolution (72 dpi) replica for each original high-resolution image. The JPEG compressed alternate image will facilitate on-screen viewing. Restrictions for using alternate images include:

■ Alternate Images in the "Alternate" array must have their "DefaultFor Printing" key set to "False".

■ The alternate image must represent the same area as its high-resolution original.

■ If the high-resolution original is edited, the alternate image must be immediately regenerated or destroyed.

10.1.2.8 | **Conformance Levels** The Standard Encryption feature is the Adobe Acrobat method of securing or limiting access rights to a file. Use of the Standard Encryption feature is limited:

■ **PDF/X-1**: Use is *restricted*. Standard encryption can be used; however, viewing and printing can never be denied and the password must be an empty string.

■ **PDF/X-1a:2001**: Use of the Standard Encryption feature is *prohibited*.

Prepress

10.2 File Exchange All potential recipients of digital files must provide information concerning their requirements with respect to standard data formats, proprietary file formats (brand and version) and ability to perform any desired edits or modifications.

10.2 | File Exchange

The provider of digital files must identify the software programs (brand name and version identification) and type fonts (style, manufacturer and version) used to create the original files. Include any other pertinent information that may assist the receiving party in opening, accessing, compensating and outputting the files such as identifying the data compression convention used. All participants prior to sending data must agree upon the method of delivery of digital files (CD-DVD, electronic transmission, etc.).

All potential recipients of digital files must provide information concerning their requirements with respect to standard data formats, proprietary file formats (brand and version) and ability to perform any desired edits or modifications.

It is strongly recommended that, in addition to the original screen and printer design type fonts, Type A suitcases be provided by the designer along with the digital file. The responsibility for licensing resides with both the design firm and the file output supplier in order to avoid copyright infringements or unauthorized duplication of type fonts. The provider must check with the supplier of fonts to make sure that the licenses held for the use of these fonts allow for use not only by the creator, but also by the output service bureau.

Either an electronic or hard copy job jacket should accompany digital files. All business information originating from the customer, such as the information encoded in a bar code, the type of bar code symbol (symbology) required, product identification number, SKU number or other such packaging identification codes should be transmitted using ANSI X12, such as the GCA SPACE/DDAP DEBIES specification. Additional information such as that identified in the EMS EFEX form should be delivered with digital files in either digital (ASCII) or hard copy format.

Until remote proofing is widely implemented and robustly controlled, a hard copy contract proof must be supplied for all digital files regardless of delivery process. This proof should include all of the required sign-off documentation. Refer to Prepress Section 15.0 for proofing information.

11.0 Job Assembly

11.1 | Image Trapping

Image trapping is accomplished through the use of chokes and spreads. This technique should be used when two colors are adjacent to each other whether the graphics are line or screen.

IMAGE TRAP TOLERANCE

WIDE WEB		PROCESS TO TO PROCESS	LINE TO LINE TO PROCESS	LINE TO LINE TO LINE
PREPRINT LINERBOARD	SBS Board	±0.0035" ±0.089 mm	±0.01" ±0.254 mm	±0.01" ±0.254 mm
COMBINED CORRUGATED	Bleached White	±0.03" ±0.762 mm	±0.03" ±0.762 mm	±0.03" ±0.762 mm
	Coated Paper	±0.015" ±0.381mm	±0.015" ±0.381 mm	±0.015" ±0.381 mm
FOLDING CARTON	SBS Board	±0.003" ±0.076 mm	±0.003" ±0.076 mm	±0.0075" ±0.1905 mm
	CRB Board	±0.003" ±0.076 mm	±0.0045" ±0.114 mm	±0.0055" ±0.14 mm
MULTIWALL BAG	Coated Paper	±0.0075" ±0.1905 mm	±0.0175" ±0.444 mm	±0.0175 ±0.444 mm
	Uncoated Paper	±0.0075" ±0.1905 mm	±0.015" ±0.381 mm	±0.03" ±0.762 mm
FILM PRODUCTS	All	±0.0075" ±0.1905 mm	±0.0075" ±0.1905 mm	±0.0075" ±0.1905 mm

NARROW WEB		PROCESS TO PROCESS	LINE TO PROCESS	LINE TO LINE
PAPER PRODUCTS	All	±0.0045" ±0.0114 mm	±0.005" ±0.13 mm	±0.005" ±0.013 mm
FILM PRODUCTS	All	±0.0045" ±0.114 mm	±0.005" ±0.13 mm	±0.005" ±0.13 mm

11.2 | Type Reproduction

11.2.1 | Text and Graphic Elements for Line Print Decks

Fine serifs, medium or small type and thin lines must comply with specifications. All text printed on a line deck must be printed in a single color. Combining tints with text and/or solids should be avoided. Check with the printer prior to producing final graphics for current specifications.

11.2.2 | Process Color Type and Graphics

When type is created with multiple colors, the dominant color must be used to hold the type shape. The lighter color(s) must be compensated to eliminate any obvious misregistration that is likely to occur in the printing process. Lighter colors used to create multi-color elements should be held back by one row of dots in all directions as measured by the screen count to be used when printing the image. Multi-color type made with process colors must be limited to three colors.

11.2.3 | Process Reversed/Knockout Text

When type is reversed out of a color and has no holding line, the use of a single color outline will greatly enhance the reproduction capabilities of the process and the impact of the final printed product as well. Fine serifs, medium and small type, and thin lines should be avoided when possible. Reverse copy printed on a line print deck should be limited to one color; type and rule lines should be confined to sizes no less than those indicated on the following charts.

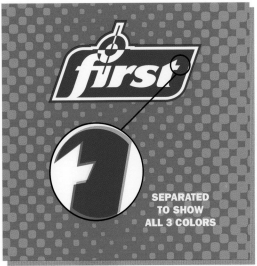

11.2.2 Process Color Type and Graphics Multi-color type made with process colors must be limited to three colors.

MINIMUM TYPE SIZE

WIDE WEB		POSITIVE SERIF	POSITIVE SANS SERIF	REVERSE SERIF	REVERSE SANS SERIF
PREPRINT LINERBOARD	SBS Board	8 pt.	6 pt.	10 pt.	8 pt.
COMBINED CORRUGATED	Bleached White	8 pt.	6 pt.	10 pt.	8 pt.
	Coated Paper	6 pt.	4 pt.	8 pt.	6 pt.
FOLDING CARTON	SBS Board	6 pt.	4 pt.	8 pt.	6 pt.
	CRB Board	6 pt.	4 pt.	8 pt.	6 pt.
MULTIWALL BAG	Coated Paper	8 pt.	6 pt.	12 pt.	10 pt.
	Uncoated Paper	10 pt.	8 pt.	18 pt.	12 pt.
FILM PRODUCTS	Polyester	8 pt.	6 pt.	12 pt.	10 pt.
	Polypropylene Clear	8 pt.	6 pt.	10 pt.	8 pt.
	Polypropylene Opaque White	8 pt.	6 pt.	10 pt.	8 pt.
	Polyethylene Clear	8 pt.	6 pt.	10 pt.	8 pt.
	Polyethylene Opaque White	8 pt.	6 pt.	10 pt.	8 pt.
	Metallized	8 pt.	6 pt.	10 pt.	6 pt.

NARROW WEB		POSITIVE SERIF	POSITIVE SANS SERIF	REVERSE SERIF	REVERSE SANS SERIF
PAPER PRODUCTS	All	6 pt.	4 pt.	8 pt.	6 pt.
FILM PRODUCTS	All	6 pt.	4 pt.	8 pt.	6 pt.

MINIMUM RULE WIDTHS

WIDE WEB		POSITIVE RULE	REVERSE RULE
PREPRINT LINERBOARD	SBS Board	0.01"	0.254 mm	0.015"	0.38 mm
COMBINED CORRUGATED	Bleached White	0.013"	0.33 mm	0.02"	0.51 mm
	Coated Paper	0.007"	0.18 mm	0.01"	0.254 mm
FOLDING CARTON	SBS Board	0.006"	0.15 mm	0.008"	0.20 mm
	CRB Board	0.006"	0.15 mm	0.008"	0.20 mm
MULTIWALL BAG	Coated Paper	0.007"	0.18 mm	0.01"	0.254 mm
	Uncoated Paper	0.013"	0.33 mm	0.02"	0.51 mm
FILM PRODUCTS	All	0.007"	0.18 mm	0.015"	0.38 mm

NARROW WEB		POSITIVE RULE	REVERSE RULE
PAPER PRODUCTS	Coated Paper	0.005"	0.13 mm	0.01"	0.254 mm
FILM PRODUCTS	All	0.004"	0.10 mm	0.008"	0.20 mm

11.2.4 | Overprint Type

Overprint type consists of type that will print over a screened area or a line color without the use of a K.O. (knock-out) or trap. Examples are black text overprinting a pale color screened area, i.e., 10% Y, 10% M, 15% C; or a solid process cyan printing over a non-process yellow line color. In these cases special attention must be given to assure the type will remain readable after anticipated dot gain. All overprint type must be limited to a single color.

11.3 | Vignette or Fade-away Edges

The lightest area of the vignette should adjoin a holding line or the edge of a graphic window. This will assure that no hard edges or dirty print appears across the vignette when the dot fades to the printer's minimum. When vignettes or fade-aways are made of more than one color, all colors must stop at the same place in order to prevent rainbowing and dirty print throughout the vignette. The printer specifies the minimum dot used along the edge of any fade-away or vignette. FIRST does not specify minimum dot by print category due to changing screen and plate technologies.

11.3.1 | Shadows

For the reproduction of shadows in process work, when possible, the use of black only is suggested in lieu of using three colors (C, M, Y).

11.3.2 | Highlights

In highlight areas, whether one color or multiple colors, dots smaller than the minimum dot based on printer specifications, should be eliminated from final compensated art. Failure to support the minimum dot will increase the likelihood of dot bridging, hard edges, excess highlight dot gain or dirty print.

11.4 | Eye Marks

Eye marks are used to stop the flow of filling material in register with the print on either the converting equipment for pre-formed packaging or on automatic loading equipment for form and fill production.

Specifications for eye mark size, location and colors vary greatly and depend upon the requirements of the converting equipment. It is the responsibility of the consumer product company and the printer to provide machine specifications, blueprint or die layouts for exact eye-mark locations to the designer or prepress provider to ensure that the printed material will correctly trigger the electric eye. The eye mark lane (running in the machine direction) should be kept clear of any patterns or copy to allow for uninterrupted visibility by the electric eye. If the eye mark requires more than one color, the underprinted colors must be made smaller by the amount required for register compensation.

11.5 | Bar Codes

11.5.1 | Bar-code Specifications

Bar-code print specifications are produced by combining three types of related specifications:

■ **Application Standards** are published by accredited standards organizations. Before explaining what application standards specify, it might be useful to know more about what they are. Simply put, bar codes are used in many different ways or "applications". For example, one bar code application is bar coding products for retail checkout lanes and

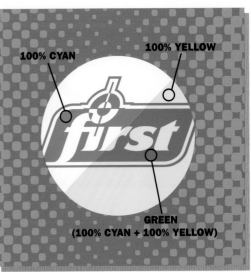

11.2.4 Overprint Type Overprint type consists of type that will print over a screened area or a line color without the use of a K.O. (knock-out) or trap.

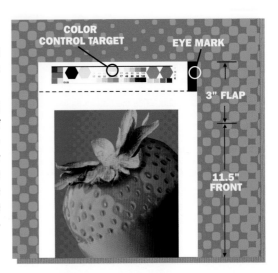

11.4 Eye Marks Eye marks are used to stop the flow of filling material in register with the print on either the converting equipment for pre-formed packaging or on automatic loading equipment for form and fill production. Specifications for eye mark size, location and colors vary greatly and depend upon the requirements of the converting equipment.

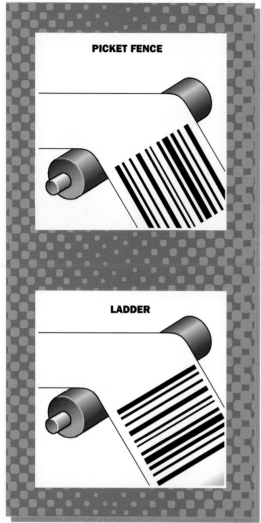

11.5.1 Barcodes Barcode orientation is critical. The top figure illustrates the bars on the UPC symbol traveling in the machine direction, while the bottom figure, illustrates the bars running across the press direction. If print slur occurs with the symbol in the picket fence orientation, the bars grow in length only and are still scannable; however the symbol printed in the cross web direction will cause the bars to grow in width, likely causing the code on the printed package to fail minimum grade specifications.

another application is bar coding shipments for conveyor lane routing in distribution centers. The specifications for the bar codes in these two application areas are different because the conditions for scanning the bar codes are very different. Accredited standards organizations (see Appendix) provide specifications in the form of guidelines and standards to assist in answering:

- What bar code type should be used?
- How to structure the data inside the bar code?
- How to print human-readable information that is inside the bar code?
- What bar code size ranges are acceptable?
- Where the bar code should be placed on the package or container?
- What are the minimum print quality requirements?

- **Print Specifications** prescribe a minimal level of capability for all printers. All specifications will fall within the acceptable specification limits of the appropriate application standard for the bar code being printed. Print specifications will assist in answering:
  - What is the minimum size for a bar code depending on selected printing press type and substrate?
  - How should the bar code be oriented given the direction the web will travel?

- **Job Specifications** should be published within the job specification for film or plate output. This type of specification should answer:
  - What output resolution should be used for film or plate production?
  - What bar-width reduction (BWR) should be used in film or plate production?

Because scanners read bar code graphics, they must be produced in a scannable color according to the specifications appropriate to the application standard, printing press type, substrate type, and film/plate output conditions. There are many considerations that apply when producing any bar code.

11.5.2 | Bar Code Type

For prepress operations that design their own bar codes, there is software that can produce a full range of bar code types. Some of the common bar code types printed by flexographic printers include:

- U.P.C. (Version A and Version E).
- U.P.C. Supplemental Symbols (2-digit and 5-digit versions).
- EAN-13.
- ITF (Interleaved 2-of-5).
- Code 128 (UCC/EAN-128).
- Code 39.

11.5.3 | Encoding Bar Code Data

A good manufacturing practice for each phase of the production process is to confirm that the human readable text associated with the bar code matches the information encoded within the symbol. It is the responsibility of the supplier providing final films or plates to ensure the bar code is properly encoded. However, it is in the printer's best interest to check the encoding for accuracy. The UCC has provided a spreadsheet for calculating check digits to the FTA and can be found in the Appendix and on the enclosed CD.

11.5.4 | Bar Code Colors

The optimum bar code color combination is opaque black ink for the bars and opaque white substrate or ink for the background. Bar codes with bars printed in opaque black, dark blue, or dark green ink and opaque white material or white, red, orange, pink, peach, or yellow ink, as the background, generally scan successfully. It is important to remember that colors with acceptable ANSI Symbol Contrast on an opaque substrate may be completely unacceptable on an opaque substrate of another color or on a translucent or transparent substrate. When printing on a transparent substrate or colored substrate, a solid, light-colored (white is optimum) background, with maximum reflectance, is recommended in the area where the bar code is to be located. It is recommended that bar code symbols should not be placed on a plate used to provide a large solid coverage of ink. This is because these plates may have requirements for extra impression and a higher volume of ink. Ink color specifications should be evaluated individually for different substrates.

Bar codes require bars with sharp edges in order for the scanner to correctly read the code. The bars and the background of a bar code must each be printed in only one color on a single print station. This is because scanning accuracy is reduced if the symbol bars are printed in two separate print stations due to variation in register. The supplier providing final compensated art must ensure that the bar code's bars and background colors are of the correct color and location on the specified layers.

11.5.4 Bar Code Colors The bars and the background in a bar code must each be printed in only one ink on a single print station, otherwise scanning accuracy is reduced due to variation in register from being printed in two separate print stations.

11.5.5 | Bar Code Size

11.5.5.1 | Overall Dimensions Bar code symbol sizes are specified in different ways. For example, EAN/UPC symbols that are scanned by omni-directional point-of-sale scanners have a fixed relationship between height and width and are specified in a range of magnifications (80% – 200%) around a nominal size. Other methods of specifying a symbol's size include providing the area reserved for the symbol (including its quiet zones) or providing the symbol's narrow element width (X-dimension). Printing a bar code below the minimum size specified by the applicable symbol specification and printing constraints specified by the printer is not supported by FIRST. All compliant printers will be able to meet the minimum bar code sizes identified.

It is necessary to specify the addressable imaging resolution whenever bar code symbols are

MINIMUM BAR CODE MAGNIFICATION		
WIDE WEB		**MACHINE DIRECTION**
PREPRINT LINERBOARD	**SBS Board**	100%
COMBINED CORRUGATED Flute Dependant	**All**	UPC: 110%–200% ITF-14: 100%
FOLDING CARTON	**SBS Board**	100%
	CRB Board	100%
MULTIWALL BAG	**Coated Paper**	115%
	Uncoated Paper	115%
FILM PRODUCTS	**Polyester**	100%
	Polypropylene Clear	100%
	Polypropylene Opaque White	100%
	Polyethylene Clear	100%
	Polyethylene Opaque White	100%
	Metallized	100%
NARROW WEB		**MACHINE DIRECTION**
PAPER PRODUCTS	**Coated Paper**	80%
FILM PRODUCTS	**All**	100%

11.5.5.2 Truncation of Bar Codes Certain symbols have a fixed relationship between their height and width, while others have minimum heights specified. Bar code truncation is a reduction of a symbol's height below the application standard or symbol specification and is not supported.

11.5.6 Quiet Zones Quiet zones allow scanners to detect when a bar code starts and stops. Quiet zones are based on multiples of the symbol's narrowest element width (X-dimension). Minimum quiet zone specifications depend on the symbol specified.

designed. This slightly adjusts the symbol dimensions before output. This is because bar codes, unlike typical graphic images, are machine-readable elements based on predictable decoding formulas. The bar code output size must be based on the resolution of the output device, most likely the film plotter or plate imaging device. The UCC refers to these adjustments as "Corrected Magnification" when applied to the symbol's overall size and "Corrected BWR" when applied to the symbol's BWR. These adjustments should also apply to the special EAN/UPC symbol characters 1, 2, 7 and 8 when output at higher resolutions. Digital bar code files should only be resized using the bar code design software package that originated them and which accounted for output resolution.

To learn more about correcting symbol dimensions to accommodate the addressable output resolution of the output device refer to UCC's "*Guidelines for Producing Quality Symbols*". Information for suppliers of bar code design software, refer to the UCC's "*Guidelines for Providers of EAN/UPC Symbol Design Software*".

11.5.5.2 | Truncation of Bar Codes Certain symbols have a fixed relationship between their height and width, while others have minimum heights specified. Bar code truncation is a reduction of a symbol's height below the application standard or symbol specification and is not supported by FIRST.

11.5.6 | Quiet Zones

The quiet zone is the area, free of printing, that precedes the left bar and follows the right bar in a bar code symbol. The quiet zones allow scanners to detect when a bar code starts and stops. Quiet zones are based on multiples of the symbol's narrowest element width (X-dimension). Minimum quiet zone specifications depend on the symbol specified. For example, the UPC-A symbol requires a quiet zone of 9X on each side, while an ITF-14 symbol (Interleaved 2-of-5 symbol specified by the UCC) requires a 10X quiet zone on each side. Bar code specifications where the quiet zone is omitted, obstructed or too small are not supported by FIRST.

11.5.7 | Bar-width Reduction

Bar widths increase in flexographic printing in a manner similar to dot gain. As the bar widths increase, the space width between the bars decreases correspondingly. It is best to print bar codes under the same conditions as dots are printed in order to minimize bar growth (plate material, mounting material, anilox roller). Just as a dot curve is typically applied to a process image to account for expected dot gain on press, a bar-width reduction is typically applied to a bar code prior to output to account for the bar growth expected on the press. The amount of BWR specified should be corrected at the symbol design stage for digital bar codes files. Refer to Print Section 20.9 for more details on bar-width reduction. Different print conditions will also result in varying bar gain during print. Refer to Print Section 20.6 for a press characterization method for bar codes or contact the printer for specific recommendations. Bar code design specifications outside the BWR specified by the printer are not supported by FIRST.

11.5.8 | Bar Code Distortion

It is not recommended to place bar codes in the cross direction because of slurring and other problems associated with this position. However, if placement in the cross direction is unavoidable and the design requires the bars in the bar code to be placed perpendicular to the direction the web is moving through the press, distortion of the bar code is necessary to account for the plate cylinder circumference. This distortion will introduce pixel-rounding errors into the bar code unless the bar code design software accounts for this input variable in the design stage (refer to the UCC's "*Guidelines for Providers of EAN/UPC Symbol Design Software*"). If it does, follow the procedures provided by the software provider. If the software does not account for distortion when the symbol is created and distortion is unavoidable, outputting the file at the highest possible resolution (e.g., 4,000 dpi) is advised to avoid introducing rounding errors.

11.5.9 | Symbol Attributes

For every film or plate that has a bar code image, prepress should record and be able to provide the printer with the following attributes:

- Bar code type.
- Bar code size (magnification).
- Bar code's BWR.
- Output resolution used to generate the film or plate.

11.6 | Template Layout
(Also known as key line, die strike, full scale drawing)

The template is the key line, mechanical or die vinyl, also referred to as conventional art. Usually a separate layer is used to identify various elements of the template.

Where applicable a template should include:

- Glue tab.
- Quiet zone.
- Non-print areas.
- Side of box (inside vs. outside).
- Varnish areas.
- Print direction.
- Copy limits.
- Seal area.
- Eyemarks.
- Printer's marks (micro dots, cross hairs, color control bars, etc.).

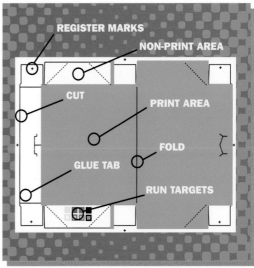

11.6 Template Layout The template must be provided by the printer. Supplied templates must include all pertinent information that must be considered during the design and prepress phase.

In a digital file, the final template must be given to the prepress provider to ensure all job elements are correctly positioned as required for the product assembly. It is the prepress provider's responsibility to bring to the attention of the customer and design firm any areas that violate quiet zones or non-image areas. When prepress providers use these areas for the placement of scales and/or targets, it is their responsibility to assure the non-print or quiet areas of the product are not violated.

If a product is to be die cut, a final die vinyl and digital file must be provided with the art before beginning final art assembly. All supplied die vinyls must indicate cuts, folds and scores as well as non-print areas. The prepress provider is responsible for verifying that the art was prepared correctly as identified on the die vinyl. If any known violations are observed, the prepress provider is also responsible for contacting the customer and design firm prior to preparing the final file for film and/or plate making. All contract proofs must contain the supplied die lines. Film overlays on the proof or blueprints are acceptable.

The design firm, in conjunction with the consumer product company, should indicate areas where color control targets may be placed to measure the conformity to specification. Refer to the Design Section 4.5 for additional template layout specifications.

12.0 Color Separations

Reference *ISO 12647-6 (Graphic Technology – Process Control for the Manufacture of Halftone Colour Separations, Proofs and Production Prints – Part 6: Flexographic Printing)* for additional information.

12.1 Gray Balance

Gray balance is critical to good color reproduction, and is a function of ink hue, ink film thickness and the percentage of dot area being printed. Color sequence, ink trapping, press characteristics and dot gain also affect gray bal-

GRAY BALANCE EXAMPLE					
FILM DOT PERCENTAGE ALL PRINT SEGMENTS					
CYAN	5%	10%	30%	70%	90%
MAGENTA	3%	7%	24%	58%	78%
YELLOW	3%	7%	24%	58%	78%
BLACK	8%	14%	35%	76%	98%

ance. Proper gray balance ensures that a tone of appropriate cyan, magenta and yellow tint values is visually perceived as neutral gray.

If process inks were perfect color filters, with each color absorbing the proper third of the visible spectrum, then cyan would absorb only red light, magenta would absorb only green light and yellow would only absorb blue light. Equal amounts of cyan, magenta and yellow ink could then be printed, and the eye would receive equal amounts of red, green and blue light. This result would be seen as a neutral gray. Unfortunately, this is not the case. Pigments that comprise the process colors are not as pure as the theory suggests; yellow typically contains ~10% magenta; magenta and cyan contain much higher percentages of the other two colors. This contamination is known as hue error. Because gray balance is achieved when we see equal portions of red, green and blue light, the amount of C, M, Y printed must be adjusted to account for this hue error. Gray balance is not achieved by printing equally sized cyan, magenta and yellow dots; this combination would print a reddish-brown. Rather, the size of yellow and magenta dots must be reduced in relation to cyan. The amount of the reduction is based on the contamination of the colors, so the combined dots absorb equal amounts of red, green and blue light.

To achieve neutral gray, solid ink density is adjusted to achieve the most saturated two-color overprints in red, green and blue. Gray balance is then realized by varying the dot sizes in neutral areas to achieve gray tones. For these reasons, color correction is always necessary in the color separation process. The dot percentages in the table are an example of gray balance. The actual dot percentages required to produce a neutral gray need to be determined on a case-by-case basis. The dot gain, density, color of process inks, and trapping characteristics of each press will determine what values to place in the film to achieve the correct printed dot areas. In addition to neutrals, gray balance affects near neutrals (flesh tones) and all but the most saturated tones in the reproduction.

12.2 | Total Area Coverage (TAC)

Also known as Tone Value Sum in ISO documentation, total area coverage (TAC) is typically measured in the darkest shadow area of a process image by adding together the dot percentages of CMYK on the final films. For example: If C, M, Y, and K each equal 75%, the total area coverage is 300%; if all four process colors were printed solid, TAC would be 400%. Because flexographic printing inks typically dry between stations, it is preferable to achieve as high a total area coverage as possible. Total area coverage is measured in the full color file prior to applying a compensation curve.

	CORRRUGATED	PAPER	FILM
WIDE WEB	270% – 300%	290% – 320%	300% – 340%
NARROW WEB	N/A	290% – 320%	300% – 340%

12.3 | Under Color Removal (UCR)

Under color removal is the balanced reduction of cyan, magenta and yellow in shadow areas. The addition of black in these reduced areas maintains the dark and near neutral shadows. UCR, used in traditional offset separations, is not always best suited for the flexographic printing process. Ideally, if the amount of color in the three process colors could be reduced while maintaining the shape and shadow detail of the image in all three colors, this would be the best application of under color removal for the flexographic printing process. UCR is done at the input/scanning or color correction stage and is measured prior to applying a compensation curve. Contact the printer for guidance.

12.4 | Gray Component Replacement (GCR)

Gray component replacement is more easily defined as an unwanted color (cyan in red or magenta in green) being replaced by black, in part or in whole as the graying component. The use of GCR is the responsibility of the prepress provider and the printer that will be printing the job. Under normal conditions, in the flexographic printing process, it is recommended that GCR be restricted to a single unwanted color. Reviewing the job with the printer or customer prior to prepress will help determine the best approach. The prepress provider and the printer should reach consensus on the amount (percent) of GCR used in an image.

When the printer is forced to print line black on the same station as the process black GCR should not be used. It is better to have a short black for the separation (skeleton black) so that the printer has more latitude in setting impression.

12.5 | FIRST Control Target

The FIRST control target contains major elements required to be monitored during make ready and should remain on the job throughout the entire production run if possible. This target is available to all members and non-members through the FTA as an electronic file. This target was originally created to fit in most eye mark tracks during job make ready and must be removed prior to saving finished goods. Based on the space available on the press form, elements of the target may have to be rearranged to fit in the space available.

The target is comprised of specific elements designed to measure color and gray balance components and parameters. Proofing and image setter control, film processor stability, dot gain compensation, plate exposure guide, dot gain values achieved during the press characterization, slur, gray balance and ink trap-

12.4 Gray Component Replacement (GCR) "GCR Short Black" This separation is a traditional offset type reproduction using a long (full range) cyan and a short (skeleton) black. The left side of the bottom image is four color and right side is Y, M, K with no cyan.

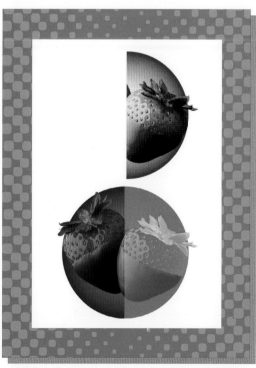

12.4 Gray Component Replacement (GCR) "GCR Short Cyan" This separation represents a 100% GCR reproduction without UCR using a long (full range) black and short (skeleton) cyan. The left side of the bottom image is four color and right side is Y, M, C with no black. The right side (top illustration) displays a 100% GCR approach to the black.

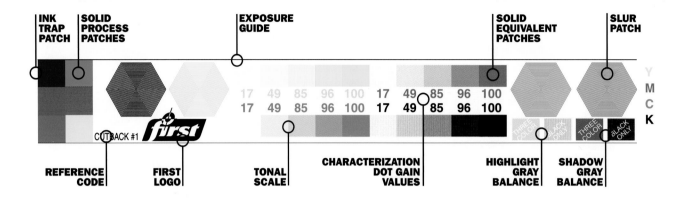

12.5 Color Control Targets The illustration above is a control target which incorporates all the necessary points of measurement required to be monitored by these specifications and is available from the FTA.

ping can all be measured. The information from this target will verify current printing conditions and flag any changes in printing conditions since the press was last characterized.

12.5.1 | Ink Trap Patch

This patch is used to verify solid ink trap. If less than 100% ink coverage produces the highest density, these scales must contain that screen value in each overprint target.

12.5.2 | Solid Process Patches

These patches should remain 100% regardless of the maximum screen value used in lieu of solids.

12.5.3 | Exposure Guide

Micro-fine rules assess proper photopolymer face exposures. This target is available in five resolutions depending upon the line screen used. It is necessary to select and incorporate the appropriate resolution control target. After exposing and processing the plate, the micro line must be straight to the touch. Failure to hold this line straight is an indication of under exposure that will lead to dirty print and bridging.

LPI	MICROLINE WIDTH
55 lpi | 22 lpcm	3.0mils | 0.08 mm
65–85 lpi | 26–33 lpcm	2.5 mils | 0.06 mm
100–120 lpi | 39–47 lpcm	2.0 mils | 0.05 mm
133–175 lpi | 52–69 lpcm	1.5 mils | 0.04 mm
200 lpi | 79 lpcm	1.3 mils | 0.03 mm

12.5.4 Slur Patch

This target monitors correct pressure settings and slur. There are two resolution slur targets; one is used for coarse screen rulings under 85 lpi, and the other is used for 100 lpi and finer.

12.5.5 Reference Code

Once a press has been characterized, this number identifies that the proper cutback has been applied.

12.5.6 Tonal Steps

From left to right the target contains 3% (or minimum dot), 10%, 30%, 70%, 100% or solid equivalent in the compensated plate (or file if directly imaged).

12.5.7 | Dot Gain Values

After the press characterization has been evaluated, the dot gain percentages actually achieved are to be inserted by the prepress provider. This will provide the press operator with the actual dot gains required to achieve a color match.

12.5.8 | Gray Balance Scales

This area of the target is used to monitor gray balance. The prepress provider must adjust these tone values so that, under normal print gains, a neutral gray in the three-color area appears the same density as the single black screen in the adjacent box for both the highlight and three-quarter tone. The prepress provider takes into consideration the density, dot gain and gray balance.

12.5.9 | Highlight Gray Balance

If the three-color area of the start-up target is not the same density or neutrality as the adjacent black tint, it is most likely due to an imbalance in dot gain. This is further reinforced if the shadow gray balance is neutral gray.

12.5.10 | Shadow Gray Balance

If the three-color area of the start-up target is not the same density and hue as the adjacent black tint, it is most likely due to:

1. Density being off target;

2. Poor ink trapping; or,

3. Shadow dot gain out of balance.

12.6 FIRST Run Target

Certain press configurations (narrow web) and package types (poly bags) may not have large enough trim areas to keep the FIRST control target on the web throughout the run. On these packages, the FIRST run target should be placed on the live area of the package to verify the density and minimum dot size remain consistent throughout the pressrun. The FIRST run target contains the minimum data necessary to monitor the run from the beginning to end. Both the FIRST control and run targets must be imaged at the same time and with the same care and accuracy as the actual image. Surprinting, plate slugs or plate build-up of the control/run target is not an accurate representation of the live image area and are therefore not acceptable.

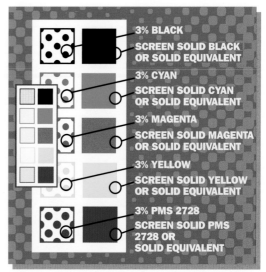

12.6 Run Targets should be placed, if possible, on the live area of the package to verify the density and minimum dot size remain consistent after the control targets have been removed. This is the minimum data necessary to monitor the run from the beginning to end.

13.0 CIELab Color Management

13.1 | Introduction

Color Management Systems (CMS) are a collection of software tools that quantify and reconcile the color differences between monitors, scanners, imagesetters, proofers and printing presses to ensure consistent color throughout the reproduction process. Typically, the available color gamut diminishes as a job progresses through the production cycle. A CMS will map colors from a larger gamut and indicate what colors are achievable in a device with a smaller gamut, such as a printing press. This process allows for realistic expectations to be set during the proofing process.

CIELab based color management uses the CIELab color space to quantify color independent of the device used to produce that color. Using the CIELab color space, colors are numerically defined, allowing the use of mathematical models and algorithms that permit color conversion based upon the measured color capabilities of an identified process. A device-independent color space enables conversion from one ingredient-based color space to another. Examples of ingredient based color systems are RGB and CMYK. RGB color ingredients refer to phosphors in a monitor, dyes in a transparency, photomultiplier tubes in scanners, or charged-coupled device (ccd) array processors in digital cameras. They can all have the same numerical RGB value but not match because of the different ingredients. CMYK color ingredients include toner powders or dyes in digital proofs, wax in thermal proofs, and different pigments in solvent, water and UV inks. The device-independent model gives the closest color match when moving from one ingredient-based system to another. Both input and output color "ingredients" are specified colorimetrically, using a spectrophotometer, and are easily compared for conversion between ingredient based color systems.

In order for CMS to be effective, a commitment to calibrate and characterize each production center and to maintain these systems must be made by every supplier contributing to the production of the package. The three most common stages of color management are:

13.1.1 | Stage 1: The Calibration of Digital Proofing Device To Current Analog Proofing System

Output the characterization target (FIRST recommends the IT8.7/4 proposed target) to film and make a proof to specifications for a selected print segment. It is important to check the dot accuracy of the films prior to proofing to assure that they meet the specification requirements. These films should then be proofed on the analog proofing system. Prior to using this proof, measure and verify that the proof is made to the manufacturer's recommendations and the values achieved are within FIRST specifications. At this point, measure and input the color values achieved in each overprint to create a spectral profile of the analog proofing system. The profile created of the analog proofing system can then be utilized to create a proof using the digital proofing system that will match the analog proof. For machine maintenance, calibration and use refer to the manufacturer's recommendations. For creating the profile implementation and use, follow the procedure recommended by the software provider.

13.1.2 | Stage 2: Characterize the Press to Create the CMS Profile

In addition to the procedure above, it is necessary to output the characterization target to film (or direct to plate) and make a plate. These plates must be made, mounted and printed under normal operating conditions to FIRST specifications. The result of this pressrun will be used to create the press's profile (characterization). The accuracy of this pressrun is paramount in the successful implementation of this stage of color management. A proof is not required for this stage. Stage 2 should not be undertaken until the press has been optimized. Refer to Print Sections 18.1 Press Optimization and 18.2 Print Optimization for more information.

The characterization target should be compensated for dot gain. When generating the characterization target, estimate the proper dot gain compensation, based upon dot gain values measured by the printer during routine pressruns (using a control or run target on jobs). After printing the target, any difference between the estimated and actual values can be corrected by applying a tonal adjustment to the plate curve. In a properly compensated characterization target, the 50% tint (in the electronic file) will reproduce on press at about 67% (as measured using a reflection densitometer calculating dot percent based on

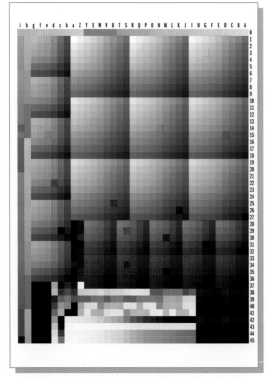

13.1.1 Calibration of Digital Proofing Device to Current Analog Proofing System FIRST recommends outputting the IT8.7/4 proposed characterization chart to film and making a proof to specifications for the selected print segment.

the Murray-Davies equation). This is important for two reasons. First, the test target is comprised of CMYK values, yet CIELab values are measured on press. For good statistical sampling, those CIELab values should be evenly distributed throughout the CIELab color space. If the 50% dot reproduces as 67% on press then there will be even distribution of color data (assuming even distribution of CMYK values in the test target). Secondly, all color management software uses mathematical modeling to calculate color values that are not specifically measured in the test target. These mathematical models will be more accurate if the CIELab data is measured in processes where the 50% dot reproduces at about 67%.

If it is unclear what the specifications are and if they have been achieved, color management is not appropriate at this time. In order to realize the benefits of moving to the next stage, the printing process must first be in control; dot gain, density, ink trap, and print contrast along with other print attributes must be routinely achieved

13.1.3 | Stage 3: Calibrating the Process from Image Capture To the Final Print Result

In addition to the procedures in Prepress Section 13.1.1 and 13.1.2, further calibration is required. Calibrate the RGB devices and combine RGB profiles with the CMYK profiles from step one and two. This will enable a facsimile on screen to match the proof or press. Palette software, when loaded with a profile, can give the CMYK for a specific press when using a spectrophotometer. A monitor calibration is needed to make images match on screen in multiple software or to simulate a press. Monitor calibrations of scanners or digital cameras are RGB. Checking the integrity of the RGB profile using a RGB gray scale is imperative.

Color management systems must be worked into current workflow systems. Some devices will not accept CIELab profiles, while others are equipped with proprietary systems. Several models of scanners cannot export unclipped or raw RGB files. An open architecture system is recommended to have the capability to move files effectively from system to system.

All digital proofs must contain the FIRST control target in addition to any scale required by the hardware or software manufacturers in order to verify the integrity of the proof.

13.2 | CMS and CIELab Applications

The first step in color management is monitoring and calibrating the processes. By capturing spectral data, a database is built that can be used to identify measurements that are out of tolerance. This database is also used to improve the process by recording the historical trends and by providing an opportunity for skilled observers to identify cause and effect relationships. Measurement, documentation, calibration and control are tools and procedures that are essential in a CMS workflow.

■ **Measurement:** the color management system, (CMS), is an electronic system that maps the color space or color gamut for any input or output device, i.e. scanner, monitor, proofing device and press. Color profiles are built by using a spectrophotometer and CMS software. These profiles can be used to move an image from one color space to another, such as RGB to CMYK, or from one press profile to another press profile. One expected benefit is that a single graphic packaging file can be

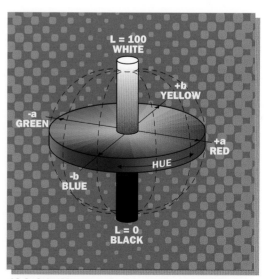

13.2 Color Management To minimize the subjective color shifts based upon the way one person is viewing the color versus another is to use a spectrophotometer. Utilizing CIELab color space, colors are numerically identified which allows the use of a mathematical tolerancing system and can minimize the variation of human perception.

13.2.1 Characterize the Press to Create the CMS Profile it is necessary to output the characterization target to film and make a plate to the specifications for the selected print segment. These plates must be made, mounted and printed under normal operating conditions to specifications, the result of which will be used to create the press's profile.

used for multiple printing segments because various profiles can be applied to the file. A CIELab profile very accurately simulates the correct ink hue, ink density, dot gain, visual appearance of ink on substrate, and print appearance at different stages of the conversion process. CIELab should be applied at the early stages of design or prepress. CMS provides for accurate contract proofs in the design/prepress stages that are used to predict the print outcome. The customer can make changes in the design, color, or materials if a result different from the contract proof is desired.

- **Calibration:** A calibration system must be in place for input, output, and measurement in the design, prepress, and print stages. CMS tools must be used in conjunction with the calibration systems already in place. Calibration of each device must be performed to provide accurate measuring results. Incoming consumables must be measured for consistency: inks, substrates, proofing materials, etc.

- **Control:** CMS is a tool that can be used to open overprints, correct gray balance, and increase the saturation of clean colors. CMS is used with analog and digital proofs. Some attributes available through digital systems using CIELab can provide more accurate proofing. Examples include: before and after lamination, nonstandard inks, print outcome with specific anilox rollers and print on various substrates. Using profiles for press simulation enables the production of a press ready file that has been modified pixel by pixel.

13.2.1 | Characterization Target

Most color management systems have their own unique test target from which the color profile (ICC profile) is created. There are industry standard targets also available such as the FIRST target (introduced in the Premier Edition of FIRST), the ECI (European Color Initiative) target and the IT8.7/4 proposed data set. In an effort to reduce the number of "standard" targets, FIRST now recommends using the IT8.7/4 proposed data set when characterizing the printing process. This data set is the result of the collaborative efforts of several standards committees and represents the best technical approach to a standard target.

There are two default layouts or "targets" based on the proposed IT8.7/4 data set. These are a "visual layout" target and a "random layout" target. Both contain exactly the same combinations of CMYK data. The random layout target should be used for print characterization. By randomizing the locations of the various CMYK combinations, ink takeout across the target area can be made more uniform and errors introduced by press anomalies will be randomized with respect to CIELab color space. The visual layout is useful for careful initial "visual" analysis of the characterization pressrun and for those applications where manual measurement is required. After a press profile is created, it is a good idea to make a proof representing the press profile. With the highly structured form of the visual layout target, it is easy to spot areas that are inconsistent with the rest of the target. This is not a substitute for actual colormetric analysis of the profile.

13.3 | Color Management System (CMS) Variables

13.3.1 | Measuring Equipment

Measurement equipment should be calibrated according to manufacturer's specifications. Measuring procedures should comply with *ANSI/CGATS.5 (1993 Graphic Technology—Spectral Measurement and Colorimetric Computation for Graphic Arts Image*s).

MEASURING EQUIPMENT: All Print Segments	
STANDARD	CGATS .5--1993
ILLUMINANT	D50 (5,000°Kelvin)
OBSERVER	2° standard observer
MEASUREMENT	Absolute (including substrate)

13.3.2 | Calibration Intervals

All production equipment must be calibrated at the manufacturer's recommended intervals. A documentation system should include all calibration steps, outcome, and corrective actions. This documentation should be used for reference and historical evaluation.

13.3.3 | Data Archives

Color characterization data must be archived. It is recommended this data be kept in a database. Nomenclature of data should include, but not be limited to, the following:

- Company.
- Date.
- Project.
- Equipment.
- Materials.
- Spectral identification of ink sets.
- Substrate characteristics.
- Press conditions.

13.3.4 | Profile Information

Profiles particular to a known press characterization should be identified via an agreed upon nomenclature:

- Date.
- Project.
- Press.
- Press speed.
- Ink set and ink order.
- Anilox Roller.
- Edited profiles should be identified. Other relevant information concerning use of GCR, UCR etc., influencing the generated profile must be included.

13.3.5 | Color Tolerancing

Color tolerancing is used to determine if the printed color, compared to a reference color, is acceptable. Typically expressed as Delta E (ΔE), the color dif-

COLOR TOLERANCING All Print Segments	
ΔE Based On CIE	Recommended
ΔE Based On CMC	Alternate

ference may be derived from one of several color difference equations. The simplest and most direct method is represented by the equation:

$$\Delta E^*_{ab} = \sqrt{\Delta L^{*2} + \Delta a^{*2} + \Delta b^{*2}}$$

Where:

$$\Delta L^* = L^*_1 - L^*_2$$
$$\Delta a^* = a^*_1 - a^*_2$$
$$\Delta b^* = b^*_1 - b^*_2$$

A more accurate color difference equation is represented by the CIE94 color tolerancing equation, which was further refined in the CIE2000 version. A third color tolerancing system is CMC (UK Society of Dyers and Colorist Color Measurement Committee) tolerancing. CIE94, 2000 (and all future versions of CIE) is referenced in FIRST as CIE tolerancing. Regardless of which version of the CIE formula is used, it is important to communicate the version with all parties involved in color management for the project. The concerned groups should agree as to the color tolerancing approach and indicate on the proof the tolerancing system used.

13.3.6 | ICC Profiles

All profiles must match the ICC format specification. A word of caution, color management systems from different vendors produce different ICC profiles. Even when reading the same test target, different programs will interpolate and expand the color data set according to their technology. Moreover, different programs using the same ICC profile may produce different results. Consistent results can best be achieved by consistency in the workflow.

13.3.7 | CMM Compatibility

The Color Management Module (CMM), sometimes called the "Color Engine" is the part of the CMS that maps one gamut to another. A CMM uses device profiles and render intents to convert the LUTs (Look Up Tables) between devices. The CMM does this by mapping the out-of-gamut colors into the range of colors that can be produced by the destination device. The CMM is a proprietary set of algorithms, meaning that results can vary depending on which "brand" of engine is used.

13.3.8 | Identifying Press Components

All system components in the press must be identified. Changes in anilox, plate, stickyback, or other components create a change in the color gamut. Production specifications should be noted in the characterization database and amended as production components change. *CGATS TR-012 (2003 Graphic Technology — Color Reproduction and Process Control for Package Printing)* identifies conditions requiring a new characterization as well as process control methods.

13.4 | Quantifying the CMS

13.4.1 | Proof-to-Press Match

A CMS uses two profiles; an input profile and an output profile. The input profile represents the colors desired and the output profile represents the colors achieved on the device being used. For example, compare an image on a computer monitor and the same image printed on a desktop printer. The input profile is the profile of the monitor (an RGB profile) and the output profile is the profile of the desktop printer (a CMYK profile). Converting between the input profile and the output profile requires a CMM (Color Matching Module) sometimes referred to as a color engine. The CMM is a set of algorithms, which calculates the dot percentages required to produce the requested color. Those calculations are typically based on regression analysis of the data contained in the input and output profiles. Consequently, there is always some error associated with the color management process; however, this error is far less than the error associated with any other color correction process, such as dot gain compensation. For matching proofs to press conditions, this error can and should be quantified. This is easily done by using the CMS to reproduce the original target used to profile the printing condition. Measure the resulting proof, color swatch by color swatch, and compare it to the original press sample. If using the IT8.7/4 proposed test target shown in Prepress Section 13.1.1, there will be 1,610 color comparisons (ΔE differences).

13.4.2 | Acceptable Difference

With 1,610 color comparisons, there will be some colors that are near perfect matches and some colors, which would be considered unacceptable matches (ΔE >3.0). The acceptable difference is where the average ΔE <2.5 (based on CIE94 tolerancing) and at least 90% of the data is ΔE <2.0.

14.0 Final Films

14.1 | Measurement and Evaluation of Film

FIRST recommends measurement of film in conformance with *ANSI/CGATS.9–(1994 Graphic Technology—Graphic Arts Transmission Densitometry Measurements—Terminology, Equations, Image Elements and Procedures)*. There are numerous definitions, equations and guidelines in CGATS.9. Some of those definitions, equations and guidelines may be found in the Glossary of this document.

14.1.1 | Transmission Densitometer Data Communication Specifications

The following information shall be included when communicating densito-metric data:

- Conformance with, or deviations from, CGATS.9.
- Densitometer manufacturer and model.
- Spectral response (Status T, E, M, A).
- Sampling aperture.
- Density: Equation (absolute or relative);
  Channel (UV/Ortho/Visual/RGB).
- Dot Area: Equation (Murray-Davies or Yule-Neilsen);
  Channel (UV/Ortho/Visual/RGB).

Before and during use, all instruments shall be calibrated in accordance with the manufacturer's recommended procedure. The transmission calibration standard shall be traceable to a standard reference.

Once the parameters listed in this section are communicated, report the color being measured. Refer to Measurement of Contract Proofs and Printed Material in Prepress Section 15.3.

14.2 | Film Negative Properties

14.2.1 | Film Densities

- The clear minimum density (D-min) area of the film should have a base orthochromatic density less than 0.05 and an ultra-violet density less than 0.10.

PLATEMAKING FILM D-min & D-max	
D-min less than Ortho/UV	0.05/0.10
D-max greater than Ortho/UV	4.0/4.0

- The black maximum density (D-max) area of the film should have orthochromatic and ultraviolet densities greater than 4.00.

■ The measurement of D-min using the ultraviolet channel on a transmission densitometer is important to assure optimum proofing and plate exposures. The higher the D-min number, the more ultraviolet light is being filtered out. Most proofing systems and photopolymer plates require ultraviolet light to accurately and consistently expose the image. Therefore, the lower the D-min value, the better.

14.2.2 | Film Thickness

■ All film should be dimensionally stable and a consistent thickness. The recommended film thickness for photopolymer flexographic plate making is 0.007" (0.18 mm) for wide web and 0.004" (0.10 mm) for narrow web printing applications.

PLATEMAKING FILM THICKNESS

WIDE WEB

PAPER/SHEET PRODUCTS	0.007"	0.18 mm
FILM PRODUCTS	0.007"	0.18 mm

NARROW WEB

PAPER/FILM PRODUCTS	0.004"	0.18 mm

14.2.3 | Handling Film Negatives

■ All film must be matte finish where specified by the raw plate material manufacturer.

■ Film must be supplied as one piece per color, identified by name of the color (Magenta, PMS 186 red, etc.).

■ All films supplied for the flexographic printing process must be negative.

■ No etching or hand color corrections may be made on supplied film.

■ Opaquing may be done on the non-emulsion side of the film. Opaquing should be minimal and thin in consistency to preclude high spots in the film that may create contact and dot gain problems during platemaking.

■ All extraneous marks smaller than a minimum dot should be opaqued or covered.

■ Excessive opaquing is unacceptable.

■ All films must be orthochromatic; no camera or soft-edged film is acceptable.

■ The film must be free of kinks and scratches.

■ Visible fingerprints, bleaching or colored markings when viewing the film's clear areas are not acceptable.

14.2.4 | Film Negative Emulsion

■ Negatives prepared for surface print must be right reading emulsion up (RREU).

■ Negatives prepared for reverse print must be right reading emulsion down (RRED)

14.3 | Dot Characteristics

Current industry data supports the reality that dot gain of two identical screen values (both considered to be round dots) from two different imagesetters will gain differently on press. Any film or direct to plate imaging device used to produce the initial characterization target should be the same make/model and software version used for all film output of live jobs. The profile of the print results is heavily influenced by the dot shape characteristics and is an intricate part of the tonal compensation.

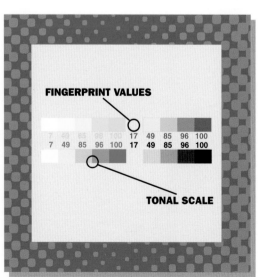

7	49	85	96	100	17	49	85	96	100
7	49	85	96	100	17	49	85	96	100

FINGERPRINT VALUES

TONAL SCALE

14.3.1 Actual Dot Size Include a control strip on the negative to confirm dot size held as expected. The control strip is a gray scale with 3% (or minimum printer), 10%, 30%, 70% and 100%.

14.3.1 | Dot Accuracy

When preparing film for the flexographic printing process, dot accuracy is extremely important, especially in the highlight tonal range. The verification of dot accuracy/integrity can be monitored only if a known dot percentage is placed on the original file/film prior to duplication or imaging. With electronically generated film, the output from the computer must represent the dot percentage of the film. If these films are to be duplicated or contacted, these scales should be used to verify contact exposure, film speed and processing conditions. The dot percentage on the final platemaking film should be within the tolerances of this chart.

DOT TOLERANCES FOR PLATEMAKING FILM						
2%	10%	25%	30%	50%	70%	75%
±0.5%	±0.75%	±1.0%	±1.0%	±2.0%	±2.0%	±2.0%

14.3.2 | Dot Shape

The dot shape that is most controlled in the flexographic printing process is a round dot. Dot gain is reduced when round dots are used, especially in vignettes and fade-aways. A round dot is defined as a dot that is round in the highlights and round in the shadows. Avoid "diamonds" in the shadows (non-printing areas) because they grow and fill-in more quickly. Failure to use round dots is cause for rejection.

14.4 | Image Screening

14.4.1 | Line Screen

Screen rulings vary based on imaging method, plate material, and print conditions (such as press width, anilox configuration and substrate). A minimum highlight dot must be maintained in all films to produce consistent plates and clean print. The minimum dot percentage may need to be increased for finer screen rulings or for printers using coarser anilox rollers. Failure to provide the minimum dot will increase the likelihood of dot bridging or excess highlight dot gain. Finer screen rulings may result in greater image detail, but may also narrow the tonal range that can be reproduced on the press. The printer must approve the use of finer screen rulings other than those specified.

For laser engraved rubber plates the maximum screen ruling is limited to 120 lpi because the material currently cannot hold dots smaller than 5% at 120 lpi under normal plating conditions. Technology is being developed to expand the process capability of laser engraved rubber but this is the current process limitation (Fall 2003). The screen ruling for digital photopolymer is restricted by the printing process not the imaging process or plate material. The lower range of line screens for photopolymer plates, both conventionally and digitally imaged, is determined by print and substrate constraints.

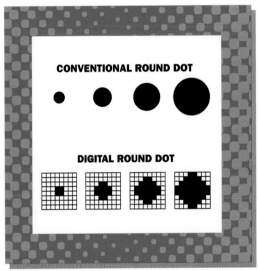

14.3.2 Dot Shape Dot gain is reduced when round dots are used, especially in vignettes or fade-aways.

Prepress

LINE SCREEN/RULING (LPI)				
WIDE WEB		**CONVENTIONAL PLATES**	**DIGITALLY IMAGED PHOTOPOLYMER**	**LASER ENGRAVED RUBBER/ CURED POLYMER**
PREPRINT LINERBOARD	SBS Board	110-133 lpi 43-52 lpcm	110-175 lpi 43-69 lpcm	110-120 lpi 43-47 lpcm
	Uncoated	100-133 lpi 39-52 lpcm	100-133 lpi 39-52 lpcm	100-120 lpi 39-47 lpcm
COMBINED CORRUGATED	Bleached White	55-100 lpi 22-39 lpcm	55-100 lpi 22-39 lpcm	55-100 lpi 22-39 lpcm
	Coated	55-110 lpi 22-43 lpcm	55-110 lpi 22-43 lpcm	85-110 lpi 33-43 lpcm
FOLDING CARTON	SBS Board	120-150 lpi 47-59 lpcm	120-175 lpi 47-69 lpcm	110-120 lpi 43-47 lpcm
	CRB Board	110-133 lpi 43-52 lpcm	110-133 lpi 43-52 lpcm	110-120 lpi 43-47 lpcm
MULTIWALL BAG	Coated Paper	75-120 lpi 30-47 lpcm	75-120 lpi 30-47 lpcm	75-110 lpi 30-43 lpcm
	Uncoated Paper	65-85 lpi 26-33 lpcm	65-100 lpi 26-39 lpcm	65-100 lpi 26-39 lpcm
FILM PRODUCTS	All	110-133 lpi 43-52 lpcm	110-150 lpi 43-59 lpcm	85-120 lpi 33-47 lpcm

NARROW WEB		**CONVENTIONAL PLATES**	**DIGITALLY IMAGED PHOTOPOLYMER**	**LASER ENGRAVED RUBBER/ CURED POLYMER**
PAPER PRODUCTS	Coated Paper	133-175 lpi 52-69 lpcm	133-175 lpi 52-69 lpcm	110-120 lpi 43-47 lpcm
	Uncoated Paper	110-133 lpi 43-52 lpcm	110-133 lpi 43-52 lpcm	100-120 lpi 39-47 lpcm
FILM PRODUCTS	All	110-133 lpi 43-52 lpcm	110-150 lpi 43-59 lpcm	85-120 lpi 33-47 lpcm

The anilox cell count should be at least four times the line screen ruling of the image to be printed. For example, when a 550 line anilox is used, the graphic line screen ruling should be no greater than 133.

$$\frac{550}{4} = 137 \quad OR \quad 133 \times 4 = 532$$

To convert from English measurement (lpi) to metric measurement (lpcm), divide the number of lines per inch by 2.54.

Example: $\frac{100 \text{ lines}}{1 \text{ inch}} \times \frac{1 \text{ inch}}{2.54 \text{ cm}} = \frac{39 \text{ lines}}{1 \text{ cm}}$

14.4.2 | Screen Angles

Screen angles and rulings should be selected to minimize moiré patterns; some moiré is inevitable. Screen angles C, M, K should be 30° apart. The yellow should be 15° between two of the colors—in most cases, the cyan and black. The nominal angle for viewing screens is 45°. However, on flexographic presses equipped with 45° or 60° anilox rollers, it is necessary to avoid using the same angle as the anilox. Usually this is accomplished by rotating all color angles by approximately 7.5°. Reference the imagesetters screening method for setting alternative angles.

It is desirable to have the dominant color (in most cases black) on the nominal angle (45°). Screen angles for two-color or three-color printing should follow the same guidelines with the dominant color at the nominal angle.

All screen angles and dot shapes should be specified in the digital file before

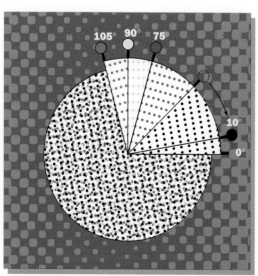

14.4.2 Screen Angles Screen angles and rulings should be selected to minimize moiré patterns; some moiré is inevitable.

68 Flexographic Image Reproduction Specifications & Tolerances

outputting film or plates (digital or laser engraved). When plates or films are made from digital data supplied by the prepress provider, it is the platemakers' responsibility to notify the prepress provider of any obvious moiré problems that develop when the screens are imaged.

14.5 | Registration Marks and Micro Dots

A printer-supplied template indicating the size and placement of registration marks supersedes the recommendations that follow.

All images must have registration marks indicating the center of the web direction as well as the centerline of the cut off direction on one-up film. For jobs that are being die cut, final assembly of the product will hide the registration marks from the consumer.

Registration marks should be solid lines with each of the colors producing precisely the same mark and in register with each other. When film is accurately registered using the incorporated marks, all elements of the job must be in register. If direct imaging, a mounters' proof is the only way to verify registration prior to press.

REGISTER MARKS Crosshair Dimensions		
WIDE WEB	**LENGTH**	**LINE WEIGHT**
PAPER/SHEET PRODUCTS	0.25" | 6.35 mm	0.01" | 0.25 mm
FILM PRODUCTS	0.25" | 6.35 mm	0.01" | 0.25 mm
NARROW WEB	**LENGTH**	**LINE WEIGHT**
PAPER/FILM PRODUCTS	0.125" | 3.18 mm	0.006" | 0.15 mm

14.5.1 | Registration Marks on Step and Repeat Files

Step and repeat files are handled differently than one-up films. The printer must confirm specific placement of register marks on stepped files. A registration mark equal in size, shape and character to the one-up file should be placed exactly in the center of the web direction. For example: if the total printed image area—including all of the various repeats across the web—equals 12" (305 mm), the mark should be placed 6" (152.4 mm) from either side.

Registration marks in the machine direction must be in the center of the repeat, taking into consideration any stagger requested by the printer. For example: if the printed product has a measurement of 4" (100 mm) and is being supplied to the printer one-up, then the center of this image is 2" (50 mm). However, if the printer has requested a half stagger, the overall dimension will be 6" (152.4 mm), making the center and the registration mark location now 3" (76 mm).

14.5.2 | Registration Marks on Die Cut Jobs

Marks that remain on the printed package need to be positioned so that, upon final assembly of the package, the registration marks will be hidden from the consumer.

14.5.3 | Auto Registration Marks

Several electronically controlled press registration devices require that the design firm, printer and/or prepress provider incorporate automatic registra-

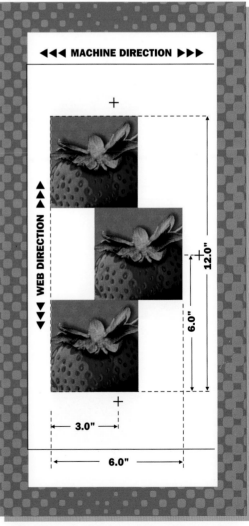

14.5.1 Registration Marks on Step and Repeat Films
This illustration indicates the proper positioning of registration marks on a step and repeat job. Note the marks are in the center of the overall dimensions.

14.5.4 Micro Dots Typical micro dots will be free standing dots that will print and remain on the printed sheet throughout the printrun.

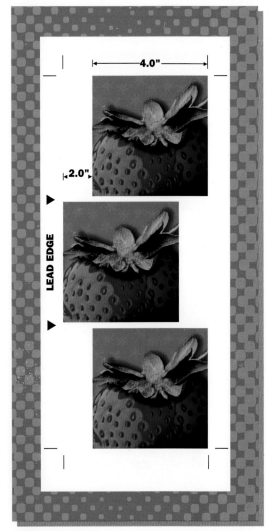

14.6 Image Stagger The above illustration shows a job stepped three across and one around with a quarter stagger. The stagger assures constant impression on all colors around the cylinder in order to minimize press bounce.

tion marks into the final file. For the specific scale, type and placement, it is the printer's responsibility to provide the information to the prepress provider prior to generation of the final file. The printer should make a digital EPS file of the special target(s) required and provide to the design firm or prepress provider during the design review process.

14.5.4 | Micro Dots

Micro dots are used in conjunction with video mounting devices. Micro dots are placed on both the left and right side of the printed material, in the center of the product's web direction, and should be 0.010" (0.25 mm) in

MICRODOT DIAMETER All Print Segments	
DIAMETER	
INCHES	MILLIMETERS
0.01	0.25

diameter unless otherwise specified by the printer. Typical micro dots will be free standing dots that will print and remain on the printed sheet throughout the printrun. When the job is in print register, the dots will overprint each other and appear to be an almost perfect dot. In some cases, due to the design, the printer may choose to knockout the micro dot by obscuring it in a solid color. In the same area of the knocked-out color, use of positive print for each of the remaining colors helps to hide the micro dot.

It is recommended that an arrow of approximately $1/16$" (1.5 mm) wide and $1/4$" (6.4 mm) long be placed approximately $1/8$" (3.3 mm) away from the micro dot, indicating its placement, so the dot is not arbitrarily removed from the files (or opaqued out of the film). It is the responsibility of the platemaker to cover the arrow so it is not made part of the plate and later printed. Only the micro dot is imaged onto the plate, remains on the product throughout the printrun, and is not cause for rejection.

14.5.4.1 | Micro Dots on Step and Repeat Files Micro dots on step and repeat files are positioned based on the total image. Usually these dots are placed across the web on the centerline of the full stepped file. The size of the design and the stepped file will determine how many dots are needed. The micro dots should be placed in areas that do not affect the design but are in strategic positions for mounting. (See illustration 14.5.4.) Micro dots must be a minimum of $1/4$" (6.4 mm) inside the live printed area of the product. The printer should be consulted for any particular placement that may be required by the individual press mounting system.

14.6 | Image Stagger

Because of the physical characteristics of printing from a raised plate, the image staggering technique is used to minimize press bounce. Within each print station, the goal is to have the plate constantly under impression. Of course, this is not always possible but staggering does help maintain an even impression and eliminates the bounce that may occur as the plates go onto impression. The printer may request a stagger of $1/3$, $1/4$ or $1/2$ of the product's overall dimension, from top to bottom. For specifics as to the treatment of staggering on stepped files, consult the printer that will be printing from the files/film/plates provided. Also be aware that each printer, although printing similar images, may require different staggering techniques.

14.7 | Calculating Distortion

When a photopolymer plate is laying flat, the top of the plate and the bottom of the plate is the same length (X=Y). However, when the plate is wrapped around a printing cylinder, the surface of the plate becomes stretched because the distance around the top of the plate is greater than the distance around the bottom of the plate ($Y_d > X_d$).

Since the plate is imaged flat and printed round, the original negative must be reduced (distorted, only in the direction it will be wrapped around the cylinder) so that upon stretching it becomes the proper size. The percent distortion is simply the ratio X_d/Y_d. X_d is the circumference of the inner circle and Y_d is the circumference of the outer circle. Circumference is $2\pi R$ ($\pi = \sim 3.14159$)

$$\% \text{ DISTORTION} = \frac{2\pi R_1}{2\pi R_2} + \frac{R_1}{R_2}$$

The values of R_1 and R_2 depend on the thickness of the plate (P), the thickness of the tape (T), the cylinder radius (C) (radius equals half the diameter) and the thickness of the Mylar® (M) used to support the plate. The thickness of the Mylar® is important because it has a very high modulus of elasticity and will not stretch when wrapped around the cylinder. Consequently R_1 is equal to the radius of the cylinder plus the tape thickness plus the Mylar® thickness. R_2 is equal to the radius of the cylinder plus the tape thickness plus the plate thickness.

$$R_1 = C + T + M$$
$$R_2 = C + T + P$$

Equation #1: $\% \text{ DISTORTION} = \dfrac{C + T + M}{C + T + P}$

Often repeat length (R_L) is provided instead of cylinder diameter. The above equation can be converted into a new equation using repeat length (Y_d).

Equation #2: $\% \text{ DISTORTION} = \dfrac{[(R_1 \div 2\pi) + (M - P)]}{R_L \div 2\pi}$

For example, a job with a repeat length of 11.5" using a 0.20" tape and a 0.067" plate will have a 96.61% distortion.

$R_L = 11.5"$
$M = 0.005"$
$P = 0.067"$

$$\% \text{ DISTORTION} = \frac{11.5 \div (2 \times 3.14159) + (0.005 - 0.067)]}{11.5 \div (2 \times 3.14159)}$$

$$= \frac{1.8302834 - 0.062}{1.8032834}$$

$$= \frac{1.7682834}{1.8032834}$$

$$= 0.9661254$$
$$= 96.61\%$$

When calculating % distortion using repeat length, tape thickness is not required for the calculation; however, it is necessary to ensure the correct tape thickness is used to account for the cylinder undercut.

For most plate material the Mylar® support is 0.005"; however, there are exceptions. Confirm Mylar® thickness with plate material manufacturer.

To assure that the proper distortion factor is applied to file/film prior to plate making, it is suggested that the files/films indicate the distorted dimension,

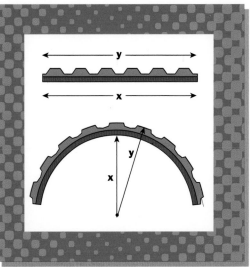

14.7 Calculating Distrotion When a photopolymer plate is laying flat, the top of the plate and the bottom of the plate is the same length (X=Y). However, when the plate is wrapped around a printing cylinder, the surface of the plate becomes stretched because the distance around the top of the plate is greater than the distance around the bottom of the plate ($Y_d > X_d$).

the distortion % and the final print dimensions. When using photopolymer plates or laser engraved rubber, image size should be maintained at 100% across the press width and be distorted in the machine direction.

When using molded rubber plates, compensation in both machine and web direction is required; the printer should provide a through-the-press distortion factor. The platemaker must determine the amount of reduction required across the press/web.

Example: For 0.125" (3.2 mm) rubber: To allow for shrinkage that takes place in the dimension across the cylinder, make art wider that the desired print dimension by 0.020" per inch (0.51 per mm).

14.8 | Final File/Film Inspection Attributes

The following attributes are to be reviewed during QC of the final files and certified by the file/film/plate supplier:

■ **Actual Dot Size:** Include a control strip on the negative to confirm dot size held as expected. The control strip is a gray scale with 3% (or minimum printer), 10%, 30%, 70% and 100% (or shadow treatment values used in lieu of solid). Measure with a transmission densitometer or have the prepress provider supply a certificate of analysis.

■ **Dot Gain Compensation Curve:** Each printer has a specification based on the press characterization. Verify that the correct compensation is applied.

■ **Bar Code Verification:** No material should be accepted for print unless it is accompanied by a bar code report. The bar code report should be scanned directly from the film supplied for plate making regardless of who makes the plates. When an assembled file is supplied for imaging to the printer or plate provider, it must be accompanied by a written report. The report should identify the human readable number for the incorporated machine-readable code and have the bar-width adjustment applied. Incoming material must be checked to verify the human readable number is correct and the proper bar-width reduction is applied.

15.0 Color Proofs

15.1 | Types of Proofs

The various proofs used in design, prepress and printing are defined below. The proof must be identified in one of the following manners to be compliant. Use the descriptions below and provide the specific information.

■ **Concept Proof:** this proof is common in the early creative stages of the project. It is typically not profiled and therefore, not used for matching color.

■ **Color Target:** this proof is not profiled using the output source profile; however, it does represent the customer's color expectations for the final printed product.

■ **Contract Analog Proof:** this proof uses film separations as an intermediate media to create an image. It is made to manufacturer's recommendations for exposing and processing (brand name of analog proofing system) and has been made according to FIRST specifications.

■ **Contract Digital Proof:** this proof uses electronic files processed by a color-imaging device. It is profiled to (brand name of digital proofing system) and has been made according to FIRST specifications.

■ **Profiled Contract Proof:** this proof represents the customer's complete content and color expectations for the final printed product and is the basis for negotiations on project performance. This proof is profiled using a color management system (CMS) and is prepared based upon profiles provided by the specific printer or prepress provider. It has been made according to FIRST specifications.

A contract proof illustrates how the printed image is expected to look when reproduced on press. It is an important quality control tool and communication device. The contract proof does not have to be a dot-for-dot reproduction, but it must be an overall visual simulation of the expected print results. Therefore, it must simulate the dot gain, color attributes, detail and contrast of the printed image.

Contract proofs represent an agreement between the printer, prepress provider, designer and the consumer product company regarding the expected appearance of the graphic reproduction on press. Following specifications, the contract proof should represent how the separations will reproduce when printed. Before a contract proof can be accurately used, the entire reproduction system must be characterized so that the proofing system is calibrated to match the printed result. Refer to Prepress Section 13.0 CIELab Color Management. Afterward, both press and proofing systems must be maintained for consistency and repeatability.

15.2 | Proofing Methods

15.2.1 | Analog Proofs

Analog proofs are made from halftone films. These may be overlay, single layer or surprint. Although analog proofs are made from films, they do not usually simulate the dot gain associated with most flexographic presses. Overlay proofs are not acceptable as a contract proof for approving process color separations, although they do an admirable job of verifying the content of film negatives, checking register and traps between colors and proofreading typeset copy for accuracy.

The most widely used contract analog proof for verifying the accuracy of color separations today is the surprint proof. Some proofing systems offer a limited number of process shades and density variations to match the color attributes of the process colors used in the printing process. Proofing films may be modified to allow the proof to simulate the dot gain of a particular flexographic printing system. All proofing densities must adhere to FIRST specifications for the intended print segment. Some prepress providers provide proofs on a wide variety of substrates to simulate the cast and brightness of the material being printed.

To correctly simulate the final printed result, proof film tone reproduction input must generally be modified from film tone reproduction used for plate making. These tone reproduction characteristics should be developed in conjunction with the printer. Analog proofs must be exposed and processed per the manufacturer's recommendations and must contain their recommended control target. In addition to the targets used to monitor the consistency of the analog proofing system, the FIRST control target must be incorporated. The manufacturer's target does not have a profile applied to it and is used to monitor the consistency of the proofing system. The FIRST control target is modified by the press profile and will match what is printed on press. These control targets must remain an integral part of the contract proof. Failure to provide a proof with incorporated targets for verification is cause for rejection.

15.2.2 | Digital Color Proofs (DDCP)

Direct digital color proofs are produced directly from digital files without halftone films. There are many different technologies used to create digital proofs including office copiers, laser printers, dot matrix, bubble jet, dye sublimation, wax, thermal transfer and ink jet. The majority of office and desktop color printers are not capable of accurately producing specifications and are not consistent enough to be used as contract proofing devices. Some DDCPs simulate a halftone dot that is used for the printing process, while others produce more of a continuous tone reproduction. There is no advantage to one over the other because the dots are not the same dots as those produced on the imagesetter. All proofing densities must adhere to the specifications for the intended print segment. Correctly calibrated DDCP systems can produce an accurate prepress proof of the anticipated printed product.

All proofing densities must adhere to FIRST specifications for the intended print segment. Digital proofs must be produced according to the manufacturer's recommendations and must contain the control target recommended by the equipment manufacturer. In addition to the targets used to monitor the consistency of the digital proofing system, the FIRST control target must be incorporated. The manufacturer's target does not have a profile applied to it and is used to monitor the consistency of the proofing system. The FIRST control target is modified by the press profile and will match what is printed on press. These control targets must remain an integral part of the contract proof. Failure to provide a proof with incorporated targets for verification is cause for rejection.

15.2.3 | Press Proofs

Press proofs require plates and possibly film (unless using direct-imaged plates). It is important that the same imaging device be used to make both the production plates and the proofing plates. All proofing densities must adhere to FIRST specifications for the intended print segment. The proof must reflect the dot gain experienced during the press characterization. If the dot gain experienced on the press proof is different from the results of the characterization two things must be done:

1. Establish what the production press dot gain is and match it on the proof press controlling it within the same tolerance established for printing.
2. Develop a curve for the production film/file to compensate for the tonal difference between the press characterization and the press proof.

All proofs must incorporate the FIRST control target. This control target must remain an integral part of the press proof. Failure to provide a proof with incorporated targets for verification is cause for rejection.

15.2.4 | Proofing Sequence

When a press proof is supplied, it is recommended that the ink lay-down sequence used for the production run be used when proofing. It is the responsibility of the provider of press proof(s) to obtain this information from the printer. Users of off-press proofing materials (analog and digital proofs) will note that manufacturers of these products often specify a particular sequence of colorant application. This is not necessarily the same as the production printing sequence.

FIRST has endorsed the identification of inks by using color index numbers to define the actual pigments. This is the first time, in any printing discipline, that inks have been identified by the base ingredients; however, automobile paints, plastics and fabrics currently use this form of identification. It is important that the proofing colors used be spectrally matched to FIRST recommended pigments.

15.3 | Measurement of Contract Proofs And Printed Materials

Measurement of printed materials consistent with *ANSI/CGATS.4 (1993 Graphic Technology—Graphic Arts Reflection Densitometry Measurements— Terminology, Equations, Image Elements, and Procedures)* and *ANSI/CGATS.5 (1993 Graphic Technology—Spectral Measurement and Colorimetric Computation for Graphic Arts Images)* is recommended. ANSI/CGATS.4 is the primary reference for evaluation of graphic arts materials using reflection densitometry. ANSI/CGATS.5 is the primary reference for evaluation of graphic arts materials by spectrophotometry.

There are numerous definitions, equations and guidelines in ANSI/CGATS.4 and CGATS.5. Some of these may be found in the Glossary of this document.

15.3.1 | Reflection Densitometer Communications Specifications

The following minimum information shall be included when communicating densitometric data:

■ Conformance with (or deviations from), CGATS.4 shall be noted.
■ Densitometer manufacturer and model.
■ Spectral response (Status E, T, etc.).
■ Sample backing.
■ Sampling aperture.
■ Polarizing filter used? (yes/no).

Before and during use, all instruments shall be calibrated in accordance with the manufacturer's recommended procedure. The reflective calibration standard shall be traceable to a standard reference (example T-Ref from GCA). Once the parameters listed in this section are communicated, report the color being measured.

DENSITOMETER PARAMETER & INFORMATION LISTING

PARAMETER	NOTED INFORMATION
DENSITY	Absolute or Relative
	Color Channel (filter) Used
DOT AREA	Solid Density
	Color Channel (filter) Used
	Equation: Murray-Davies or
	Yule-Nielsen (include "n" factor)
DOT GAIN	Film Printing Dot Area
	Equation: Murray-Davies or Yule-Nielsen (include "n" factor)
TRAP	Overprint(s) Measured
	Lay down sequence
	Equation: Brunner, newsprint, apparent
PRINT CONTRAST	Film Printing Dot Area
	Paper (included/excluded)

The Murray-Davies equation is preferred; both are mentioned in the event that a company is using the Yule-Nielsen equation. The remainder of this publication refers to the Murray-Davies equation.

15.3.1.1 | Spectral Response There are many different densitometric spectral responses used in the graphic arts. When communicating a specified density value, it is important to report the spectral response used. The density value obtained is a function of the spectral characteristics of both the material being measured (e.g., inks, dyes, etc.) and the spectral response. The values obtained with different response functions (Status E, Status T, etc.) may be similar or significantly different, depending on the particular material being measured. It is important for the densitometer to be calibrated using a T-ref standard calibration target. The T-ref calibration target ensures the densitometer (using the Status T spectral response) is operating within specifications.

■ **Status T** is the preferred spectral response in North America. It is defined to closely match the characteristics of graphic arts materials normally used in the United States, such as ink-on-paper printed materials, off-press proofs and original art to be color separated.

■ **Status E** is defined to closely match the characteristics of graphic arts materials normally used in Europe, such as ink-on-paper printed materials, off-press proofs and original art to be color separated.

15.3.1.2 | Printed Sheet Backing for Reading Densitometer Values Because flexographic substrates usually are translucent and not opaque, images printed on the backside of the substrate (or contents of the package) will affect measurements. If a white backing is used, some of the light transmitted through the paper will reflect back to the measuring instrument. The best method to minimize back-reflected light is to use a black backing material. The backing material should be spectrally non-selective, diffuse-reflecting, and have an ISO density greater than 1.5. The choice of black backing was made to reduce density variability introduced by the backing material or image existing on the backside.

15.3.1.3 | Solid Ink Density of Contract Proofs & Printed Materials Solid ink density values on dry proofs shall fall within ±0.07 for M, C and K and within ±0.05 for Y of the desired density values for the intended print segment. As an example, if the magenta proof density is +0.07 (the target), the remaining colors must be proofed at or above their respective target density to maintain balance.

SOLID INK DENSITY TARGETS				
WIDE WEB	CYAN	MAGENTA	YELLOW	BLACK
PAPER PRODUCTS	1.25	1.25	1.00	1.50
FILM PRODUCTS	1.25	1.20	1.00	1.40
NARROW WEB	CYAN	MAGENTA	YELLOW	BLACK
PAPER PRODUCTS	1.35	1.25	1.00	1.50
FILM PRODUCTS	1.25	1.20	1.00	1.40

FIRST has identified process and line pigments by the color index number. Proofing pigments need to match the inks being used. Using the pigment (referenced by the color index number) will prevent metamerism. If the proofing method used does not utilize pigments, the C.I.# of the pigments being used by the printer will facilitate the identification of the best match available for the given proofing colorant. Refer to Print Section19.3.2 & 19.3.3 for FIRST recommended pigments.

15.3.1.4 | Total Dot Gain (Tonal Value Increase) of Proofs Failure to monitor and maintain accuracy of the contract proof will result in inaccurate and inconsistent proofs, rendering them unusable for the printer and consumer product company to approve color.

FIRST control and run targets, to be printed and used for calibration purposes, must be imaged and plated (when providing press proofs) using the same devices and materials as live production. A variation in dot shape and material can significantly alter print results.

■ **Press Proofs:** In order to ensure properly balanced tone reproduction, it is recommended that the total dot gain be based on the press profile/characterization produced by the printer for whom film is being prepared. For press proofs, the allowable variation on the 30% and 70% original film value is ±5% of the dot area achieved during the characterization. For example, if the magenta proof dot gain is +5% the target, the remaining colors must be proofed at or above their respective target dot gains to maintain balance.

■ **Prepress Proofs:** All proofs must be made to the manufacturer's specifications using their recommended target for verification. The target should be outside the live image area of the graphics and must remain on the finished proof. The dot area on each of the colors containing a screen tint must be measured using the Murray-Davies equation for dot area measurement outlined in CGATS.4. The absolute value of apparent dot area must be consistent with the supplier's recommendations for the respective proofing system. This chart is provided as an example. Actual values must be based upon the printers' press characterization.

EXAMPLE PRESS/PREPRESS PROOF DEVIATION

	FILM VALUE	PREDICTED DOT GAIN	ACTUAL DOT GAIN	DEVIATION FROM TARGET
CYAN	50%	72%	72%	0
MAGENTA	50%	72%	70%	−2
YELLOW	50%	72%	68%	−4
BLACK	50%	72%	73%	1

15.3.2 | Spectrophotometry Guidelines
ISO 2846-5 (Graphic Technology – Colour & Transparency of Printing Ink Sets for 4-Colour Printing Part 5: Flexographic Printing) defines the standard spectrophotometric instrument settings.

ISO 2846-5 Spectrophotometer Settings

GEOMETRY 0°/45° or 45°/0°

OBSERVER 2° standard observer

ILLUMINANT D50 (5,000° Kelvin)

15.3.2.1 | Colorimetric Guidelines Colorimetric parameters shall be calculated using the equations of CGATS.5; specific parameter calculation details may be found in that publication. In general, the most commonly used colorimetric parameters are CIE L*, a*, b*, C*ab, h*ab.

■ **L★** describes the lightness of a sample. Lower values are perceived as darker; higher values are perceived as whiter.

■ **a★** describes the red/green dimension of a sample. The more positive the a* value, the more red the sample; the more negative the a* value, the more green the sample.

■ **b*** describes the yellow/blue dimension of a sample. The more positive the b* value, the more yellow the sample; the more negative the b* value, the more blue the sample.

■ **C*ab** (Chroma) and **h*ab** (hue) are derived from a* and b* and are an alternative way of specifying the color of a sample.

15.3.2.2 | **Communicating Spectrophotometric Data**   When communicating colorimetric, or spectral, data in accordance with CGATS.5, the data should be accompanied by the following information:

■ Measurements and computations in conformance with CGATS.5
■ Originator of the data
■ Creation date of the data
■ A description of the purpose or contents of the data being exchanged
■ A description of the instrument used, including, but not limited to, the brand and model number
■ Measurement source (light source and filter) conditions used
■ Wavelength interval used
■ When density data is reported, the spectral product's weighting function (status or type response) used shall be identified.

Before use, all instruments shall be calibrated in accordance with the manufacturer's recommended procedure. The reflective calibration standard shall be traceable to a standard reference.

15.4 | Proof Compliance Cover Sheet/Label

A cover sheet or label should accompany the proof submitted for color match at press and approved by the customer. The cover sheet or label should state which proofing product or system was used, and the company supplying the proof (contact name, telephone and fax numbers).

If this proof is to be used for color approval as a contract proof, the cover sheet must also contain information required to verify the proof's compliance to the technical attributes required for that proofing type. Refer to Prepress Sections 15.3.1 & 15.3.2.2.

15.5 | Viewing of Artwork, Proofs and Printed Material

Accurate, consistent visual perception of color requires the image to be viewed in a standard, chromatically neutral, controlled environment. If the printer, separator, and customer standardize viewing conditions, color discrepancies can be minimized.

A color viewing booth is used to view printed images, proofs, or transparencies, under a controlled and standard light source. ANSI 2.30 1989 set specifications for proper viewing conditions.

15.5 Viewing Artwork, Proofs and Printed Material
Accurate, consistent visual perception of color requires that the subjects be viewed in a standard, chromatically neutral, controlled manner.

ANSI 2.30 – 1989: COLOR VIEWING CONDITIONS

PARAMETER	SPECIFICATION
LIGHTING	5,000° Kelvin bulbs
LIGHT SOURCE	Color Rendering Index: ≥ 90
VIEWING SURFACE	Luminance: =204, ±44 foot candles
VIEWING AREA COLOR	Neutral Gray: Munsell N8 or equivalent
ANGLES OF ILLUMINATION	Minimize glare

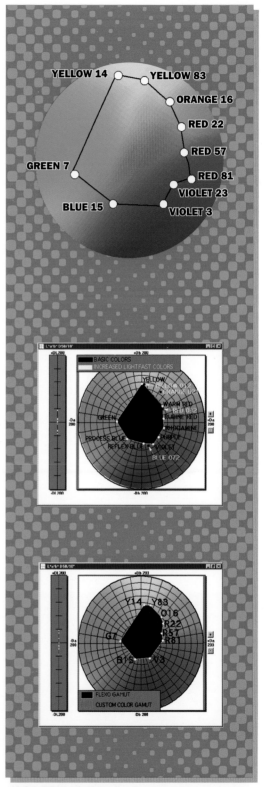

15.6 | Proofing For Expanded Color Gamut Printing

Proofing for expanded color gamut printing can be as diverse as the systems used to expand the gamut itself. At the very least, any proofing device used must be able to match the expanded gamut of the color separation being reproduced on press, with the chosen ink set. Expanded gamut refers not only to the outer edges of the color gamut with the most saturated colors but also to the purest pastels and semi-saturated colors that are often missing using traditional CMYK technology.

15.6.1 | Proofing Devices for Expanded Color Gamut

A whole range of devices have been used with success, from analog devices with special ink colors, to digital proofing with CMYK and expanded CMYK ink jets and digital halftone devices using laser ablatable or thermal transferable ink sheets.

Digital ink jet proofers using only CMYK, use very pure single pigmented inks. These pigments are purer than the typical CMYK inks that are used commercially in flexographic printing today. Because of the purity and saturation of these inks, and often the addition of a light cyan fifth and a light magenta sixth ink, the proofing device is capable of reproducing a much wider color gamut. These devices may be acceptable for some expanded color gamut proofing applications.

15.6.2 | Expanded Gamut Color Space and Color Matching

There are numerous approaches to increasing the printed color gamut. Whatever ink set is chosen, a characterization target must be printed. There are no industry standard targets for profiling the expanded gamut space. There are targets available from specific vendors: these targets contain patches for CMYK as well as targets for the additional inks. Once the data is analyzed with a spectrophotometer, a color gamut range can be mapped. This same mapping can also be done with a target printed from the proofing device, and a correlation of the color space between the press and proofer can be determined.

Expanded color gamut systems contain software that enable the printer to determine the specific colors capable of being reproduced on press given their chosen ink set and print capabilities. Once the proofing device is correlated to the press, a proof can illustrate the special color matches that are achievable on press, based on L*a*b value comparisons.

15.6.3 | Selecting Expanded Gamut Inks

Expanded color gamut can be achieved using commercial systems with predefined ink sets or custom ink sets chosen by the user. The gamut of an ink set will only expand so far by increasing ink density, as the hue angle of the ink tends to curve away from pure with increased ink film thicknesses. The color gamut can be further expanded by increasing the whiteness and reflectance of

15.6.2 FIRST Ink Pigments The gamut shown in the top illustration is created by plotting FIRST recommended line pigments. The middle graph illustrates the change in the color gamut created by adding additional pigments. The bottom graph compares the color gamut created with FIRST line pigments to the gamut created with the Pantone® bases (lithographic). All pigments were proofed in a water-based ink formula on Leneta stock for demonstration purposes only.

the substrate, or more dramatically, by adding extra ink sets. With regard to adding extra ink sets, single pigment inks are recommended. The logical inks to add to C, M, Y are pigments that are halfway between those values. Based on the closest hue values to the halfway point, the best ink choices are Violet 3, Red 2 and Green 7. Other colors used to expand the color gamut include:

■ Red, Green, Blue.

■ Orange, Green, Violet.

■ Orange and Green.

■ Other colors chosen for a specific pictorial enhancement.

■ Using brand colors for pictorial enhancement (i.e, "Shelly's Cola Red").

15.6.4 | Screen Angles and Using Expanded Color Gamut Printing

Another issue for consideration when printing more than four colors is the choice of screen angles. The best solution is to place extra ink colors on the same angle as the opposing complimentary colors. So in the case of violet, red and green the green should be placed on the magenta angle, the red should be placed on the cyan angle and the violet should be placed on either the yellow or black angle.

15.6.5 | Color Management Systems and Expanded Color Gamut Printing

The most problematic issue for conducting an expanded gamut printing trial has been the implementation of color management. One way to implement color management is through the use of ICC color profiling. Some of the current color profiling software does not have a consistent system for creating multi-process profiles for custom color choices. It is necessary to select software that can use custom colors and custom scripts. The ICC format supports up to ten colors: however few RIPs will support more than four colors. Current color profiling software solutions do not feature industry approved standardized targets with color chips or swatches of pure additional inks and/or overprints of the additional inks with each other and the normal process hues. Additionally, many current software solutions assume that the spectrophotometer is only reading CMYK inks when evaluating the existing targets. The evaluation process of expanded gamut printed material is not fully developed. Although expanded gamut printing can reproduce a more desirable product, the ability to control the color consistency will continue to be an important.

16.0 Printing Plates

16.1 | Introduction

This section provides information on the manufacturing methods, specifications and tolerances of the various types of flexographic printing plates. This knowledge will aid the print production team in selecting the most appropriate printing plate to best produce the design.

A review of incoming films is crucial to successful plate making. A list of critical attributes of final files/films is detailed in Prepress Section 14.8. It is recommended that these attributes be included on a certificate of analysis by the file/film supplier or performed in-house as an incoming materials inspection.

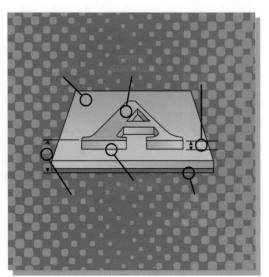

16.0 Printing Plates The above illustration identifies plate attributes discussed in this section.

16.2 | General Specifications

- All plates for one print job are to be made from the same batch of raw material.
- Caliper tolerances are to nominal thickness from the raw material manufacturer.
- During plate processing, main exposures are to be made using the exposure target. This is to control and monitor accuracy of line widths and halftone dot integrity.

16.3 | File Preparation for Digitally Imaged And Laser Engraved Plates

16.3.1 | File Preparation

By employing these recommendations, files can be processed efficiently and reliably by the RIP (Raster Image Processor) on a PC, Apple or workstation.

- **Files must be true PostScript:** Avoid the use of EPS (Encapsulated PostScript) files. EPS files use a subset of PostScript. They are usually images, which have been created for incorporation in another document. EPS files do not contain certain important information for output, such as page size.

  True PostScript is normally produced by "printing" an image to a file. For this reason they are sometimes known as "print" or "print-to-disk" files. They can usually be made from any application by selecting an appropriate printer driver. Choose a driver who supports custom page sizes, such as "Generic imagesetter" or "Linotronic".

- **Files must be trapped and color separated:** For laser engraving, it is necessary to create a separate postscript file for each color in the job. Color separation must therefore be carried out before the PostScript is sent to the RIP. In QuarkXpress, for example, make sure that the "Print Separations" box is checked; in Adobe Illustrator the Separator function must be used. The separated PostScript can either consist of a single file, with a "page" for each color, or a set of files, each color having its own file. The single file option is normally more convenient and generates less data. However if a job contains both linework and tonal separations, these should not be mixed within a single PostScript file.

- **Files should be the correct size:** The size of an image produced by the RIP is normally determined by the page size contained within the PostScript file. In most applications the PostScript page size is set not by the document page size, but by the "printer" page size. Before generating PostScript make sure that the paper size is set to the desired image size. For example, using QuarkXpress, if the "Document Setup" dialog is used to set a custom page size of 125 mm x 100 mm (5" x 4"), the PostScript will still have the default page size, usually US Letter or DIN A4. The printer paper size is set in the "Print Setup" dialog. If a roll-type printer description, such as "Generic Imagesetter" or "Linotronic", has been selected it is only necessary to set the "Paper Width". Height will be set automatically.

  There is a limitation on the PostScript page sizes generated by many common applications, including Adobe Illustrator and QuarkXpress. Page size can only be set in increments of whole points ($1/72$", approximately 3.5mm). Any page sizes entered, which do not convert to an

16.3.1 File Preparation For laser engraving, it is necessary to create a separate postscript file for each color in the job. Color separation must therefore be carried out before the PostScript is sent to the RIP. In Adobe Illustrator the Separator function must be used.

exact number of points, will be rounded. This limitation can be overcome by using the page size override feature in the RIP to set the exact page size for each job, or by outputting the job oversize and cropping the files later using, for example, ImageMaster or Adobe PhotoShop. Some dedicated prepress applications do not have this limitation and can output exact page sizes.

■ **Fonts must be available:** Any fonts used in an image must be available at the time the job is processed by the RIP. Fonts, which are used regularly, should be installed on the RIP-Server. Other fonts should be included in the PostScript file.

■ **Comparing "Mask Ablation" and "Direct Engraving" files:** Mask Ablation creates "holes" in the carbon mask where dots are to be imaged on the plate via UV exposure. The "holes" in the mask, where dots are to be imaged on the plate, are created by ablating (removing) the carbon masking material with a laser. Direct engraving creates dots directly on the plate by ablating (removing) the plate material in the non-image area with a laser. Thus corresponding files for each will be opposite each other, much like film negatives and positives.

16.3.2 | File Transfer: 1-Bit TIFF

The use of 1-BIT TIFF(s) is common in digital platemaking applications. These rastered files are digitally stable and cannot be altered unless opened within some type of raster imaging software program. A 1-BIT TIFF is essentially a digital negative created by the same RIP (Raster Image Processor) that would be used to create film for an imagesetter. Normally, 1-BIT TIFF(s) are written as individual colors in the same way a film negative would be used to describe individual colors. 1-BIT TIFF(s) contain only black and white (positive or negative) information. All screening information is inherent to the file. This information is used directly by the platemaking device to image a digital plate.

■ Compression: File compression and FTP transfer can be used to efficiently move data between facilities. The different formats represent different levels of compression. Do not send uncompressed files and do not use TIFF built-in compressions. This is not the best way to compress the file; use a separate tool such as "WinZip".

■ Proofing: Traditionally, film negatives are proofed to evaluate job content for accuracy of elements. It is strongly recommended by FIRST that the producer of the 1-BIT TIFF have the ability to proof the content of these files in the same manner for the same reasons traditional negatives are checked. There are several manufacturers that make software that allows the composite viewing of these screened files in a soft proof environment. Screen ruling, screen angle, and other measurement tools are built into these systems.

Several manufacturers of inkjet RIPs also allow the compositing of screened 1-BIT TIFF(s) for output to a DOD (drop on demand) inkjet device. However, accuracy of these proofs can be compromised when pushing beyond the capabilities of the inkjet device. Out of gamut color and spot color overprinting are two potential problems. Using 1-BIT TIFF(s) with ink jet devices limits the control of proofing to only nine colors. A custom file must be generated for proofs and cannot be proofed across multiple proofing systems.

■ Required Parameters: All job parameters such as screen ruling, screen angles, image trapping, distortion and dot gain compensation are required to be known and incorporated by the generator of the 1-BIT

TIFF. These are most often final plating files so all stepping parameters, bearer bars, density blocks, registration marks, etc. must be included. In a digital platemaking work flow specific criteria, such as calibration for minimum dot (bump curve) and resolution of output device, need to be defined and coordinated between the generator of the 1-BIT TIFF and the platemaker.

■ Resolution: Images can be saved at higher resolutions than the minimum stated below. Higher resolutions will have very little if any visible difference on most jobs and will create files that are larger than required slowing down the production pipeline. Some 1-BIT TIFF RIPs have the ability to save continuous tones at one resolution and linework at a different resolution within the same file.

SUGGESTED MINIMUM RESOLUTION

CONTINUOUS TONE IMAGES ONLY	1,200 dpi
CONTINUOUS TONE AND LINEWORK	1,800 dpi
FINE LINE COPY	2,400 dpi

16.3.3 | Pre-RIP Settings Prior to Imaging

The following attributes of a job require proper data input prior to ripping the electronic file to the digital imager or laser engraver. Specifications may vary by equipment manufacturer.

■ **Circumference:** Assures the job size will be correct in both dimensions on the imaged plate. This setting also assures screens image correctly around the circumference of the cylinder. A setting for circumference is not necessary for all imagers.

■ **Resolution:** Specifies the DPI (dots per inch) or PPI (pixels per inch) for the electronic file to be imaged on the laser device. Resolution will vary depending upon the imaging unit and the screen ruling.

For high-quality direct laser engraving of fine linework and screens a resolution of 635 dpi is an excellent choice for image resolution. Higher resolutions only bring benefits in special cases, such as when engraving pin register holes where positioning is critical. Higher resolution files might take proportionately longer to engrave. It is recommended to consult with the image engraving company in order to coordinate resolution.

■ **Distortion:**

■ For photopolymer plates processed flat and subsequently mounted on a cylinder or sleeve, a distortion factor must be applied to compensate for the change in image size when the plate is mounted around the print cylinder. Refer to the appendix or Prepress Section 14.7 for additional information on calculating distortion factors.

■ For photopolymer plates/sleeves that are imaged and processed on the same cylinder/size as used to print, a distortion factor is not applied; the distortion is automatically based upon the circumference.

■ **Dot Gain Compensation:** An adjustment applied to the final electronic file, determined by identifying the total dot gain expected in the printing process as measured by the press characterization (Print Section 18.3). Dots, positive and reverse line elements are all affected by dot gain and should be compensated accordingly. For some laser engraving systems, this curve can be entered as one parameter of the system's internal dot generation and applied to a 100% file during plate engraving.

16.3.3 Calculating Distortion When a photopolymer plate is laying flat, the top of the plate and the bottom of the plate is the same length (X=Y). However, when the plate is wrapped around a printing cylinder, the surface of the plate becomes stretched because the distance around the top of the plate is greater than the distance around the bottom of the plate ($Y_d > X_d$).

■ **Bump** (Highlight Compensation Curve): Used for digitally imaged photopolymer plates only; does not apply to laser engraving. To avoid imaging dots in the mask, which are too small to allow full dot formation on the plate during UV exposure, it is possible to apply a "bump" to increase the size of the minimum dot. The minimum dot should be at least 30 microns in diameter. If the minimum dot in the file is large enough, a bump may not be required. The bump curve will vary with screen ruling. The finer the screen ruling, the greater the bump required to image the minimum dot.

■ **Line Screen:** Refer to Prepress Section 14.4.1 for print segment specifications.

■ **Seamless Sleeves:** Because a seamless image requires a perfect "pixel-to-pixel" match all the way around the cylinder, it may be necessary to adjust the line screen prior to imaging. Considerations need to be made for circumference and file resolution.

16.4 | Digitally Imaged Photopolymer Plates

The digitally imaged photopolymer plate is processed without the use of photographic film. The sheet photopolymer material is supplied to the platemaker with a carbon black layer on the surface that is imaged from an electronic file using a laser, which removes (ablates) the carbon black layer in the image areas of the design. After ablation, the carbon black layer acts as a mask, blocking the ultra-violet light, during the platemaking exposure process. The plate is back exposed, main exposed, washed out, dried, detacked and finished just as with a conventional sheet photopolymer plate.

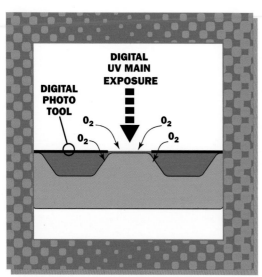

16.4 Digitally Imaged Photopolymer Plates The digitally imaged photopolymer plate is processed without the use of photographic film. The plate is back exposed, main exposed, washed out, dried, detacked and finished just as with a conventional sheet photopolymer plate.

DIGITALLY IMAGED PRESS READY PLATE & SLEEVE SPECIFICATIONS	
HALFTONE DOT RANGE ON PLATE	1% to 98% @175 lpi (69 lpcm) line screen and lower
MINIMUM RULE WIDTH	0.004" (0.102 mm)
MINIMUM POSITIVE/ REVERSE TYPE	3 pt. (0.042" = 1.067 mm)
PLATE CALIPER UNIFORMITY	**Within a Plate:** ±0.00075" (0.019 mm) **Within a Job Plate Set:** ±0.001" (0.025 mm)
SLEEVE/ROLL UNIFORMITY	**Total Indicated Runout:** ±0.001" (0.025 mm) **Microfinish:** <0.000025" Ra
PLATE SIZES PLATE OR ROLL As available from supplier	**Gauges =0.125" (3.18 mm):** from roll stock up to 50" x 360" (127cm x 914cm) **Gauges >0.125" (3.18 mm):** from roll stock up to 50" x 180" (127cm x 457cm)
FLEXO PLATE THICKNESS	from 0.030" to 0.280" (0.075 mm to 7.11 mm)
SLEEVE/ ROLL SIZES FACE LENGTH	Capabilities to >150" (3,810 mm)
SLEEVE MAXIMUM REPEAT	Capabilities to 62" (1,575 mm)

16.4.1 | Mask Specifications

16.4.1.1 | Carbon Density Specifications: The carbon black mask should have a density greater than 3.0, have a uniform consistency of coating, and be free of visual defects such as pinholes, scratches, abrasions and smudges prior to ablation. After ablation, the carbon black opening "stain level" should have a density of 0.06 or less on a transmission densitometer.

CARBON DENSITY SPECIFICATIONS		
PRIOR TO ABLATION	**CARBON MASK: D-MAX**	>3.0
POST ABLATION	**CARBON OPENING: STAIN LEVEL**	<0.06

16.4.1.2 | Mask Ablation on Carriers or Sleeves Guidelines for preparing to image on carriers or sleeves:

- Backflash the digital photopolymer plate prior to placement on the sleeve or cylinder. This exposure will determine the relief of the image. Verify relief height with the printer. In general, there is less relief when imaging on a carrier or sleeve.
- Uniformity of coating for the carbon black mask layer should be consistent. Variation in the stain will create problems with process printing such as inconsistent dot size and shape.
- As sleeve diameters vary, a consistent main exposure is important for highlight dot reproducibility.

16.4.1.3 | Mask Imaging Inspection

- Prior to imaging, check mask layer for any visible scratches, abrasions or marks. Plate material should be clean and flat.
- After imaging and prior to UV face exposure, re-inspect for damage to the mask layer. Flaws in the non-image area of the mask can be corrected with tools such as high-density opaque or red litho tape. Be sure to remove tape prior to plate processing.
- After UV face exposure, the device calibration target should be measured using a transmission densitometer. Check the 100% area to ensure complete clearing. The minimum dot should not vary more than ±1%. Should the scale exhibit 2% or more variation, the imaging process should be checked. Process checks may include the imaging equipment, set-up parameters, flash lamp and raw material.

The device calibration target is a tone scale, without a bump curve, which identifies where dots begin being fully formed at printing height in the digital imaging process. The scale should include, but not be limited to, values between 0 – 10%, 25%, 50%, 75%, 90% and solid. A device calibration target should be placed in a void or non-print area for each plate being imaged.

16.4.2 | Plate Processing

- Vacuum is not required and not recommended during ultraviolet light exposure.
- If digital plates are manufactured with a point light source, maximum light diffusion should be used in combination with extended exposure times to avoid loss of fine detail such as highlight dots.

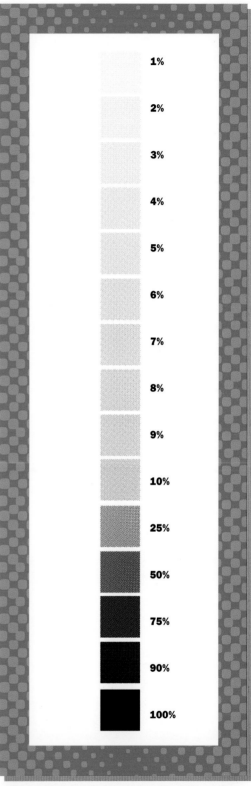

16.4.1.3 Mask Imaging Inspection The device calibration target is a tone scale, without a bump curve, which identifies where dots begin being fully formed at printing height in the digital imaging process. The scale should include, but not be limited to, values between 0–10%, 25%, 50%, 75%, 90% and solid. A device calibration target should be placed in a void or non-print area for each plate being imaged.

16.4.3 | Finished Plate Characteristics

■ **Relief Specifications:** Digital photopolymer plates image with a unique dot profile and structure. Digital dots have a straighter shoulder than conventional dots and therefore, require less relief to assure maximum dot support. Variances in cylinder build-up, press tolerances, or press operation may impact relief requirements for a particular application.

TARGET RELIEF SPECIFICATIONS FOR DIGITAL PHOTOPOLYMER PLATES AND SLEEVES

TARGET RELIEF	PLATE THICKNESS: ENGLISH MEASUREMENT (inches)						
	0.030	0.045	0.067	0.107	0.112	0.125	0.155
PLATES	0.023	0.023	0.020	0.025	0.025	0.030	0.035
SLEEVES	0.020	0.020	0.020	0.022	0.022	na	na

TARGET RELIEF	PLATE THICKNESS: METRIC MEASUREMENT (millimeters)						
	0.762	1.14	1.20	2.72	2.84	3.18	3.94
PLATES	0.584	0.584	0.584	0.635	0.635	0.762	0.889
SLEEVES	0.508	0.508	0.508	0.559	0.559	n/a	n/a

■ **Print Height:** All imaged areas must be at full printing height. There should be no recessed dots on a digital photopolymer plate. Inadequate plate exposure can result in fine details, such as highlight dots, not achieving full printing height. Measure the height of the minimum dot target with a micrometer and compare to a solid area.

■ **Caliper:** See Prepress Section 16.10.2 for measurement method and 16.4 chart for specifications.

■ **Dot Accuracy:** The FIRST Control Target (Prepress Section 12.5) should be used to verify dot accuracy after platemaking. One element of the FIRST color control target is a tone scale; with a bump curve and dot gain compensation applied. Use a calibrated "Flexo Plate Analyzer" (Prepress Section 16.10.3) to measure the screen values to assure dot accuracy.

DOT TOLERANCES FOR DIGITAL PLATEMAKING

2%–9%	10%–24%	25%–39%	40%–49%	50%–98%
±0.5%	±1.0%	±1.5%	±1.75%	±2.0%

16.5 | Laser Engraved Rubber/ Cured Polymer Plates and Sleeves

The digitally engraved rubber, or cured polymer, platemaking process is a direct-to-plate system that does not use photographic film, etched molding masters, conventional rubber vulcanization or subsequent processing steps. Rubber/polymer sheets or seamless covered sleeves are supplied to the platemaker fully "cured" and ready for the one-step production of the digitally imaged plate or sleeve. The image files are sent to a laser that ablates (removes) the rubber/cured polymer from the non-image areas of the design. No processing steps after laser engraving of the plate material is required.

The laser engraved rubber process can also be used to produce seamless rolls (sleeves). In this process, a rubber compound is adhered to either a removable sleeve or directly to a plate cylinder. The laser is then used to engrave the image into the rubber roll. Caution is advised when using demountable sleeves; the process of adhering the rubber to the sleeve involves heat that may distort certain types of sleeves. Not all sleeve types can be used in the seamless process.

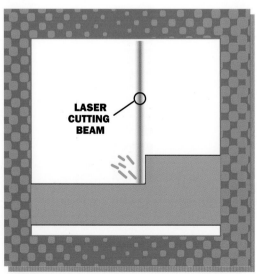

16.5 Laser Engraved Rubber/Cured Polymer Plates and Sleeves The digitally engraved rubber, or cured polymer, platemaking process is a direct-to-plate system that does not use photographic film, etched molding masters, conventional rubber vulcanization or subsequent processing steps.

LASER CUTTING BEAM

LASER ENGRAVED PRESS READY PLATE & SLEEVE SPECIFICATIONS

HALFTONE DOT RANGE ON PLATE	5% @120 lpi (47 lpcm) line screen
MINIMUM RULE WIDTH	0.004" (0.102 mm)
MINIMUM POSITIVE/ REVERSE TYPE	3 pt. (0.042" = 1.067 mm)
PLATE CALIPER UNIFORMITY	**Within a Plate:** ±0.00075" (0.019 mm) **Within a Job Plate Set:** ±0.001" (0.025 mm)
SLEEVE/ROLL UNIFORMITY	**Total Indicated Runout:** ±0.001" (0.025 mm) **Microfinish:** <0.000025" Ra
PLATE SIZES PLATE OR ROLL As available from supplier	**Gauges =0.125" (0.318cm):** from roll stock up to 50" x 360" (127cm x 914cm) **Gauges >0.125" (0.318cm):** from roll stock up to 50" x 180" (127cm x 457cm)
FLEXO PLATE THICKNESS	from 0.030" to 0.280" (0.075 mm to 7.11 mm)
SLEEVE/ ROLL SIZES FACE LENGTH	Capabilities to >150" (3,810 mm)
SLEEVE MAXIMUM REPEAT	Capabilities to 62" (1,575 mm)

16.5.1 | Finished Plate/Sleeve Characteristics

■ **Relief Specifications:** Digital imaging results in finer highlight and quarter-tone dot profiles than plates produced through conventional engraving to molded matrix to molded rubber platemaking. Digital dots have a straighter shoulder than conventional dots and therefore, require less relief to ensure maximum dot support and lengthened plate life. Variances in cylinder build-up, press tolerances, or press operation may impact relief requirements for a particular application.

TARGET RELIEF SPECIFICATIONS FOR DIGITAL PHOTOPOLYMER PLATES AND SLEEVES

PLATE THICKNESS: ENGLISH MEASUREMENT (inches)							
TARGET RELIEF	0.030	0.045	0.067	0.107	0.112	0.125	0.155
PLATES	0.023	0.023	0.020	0.025	0.025	0.030	0.035
SLEEVES	0.020	0.020	0.020	0.022	0.022	na	na

PLATE THICKNESS: METRIC MEASUREMENT (millimeters)							
TARGET RELIEF	0.762	1.14	1.20	2.72	2.84	3.18	3.94
PLATES	0.584	0.584	0.584	0.635	0.635	0.762	0.889
SLEEVES	0.508	0.508	0.508	0.559	0.559	n/a	n/a

■ **Print Height:** Check to ensure that all imaged areas are at full printing height. Although recessed dots are not recommended by FIRST, some software packages allow discretionary engraving of controlled "below-the-surface" dots in fine highlight areas. If used, verify imaged areas above 10% where dots are at full printing height.

■ **Caliper:** Refer to Prepress Section 16.10.2 for measurement method and 16.5 chart for caliper specifications.

■ **Dot Accuracy:** The FIRST Control Target (Prepress Section 12.5) should be used to verify dot accuracy after laser engraving. One element of the FIRST control target is a tone scale with the press gain compensation applied. Use a calibrated Flexographic Plate Analyzer (Prepress Section 16.10.3) to measure the screen values to assure dot accuracy.

DOT TOLERANCES FOR LASER ENGRAVED PLATES				
2% – 9%	10% – 24%	25% – 39%	40% – 49%	50% – 98%
±0.5%	±1.0%	±1.5%	±1.75%	±2.0%

16.6 | Liquid Photopolymer Printing Plates

In the liquid photopolymer platemaking process, the photographic negative is placed on the plate exposure unit with the emulsion side of the film up. A cover film is placed over the negative and air is removed by a vacuum. A layer of liquid photopolymer resin and a polyester backing sheet are applied on top of the cover film and negative. The exposure unit is closed and the material is exposed with UV light. The photopolymer is hardened by the ultraviolet exposure from two banks of lamps. The top lights create the floor (back exposure) and the bottom lights set the image from the negative into the plate material (main exposure). Photopolymer not exposed to light remains a liquid and can be recycled for future use. The exposed plate is washed out in a detergent and water solution that removes unexposed polymer in the non-image areas. The printing plate is then dried in a hot air dryer and finally post exposed. A germicidal exposure finishes the plate to a tack-free surface.

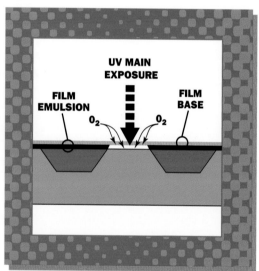

16.7 Photopolymer Printing Plates In the photopolymer platemaking process, the photographic negative is placed on the plate exposure unit with the emulsion side of the film up.

LIQUID PHOTOPOLYMER PRINTING PLATE SPECIFICATIONS	
HALFTONE MINIMUM DOT	2% @150 lpi (59 lpcm) line screen and lower
MINIMUM RULE WIDTH	0.008" (0.20mm)
DUROMETER	25 Shore A to 50 Shore A

THICKNESS UNIFORMITY	On A Plate:
	    –0.125" (3.2 mm): ±0.0005" (0.013 mm)
	    >0.125" (3.2 mm): ±0.001" (0.025 mm)
	Within A Set of Plates:
	    –0.125" (3.2 mm): ±0.0015" (0.038 mm)
	    >0.125" (3.2 mm): ±0.001" (0.05 mm)

16.7 | Sheet Photopolymer Printing Plates

Sheet photopolymer printing plates are made from pre-cut sheets of photopolymer material that is made at a specified thickness. The plates are exposed through a matte finish negative. An overall exposure is made through the back of the material (back exposure) determining the relief of the image. A main exposure is made, under vacuum, through the film negative onto the front of the material after removing the cover sheet. The non-exposed material is washed away in a solvent leaving a relief image in the plate material. Solvents are removed from the plate in a dryer. The final steps are post-exposure and finishing.

Because the sheet photopolymer material is pre-manufactured, the specifications and tolerances of the finished plate are determined by the raw material specifications of the manufacturer. The plate maker controls the plate manufacturing process so that the finished plate remains within the nominal specifications of the raw materials. The control target is used during the main exposure to control the integrity of the image in the material. Exposure tests are made to determine the length of exposure required to control plate relief. The control target contains exposure rules to check proper exposure of the photopolymer. The width of the rule is approximately equal to the diameter of a 3% dot. As such, five different targets are provided for different screen rulings (Refer to Prepress Section 12.5.3). After exposure, the lines should be straight both visually and to the touch.

SHEET PHOTOPOLYMER PRINTING PLATES SPECIFICATIONS	
HALFTONE DOT RANGE ON PLATE	2% @200 lpi (79 lpcm) line screen and lower
MINIMUM RULE WIDTH	0.008" (0.2 mm) for plates up to 0.125" (3.2 mm); 0.015" (0.4 cmm) for plates over 0.125" (3.2 mm)
PLATE SIZES (RAW MATERIAL)	up tp 50" x 80" (132 cm x 203 cm)
THICKENESS	0.045" (1.1 mm) 0.067" (1.7 mm) 0.107" (2.7 mm) 0.112" (2.8 mm) 0.125" (3.2 mm) 0.25 " (6.4 mm)
CALIPER UNIFORMITY	**Within a Plate:** ±0.0005" (0.013 mm) on a plate up to 0.125" (3.2 mm) **Within a Set of Plates for One Job:** ±0.001" (0.025 mm) within a set of plate up to 0.125" (3.2 mm) ±0.0015" (0.04 mm) within a set of plates over 0.125" (3.2 mm)

16.8 | Continuous Photopolymer Covered Printing Sleeves

Bonding specially prepared sheet photopolymer materials to a sleeve produces the continuous photopolymer covered printing sleeve. The sleeve needs to be of a stable material and be within the caliper and run-out tolerances of the final product specifications. When the photopolymer material has been bonded to the sleeve, it will exhibit a totally seamless image across and around the sleeve.

After bonding the sheet photopolymer to the sleeve, the plate height will not be correct in caliper for the finished product. The diameter of the sleeve is oversized and will show some imperfections in the surface of the material. The photopolymer surface is then finished and ground to the specified repeat for the job. The flexibility of the process allows the finished diameter to vary by several thousandths of an inch above, at, or below the pitch diameter of the cylinder based upon the requirements and specifications of the customer.

CONTINUOUS PHOTOPOLYMER COVERED PRINTING SLEEVE SPECIFICATIONS	
HALFTONE MINIMUM DOT	2% @150 lpi (59 lpcm) line screen and lower
MINIMUM RULE WIDTH	0.008" (0.2mm)
TOTAL INDICATED RUN OUT (TIR)	±0.0005" (0.013 mm) within a sleeve

16.9 | Molded Rubber Printing Plates

In the molded rubber plating process, a film negative is made of the image. An exposure of the film negative is made of magnesium or copper that has been coated with a light sensitive coating. The metal is placed in a wash-out solution that removes the metal in the non-image areas leaving a relief image of the copy. The metal engraving is used to make an impression into a thermal setting matrix material. A charge of non-vulcanized rubber is placed into the matrix and under heat and pressure a rubber plate is made from the image in the matrix. The total plate thickness and the relief of the image is controlled by spacers or bearers that are built up between upper and lower heated platens in the plate molding press. The control of bearer thickness, heat, pressure, and processing time determine the quality of the finished plate.

MOLDED RUBBER PRINTING PLATES SPECIFICATIONS	
HALFTONE: MINIMUM DOT	3% @120 lpi (47 lpcm) line screen and lower
MINIMUM RULE WIDTH	0.010" (0.25 mm)
DUROMETER	25 Shore A to 50 Shore A
THICKNESS UNIFORMITY	**On A Plate:** −0.125" (3.2 mm): ±0.0005" (0.013 mm) >0.125" (3.2 mm): ±0.001" (0.025 mm) **Within A Set of Plates:** −0.125" (3.2 mm): ±0.0015" (0.038 mm) >0.125" (3.2 mm): ±0.001" (0.05 mm)

If rubber plates are to be ground, the molded thickness should be ±0.002" (0.05 mm) within the plate. Plate thickness variations beyond 0.004" (0.10 mm) cannot be corrected by grinding due to image distortion. It is not recommended to grind process plates due to distortion of process dots.

16.10 | Printing Plate Measurement and Control

PROPERTIES TO MEASURE	MEASUREMENT DEVICE/TOOL
DUROMETER	Shore A Gauge only for material <0.250" (6.4 mm)
TOTAL CALIPER	Plate Micrometer
PLATE RELIEF	Plate Micrometer
MINIMUM DOT EXPOSURE	Flexo Plate Analyzer
MAXIMUM DOT EXPOSURE	Flexo Plate Analyzer *(maximum dot exposure not yet available)*
LINE WIDTH	Microscope

16.10.1 | Shore A Gauge

The Shore A gauge is an instrument for measuring the durometer or hardness of plate materials. The instrument is a hand held gauge with an indentor attached to a dial scale. A test block is supplied with the Shore A gauge to test the calibration of the instrument. The test block is matched with the serial number of each instrument and is stamped with a durometer reading for calibration. When properly calibrated, the instrument should read within plus or minus one point of the number stamped on the test block.

When using the Shore A gauge, a minimum area of 2" x 2" (50 mm x 50 mm) is required to get an accurate reading. The durometer gauge is held perpendicular to the surface to be measured. The indentor is depressed into the plate material. The durometer reading is indicated on the scale of the instrument. A minimum plate caliper of 0.250" (6.4 mm) is required for using the Shore A gauge.

Readings are only taken in the solid area of the plate. It should not be attempted to take readings on process areas of the plate due to distortion of the plate material.

16.10.2 | Plate Micrometer

Plate micrometers are used to measure the thickness uniformity and relief of flexographic printing plates with either analog or digital readings. The instrument is calibrated using a precision machine block inserted between the surfaces. Accuracy of calibration should be within ±0.0005" (0.013 mm) of the calibration block.

When measuring caliper and relief with the plate micrometer, readings should be made in areas that are at least 1" x 1" (25 mm x 25 mm) in area. Multiple measurements should be taken across the plate to determine the uniformity of plate thickness. Digital plate micrometers equipped with a printer can output statistical data of the plate measurements. To confirm the plates comply with certification requirements, the printer should check this data.

When measuring the plate uniformity both within a plate and from color to color, solids must be compared to solids and screened areas to screened areas for consistency. There may be a difference in the finished plate height between screened areas and solid areas.

16.10.2 Plate Micrometer Plates should be inspected and measured on a micrometer, with gauge readings marked on the plates for use by the mounter during layout.

16.10.3 | Flexographic Plate Analyzer

The flexographic plate analyzer is a device that measures halftone dot size. A high-resolution video camera allows for precise measurement. This device must read halftones regardless of the contrast, color or graining of the image. Excellent correlation may be possible with conventional densitometers when measuring film to plate. Stochastic or FM screen images can also be verified for quality.

16.10.4 | Microscope

A conventional gravure microscope with a scale can be used to measure halftone dot size, rule widths, and plate relief. The microscope can be used to measure in thousandths of an inch or in microns depending on specifications. To measure plate relief, first the microscope is focused on top of the image of the plate and then zeroed. Next, the microscope is focused on the floor of the plate. Readings are taken from the scale on the microscope. Multiple readings should be taken to determine the uniformity of the relief across the plate surface.

16.10.5 | Exposure Guide

During the main exposure process of platemaking photopolymer plates, the control target is imaged within each plate exposure. The control target is used as the exposure guide containing positive line and halftone scales. The line screen value of the control targets should correspond with the line screen value used in the image. The imaged exposure guide can be measured to determine uniformity of the printing plate to specifications.

For Example: If 133 line screen is used the exposure rules will be 0.0015" (0.11 pts.) thick. This line weight corresponds approximately to the diameter of a 3% dot at 133 line screen.

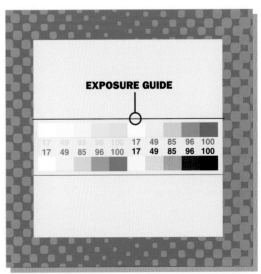

16.10.5 Exposure Guide The control target is used as the exposure guide containing positive line and halftone scales. The imaged exposure guide can be measured to detemine uniformity of the printing plate specifications.

16.10.6 | Reasons for Various Control Targets

There are five control targets for two reasons. One is the aforementioned exposure rule, which varies in width with screen ruling. The second is to provide a coarse and fine slur target for different screen rulings. The five targets and the screen rulings are:

LINE SCREEN	EXPOSURE LINE WEIGHT THICKNESS	SLUR TARGET
55 lpi (22 lpcm)	0.22 pts. (0.078mm)	Coarse
65 – 85 lpi (26 – 33 lpcm)	0.18 pts. (0.064mm)	Coarse
100 – 120 lpi (39 – 47 lpcm)	0.14 pts (0.049mm)	Fine
133 – 175 lpi (52 – 69 lpcm)	0.11 pts. (0.039mm)	Fine
200 lpi (79 lpcm)	0.09 pts. (0.032mm)	Fine

17.0 Introduction

The science of print reproduction requires measured, controlled, optimized, repeatable results. This section is a guide to achieving specifications on press. Step by step procedures outline proven methods for repeatable, consistent, profitable flexographic process and line printing. To skip or shortcut any element is to invite failure.

17.1 | Mechanics of Achieving and Maintaining Print

Two basic sections comprise the print section. The initial section focuses on the mechanics of physically achieving quality print. The following section addresses significant print variables that are critical to managing and maintaining print results.

When a press is in its best possible condition mechanically, its performance is optimized. A press running with worn or non-functioning parts cannot print consistently and therefore becomes an uncontrolled variable. The Press Optimization section describes how to make a press operate at its peak performance. Print optimization determines the best combination of plates, anilox, ink, etc., through methodical testing. Print characteristics such as dot gain, register and trap are specific to every combination of materials used on press. These print characteristics are quantified by "characterizing the press" for a given set of variables (combination of plates, anilox, stickyback, ink, etc.). The designer and color separator use the characterization data to select the type of graphics and to compensate the graphics so the print outcome is consistent and able to match the contract proof.

The second basic segment covers significant print variables that are critical in managing and maintaining the print results. These are:

- Contract Proofs.
- Substrates.
- Inks.
- Plate Mounting.
- Sleeve Systems.
- Anilox Rollers.
- Doctor Blades.

Print specific information is provided on bar codes as well as considerations for specialty print applications.

18.0 Controlling the Press and Print Outcome

18.1 | Press Optimization

The objective of press optimization is to determine if the press is mechanically holding impression settings and register and evenly delivering ink. Print trials should be conducted to test the various press settings and mechanical components to verify the press is consistent and able to hold its settings.

New presses are likely performing at the top of their capabilities. However, with day-to-day use, wear is inevitable. The changes from wear occur slowly and may go unnoticed unless measurements are routinely taken and compared to original performance specifications. Press optimization is attempting to address all the issues that can hinder press performance. Unquestionably, a regular maintenance program helps keep a press in optimum condition.

Flexographic press designs are very diverse and driven by market segment. When determining what to expect for optimum capability, consult with the press manufacturer. The press should be optimized when it is installed and whenever press variability is introduced (new gears, rollers, dryers, etc).

The following are some of the most common mechanical problems on press that influence print quality and prevent consistent quality results.

18.1.1 | Gear Condition

Worn plate cylinder gears create backlash and register problems. Backlash appears as slurred dots and barring (gear marks) in the image—especially in vignettes. The gear teeth should be cleaned and regularly examined for wear. Wear often appears as a sharpening of the top of the gear tooth. Worn gears of other components in the plate cylinder gear train can also have a negative effect. The vibration created by worn gears affects the quality of the printed image.

18.1.2 | Impression Cylinder or Central Impression Drum

The TIR (total indicated runout) of the central impression drum (or impression cylinders) affects the ability to achieve consistent kiss impression. If a drum or impression cylinder has excessive runout, part of the print will either skip or be over impressed. Central impression (CI) drums, if not properly cooled, will expand and contract with changes in temperature that inhibit achieving optimum impression settings. Press dryers and pressroom temperature can affect the CI drum. The print results appear as heavy and then light or may print in the area of the center of the drum first. To control the temperature, make sure water is flowing through the cooling coils. Prolonged running of an uncontrolled drum may cause permanent warping. For presses with individual impression cylinders, TIR problems come mainly from worn bearings or bushings. Use a dial indicator to measure TIR. Original equipment manufacturers have established specifications for their presses.

18.1.2.1 | Dial Indicator

This tool is used to measure total indicated runout (TIR), the recommended increment is 0.0001" (0.0025 mm). This tool can also be used to measure deck repeatability (how accurately the anilox and plate cylinders return to the "exact" same position after rotating several times or going off/on impression.

18.1.3 | Parallelism

The impression cylinder, plate cylinder, anilox roller, drive rolls and idler rolls must be in alignment and parallel. When the anilox roller or impression cylinder is not perfectly parallel with the plate cylinder, one side of the print cylinder will begin to print before the other.

Another consideration is alignment of drive, nip and idler rolls in the web or sheet path. When not aligned they create baggy web edges, wrinkles, drifting substrate and inconsistent register. The anilox roller and doctor blade chamber (or rubber roller) must also be in alignment with each other and the print cylinder for consistent, even ink metering.

18.1.2 Impression Cylinder or Central Impression Drum
The TIR (total indicated runout) of this component affects the ability to achieve consistent kiss impression. If a drum or impression cylinder has out of balance runout, part of the print will either skip or be over impressed.

18.1.4 | Tension Controls

Tension plays a major part in register—especially on extensible films. Make certain in-feed and out-feed tension controls are fully operational and calibrated.

Shaftless presses, with individual servo motors, possess increased tension control throughout the press.

18.1.5 | Wear

Worn, dirty deck screws and ways cause impression setting and repeatability problems. These vital parts must be kept clean and oiled for smooth operation. Plate and anilox cylinder bearings or bushings in poor repair also do not allow proper impression setting. Plates must often be over impressed to avoid the bounce caused by play in worn bearings. The result is slurred dots and banding effects. It is necessary to replace all worn bearings for optimum press performance.

18.1.6 | Drying Systems

The dryers must be clean, the nozzles clear and the airflow balanced for maximum velocity. Unbalanced dryers may cause air to escape and blow on the plates. This causes dirty print and reduced color density. Adjusting the airflow (velocity) down too low causes poor ink trap and drying

These are only some of the press mechanics requiring optimization. Evaluate the entire press for mechanical consistency and follow the press manufacturer's recommendations.

When the press is in the best condition possible, the challenge is to maintain it. Regular press maintenance lends consistency to its performance. A daily, weekly, monthly and annual formal maintenance procedure is required.

18.1.5 Wear Plates must often be over impressed to avoid the bounce caused by play in worn-out bearings. This can result in banding or slurred dots. They way to correct this is by replacing all worn bearings.

18.2 | Print Optimization

The objective of print optimization is to determine the optimum combination of incoming materials such as plates, stickyback, anilox rollers, ink, substrate, etc. to achieve the best possible print results on a given press. After testing to determine what combinations are optimum for various types of graphics (process vs. line vs. solids), it is important to standardize the combinations and consistently use the same set of materials. Changing the components will change the characterization outcome and make the existing data used by designers, prepress providers and printers incorrect. This may result in the inability to match the contract proof and achieve acceptable print quality on press.

18.2.1 | How to Optimize

Begin the optimization process by testing the materials currently in use. Run a single color trial using magenta or cyan. If the recommended specifications are attained, the current combination of materials is acceptable. If not, it is time to optimize.

While there are several approaches to print optimization, a collaborative effort with suppliers is advised. Begin by running a series of plate types. Test each plate separately with each mounting material type. Refer to Print Section 19.4.1.

Plate type, mounting materials, ink and anilox volume are all key elements influencing dot gain and density. For example, if the printed image achieves density well above the target for that color, a lower volume anilox roller should be used. With the lower volume anilox, dot gain and density decrease. Less gain is good but target density must be obtained.

If a certain plate and lower volume anilox achieves the dot gain required but not the color density, consult the ink supplier for possible ink formulation adjustment. Test all process colors: cyan, magenta, yellow and black, to make sure they all perform to specifications. Optimizing ink strength to obtain target densities with a lower volume anilox roller is one approach.

Some printers run a banded anilox roller to determine the optimum combination of ink and anilox cell volume and cell count. A single anilox is engraved with several bands of different line screens and volumes. An identical test target is run on each band. The lowest volume band achieving slightly higher than target density while incurring minimum dot gain is the optimum anilox specification. A banded anilox can be run with several ink strengths to identify the optimum combination of anilox engraving and ink strength.

It is important to verify that the chosen materials perform as expected in everyday production. Without supervision, have several trained press crews, not previously involved in the press optimization, run the test and achieve the same results. This will confirm that the results are repeatable in the production environment. This test also establishes whether the training and skill level of a crew are sufficient enough to print to the desired specifications.

Similar press tests can be designed to evaluate any combination of press variables desired. It is important to appoint a qualified person to design the test, organize all of the materials (order a banded anilox, coordinate ink samples, stickybacks, etc.), label the samples as they are printed, accurately measure the print samples and interpret the results. Without sufficient control of the pressrun and meaningful evaluation of the data generated, the pressrun is of little value. The scope of the test can quickly become unmanageable if too many variables are evaluated at one time. Begin the print optimization process by identifying primary materials that affect print quality. The following items have a measurable influence on print results and image quality.

18.2.2 | Platemaking Film

Films generated on different output devices have significant enough variation to cause a change in print results (Refer to Prepress Section 14). Some of the variables are:

- Dot shape (significant influence on dot gain).
- Screen quality.
- Screen resolution.
- Consistency and tolerances of screen percentages.
- Matte finish.

Using a single source film/plate output device is the best option, but not always possible. When using a new output device it is important to adjust for output variables by characterizing/profiling the press again with the new suppliers test plate. An alternative is to use existing characterization data. A new film/plate supplier may have the same imagesetter as the previous supplier. Verifying the accuracy of dot percent between suppliers will validate the previously run characterization, providing the print has remained consistent. A third option is to run uncompensated control targets, side by side, from the existing and new output device. Evaluate the difference in dot gain and adjust future dot gain compensation accordingly. It is important to document which imagesetter/platesetter was used to produce the characterization target.

18.2.3 | Plate Type

A wide range of materials and parameters exist for producing quality flexographic printing. Differing plate materials result in varying ink release characteristics. See Prepress Section 16 for more information on platemaking specifications and tolerances. Key plate variables affecting print results include:

18.2.2 Platemaking Film Films generated on different output devices have significant enough variation to cause a change in print results. Keep a record of which imagesetter/platesetter was used to produce the characterization materials.

- Type of plate material: ink release and imaging traits vary widely among the many materials available. Even within a category of material, such as photopolymer, the print characteristics vary dramatically by type of material (polymer).
- Durometer of the plate: affects impression pressure, dot gain, plate durability and the effectiveness of mounting materials.
- Plate caliper (thickness): influences imaging traits and tonal range. Usually thinner plates cause less image distortion. The industry trend is toward thinner plate materials for this reason.
- Plate uniformity: monitor photopolymer exposure times to assure consistent imaging caliper. Once a specific plate material is selected, use it consistently. Plates must have uniform caliper to avoid over impressing or underlaying to eliminate low spots.
- Relief: influences minimum dot size held on the plate while also affecting how the image distorts. Too deep a relief results in cupping when the plate is wrapped around the cylinder.
- Plate processing method: polymer plate quality is affected by the method used for imaging the polymer, plate exposure, plate wash, plate drying and the degree of post exposure. Rubber plates require consistency of the engraving material and careful monitoring of the molding process.

18.2.4 | Mounting Materials

The materials used to mount plates to the print cylinder or carrier sheet can create caliper deviations or change the overall hardness of the plate/mount combination. It is important to select a specific mounting material for each print application. Changing mounting materials will affect the print outcome and often re-characterization is required. Refer to Print Section 19.4.

18.2.5 | Substrate

Fluctuations in characteristics within a particular substrate or changing to a different substrate will likely produce differing print results. Control of key variables by the substrate manufacturer is critical. Refer to Print Section 19.2.

18.2.6 | Ink

Many performance properties of an ink affect the printed result. Because ink properties vary dramatically depending on application, substrate and end use requirements, it is impossible to list all the specifics. Work with the ink supplier to identify key properties of the ink that should be included in a "Certificate of Analysis" or internal incoming material testing protocol. Refer to Print Section 19.3.

18.2.7 | Anilox Rollers

Ink and anilox rollers are dependent upon one another. A change in one affects the performance of the other. It is important to consider both in tandem when optimizing the printing process. Refer to Print Section 19.6.

18.2.8 | Ink Metering System

- Proper alignment and good repair of the print deck components should take place during press optimization. Variables include ink metering doctor blades, rubber rolls, or a combination of both. Refer to Print Section 19.7 for more information on doctor blades.

18.2.4 Mounting Materials Select a specific mounting material for each print application. Changing mounting materials will affect the print outcome and often recharacterization is required.

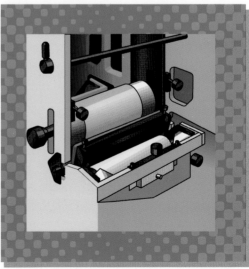

18.2.8 Ink Metering Proper alignment and good repair of the print deck components should take place during the press optimization. Variables include ink metering doctor blades, rubber rolls, or a combination of both.

FIRST Characterization Target

18.3 Print Characterization It is important that the characterization target for a typical project is output by the prepress provider at the proper screen count, using the same imagesetter, plate type and other ingredients that have been the result of press optimization.

18.3 | Print Characterization

There are many terms used to describe print characterization including: press characterization, press profile, and fingerprint. The objective of the characterization process is to measure and record the ongoing print characteristics of a particular press with specific settings and materials. The data from the characterization is provided to the designer and prepress provider for selection of graphics and compensation to the characterization results. The press crews also use this data as specific targets and numbers to achieve during all production runs. Any deviation of production outcome from characterization data should be checked to determine what changed to cause the deviation.

The process of characterization implies a commitment to apply characterization data and to use control targets on all future pressruns. Routinely measuring and maintaining the print data within tolerances of the characterization data authenticates the repeatability of the print. This provides the ability to predict print results and to match the contract proof.

18.3.1 | The IT8.7/4 Proposed Characterization Data Set

Most color management systems have their own unique test target from which the color profile (ICC profile) is created. There are industry standard targets also available such as the FIRST target (introduced in the Premier Edition of FIRST), the ECI (European Color Initiative) target and the IT8.7/4 proposed data set. In an effort to reduce the number of "standard" targets, FIRST now recommends using the IT8.7/4 proposed data set when characterizing the printing process. This data set is the result of the collaborative efforts of several standards committees and represents the best technical approach to a standard target.

There are two default layouts or "targets" based on the proposed IT8.7/4 data set. These are a "visual layout" target and a "random layout" target. Both contain exactly the same combinations of CMYK data. The random layout target should be used for print characterization. By randomizing the locations of the various CMYK combinations, ink takeout across the target area can be made more uniform and errors introduced by press anomalies will be randomized with respect to CIELab color space. The visual layout is useful for careful initial "visual" analysis of the characterization pressrun and for those applications where manual measurement is required. After a press profile is created, it is a good idea to make a proof representing the press profile. With the highly structured form of the visual layout target, it is easy to spot areas that are inconsistent with the rest of the target. This is not a substitute for actual colormetric analysis of the profile. Refer to Prepress Section 13.0 CIELab Color Management for additional information.

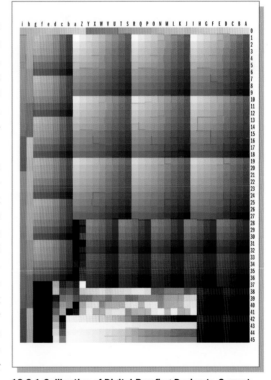

18.3.1 Calibration of Digital Proofing Device to Current Analog Proofing System FIRST recommends outputting the IT8.7/4 Proposed Characterization Data Set to film and making a proof to specifications for the selected print segment.

18.3.1.1 | Elements of the IT8.7/4 Proposed Characterization Data Set

■ **Solid Ink Density:** Used to measure the solid ink density and hue error of yellow, magenta, cyan, and black.

■ **Tonal Scales:** Patches containing known dot areas of the four single colors (CMYK). Twenty dot values are measured for each process color. Comparing the tonal value on film to the tonal value printed for each patch, a cutback curve (dot gain compensation) can be generated.

■ **Trap or Overprint of Solids:** Two color overprints are used to measure ink trap. Red, Green and Blue overprints are included in the target.

■ **Gray Balance, Highlight and Shadow:** Gray balance is a measurement of Y + M + C vs. K. The target includes highlight, quartertone, midtone, three-quartertone and shadow gray balance patches. As an exam-

Print

ple, the quartertone gray balance comparison uses two patches. One has 25% black ink; the second one has 23% C + 16% M + 16% Y (example) ink combining to achieve a quarter-tone neutral gray.

■ **CMYK Overprints:** Randomly distributed overprint patches of various combinations of dot percentages of the process colors (CMYK). These patches are used to build ICC profiles and can be measured and used to compare and correlate the color match of one device to another device. Refer to Prepress Section 13.0 for additional information.

18.3.2 | Other Elements for Consideration On a Characterization Test Plate

In addition to running a characterization target, other elements may be included on the test plate to capture additional "characterization" information (depending on the size of the web).

■ UPC Magnification and Bar-Width Reduction (BWR): To determine optimum BWR for a given magnification, refer to Print Section 20.6.

■ Linear Blends: Used to visually determine the minimum and maximum printing dot.

■ Positive and Reverse Lines: Used to determine minimum printing line widths for positive and reverse rules.

■ Registration Marks/Microdots: Used to determine accuracy and consistency of registration.

■ Slur Targets: Provides a visual indication of slur.

■ Vignettes or Gradated Screens: Include several line screens to determine optimum line screen for vignettes.

18.3.3 | Controlling the Characterization Process

Variables to verify and control include:

■ FIRST specifications for applicable industry segment.
■ Ink color match.
■ Correct ink color sequence and viscosity range.
■ Plate, ink, anilox, mounting material, etc. are made to manufacturers' specifications and tolerances.
■ Calibrated measuring tools.
■ The appropriate measurements taken, recorded and used to make adjustments.
■ Characterization is run at projected production speeds.
■ Each substrates is characterized individually.

18.4 | Good Pressroom Practices For Maintaining Specifications

As stated previously, control and consistency are vital to success. Good pressroom practice is simply organizing various procedures and support equipment to ensure consistency. This section discusses some of the most important systems and issues.

18.4.1 | Accurate Densitometry

A daily check of all densitometers to a T-Ref standard and logging of the results is recommended. If out of specification, calibrate the densitometer according to manufacturer's instructions. Having one person assigned to scheduled densitometer verification is recommended. (See Appendix for T-Ref ordering information from the GCA and Print Section 18.5.2 for more information).

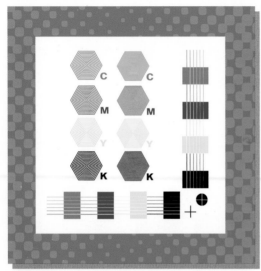

18.3.2 Elements of the Characterization Target include registration marks, positive and reverse lines and slur targets.

18.4.2 | Anilox Cleaning Equipment and Procedure

Even with on-press cleaning during press wash-ups, invariably anilox cells plug with dried ink. When plugged, the volume or ink capacity of the roller erratically decreases. This plugging causes a change in the rollers' printing characteristics. Many systems and techniques exist for cleaning anilox rollers; regardless of the system used, cleaning rollers to maintain consistent cell volume is critical to achieving specifications. Refer to Print Section 19.6.6. Cleaning methods include:

- Cleaning compounds and brushes.
- Ultrasonic.
- Bicarbonate of soda or poly bead bombardment.
- Caustic soak with high-pressure water rinse.

18.4.3 | Anilox Identification System

Maintain a data sheet for each roller; recording manufacturer, cell count, cell volume, screen angle, age, location and cleaning history.

18.4.4 | Job History Information

Generate a run condition sheet for each job. When filled out at the completion of the run, this sheet documents press conditions for future reference. The record includes information on variables affecting the run and appearance of the image. Document the following:

- Anilox roller cell count, volume and identification number.
- Color sequence.
- Dryer temperature.
- Gear, cylinder and sleeve package (including repeat length).
- Ink type, viscosity and pH (for water inks).
- Mounting material (stickyback, carrier sheet, etc.).
- Plate material.
- pressrun speed.
- Substrate.
- Tension or caliper settings.

As issues arise during production, add them to the list. Beware of including too much information that makes the sheet difficult to fill out and use.

18.4.5 | Documentation of Incoming Materials

Work with suppliers to develop a program using certificate of analysis (COA) or certificate of compliance (COC) or similar documentation. For all incoming materials, list every variable requiring verification or inspection. A certificate of analysis (COA) or certificate of compliance (COC) attached to each shipment confirms, guarantees and documents that the product meets specifications.

Often printers opt to spot check all materials, even if the material is supplied with a COC (certificate of compliance) or COA (certificate of analysis). Procedures should be established to monitor and verify the consistency of incoming materials. This practice ensures the material supplied will produce the expected result prior to using it during production. If a problem is identified, the material can be corrected or replaced before it is needed in production.

18.5 | Print Evaluation Equipment & Methods

Use the same set-up conditions as was used to print the characterization. Replicating the materials, press conditions and numbers used for the print characterization pressrun are essential to successful, profitable printing.

18.5.1 | Color-viewing Booth

Accurate, consistent visual perception of color requires the image to be viewed in a standard, chromatically neutral, controlled manner. If the printer, separator, and customer standardize viewing conditions, color discrepancies can be minimized.

A color-viewing booth is used to view printed images, proofs, or transparencies, under a controlled and standard light source. ANSI 2.30 1989 set specifications for proper viewing conditions.

18.5.1 Color-vewing Booth Accurate, consistent visual perception of color requires that the subjects be viewed in a standard, chromatically neutral, controlled manner.

ANSI 2.30 – 1989: COLOR-VIEWING CONDITIONS	
PARAMETER	**SPECIFICATION**
LIGHTING	5,000° Kelvin bulbs
LIGHT SOURCE	Color Rendering Index: ≥ 90
VIEWING SURFACE	Luminance: =204, ±44 foot candles
VIEWING AREA COLOR	Neutral Gray: Munsell N8 or equivalent
ANGLES OF ILLUMINATION	Minimize glare

18.5.2 | Reflection Densitometer–Measuring Process Colors

ANSI/CGATS.4 (1993 Graphic Technology—Graphic Arts Reflection Densitometry Measurements—Terminology, Equations, Image Elements, and Procedures) is the standard used for the measurement of printed materials using a densitometer. Verify the densitometer used meets the following criteria:

- Status T wide-band filter is the preferred spectral response in North America. It is defined to closely match the characteristics of graphic arts materials normally used in the United States.
- Aperture size: 3.5 mm
- Accurately reads a standard reference such as T-Ref to ±0.02. The T-ref provides a calibrated standard on a laminated sheet with white, black, cyan, magenta and yellow circles with the associated readings for each color available from GCA. Refer to the Appendix for GCA contact information.
- Rugged enough for the pressroom environment

DENSITOMETER PARAMETER & INFORMATION LISTING	
PARAMETER	**NOTED INFORMATION**
DENSITY	Absolute or Relative Color Channel (filter) Used
DOT AREA	Solid Density Color Channel (filter) Used Equation: Murray-Davies or Yule-Nielsen (include "n" factor)
DOT GAIN	Film Printing Dot Area Equation: Murray-Davies or Yule-Nielsen (include "n" factor)
TRAP	Overprint(s) Measured Lay down sequence Equation: Brunner, newsprint, apparent
PRINT CONTRAST	Film Printing Dot Area Paper (included/excluded)

The Murray-Davies equation is preferred; both are mentioned in the event that a company is using the Yule-Nielsen equation. The remainder of this publication refers to the Murray-Davies equation. For additional information on densitometry refer to Prepress Section 15.3 and to "Introduction to Densitometry – Users Guide to Print Production Measurement Using Densitometry" published by the Graphic Communications Association (GCA contact information is listed in the Appendix).

18.5.2.1 | Solid Ink Density and Balance The table below defines the solid ink density target for each process color. All process colors must balance with each other for proper image reproduction and neutral gray balance. Maintain the density for M, C, K within ±0.07, and yellow within ±0.05. As an example, if the magenta ink density is +0.07 (the target), the remaining colors must be printed at or above their respective target density to maintain balance. Refer to Print Section 19.3.2 for information regarding FIRST recommended process ink pigments and L*a*b values.

SOLID INK DENSITY TARGETS				
WIDE WEB	**CYAN**	**MAGENTA**	**YELLOW**	**BLACK**
PAPER PRODUCTS	1.25	1.25	1.00	1.50
FILM PRODUCTS	1.25	1.20	1.00	1.40
NARROW WEB	**CYAN**	**MAGENTA**	**YELLOW**	**BLACK**
PAPER PRODUCTS	1.35	1.25	1.00	1.50
FILM PRODUCTS	1.25	1.20	1.00	1.40

18.5.2.1.1 | Opacity of White Ink or Substrate Color is affected by the way light is reflected from the substrate or white ink under the printed area. Variations in how the light reflects changes the image appearance even though the printed process color densities may not have changed. Monitor the substrate and white ink opacity by developing a target reading using an opacity meter or densitometer. An opacity meter measures the opacity of a substrate or white ink. Opacity variance can drastically affect the process-printed image. An alternative tool for measuring opacity is a densitometer. Measure the white opacity over the black plaque using the densitometer filter for black. The lower the number is on the meter, the higher the opacity. Refer to Print Section 19.3.4.3.6 for opacity testing information.

18.5.2.2 | Dot Gain (Tonal Value Increase) Proper tone reproduction depends on correct compensation for dot gain according to the measurements taken during the print characterization. The dot area readings from the current printed control target should match the readings from the print characterization. Measure dot gain (dot area) with a reflection densitometer set to the Murray-Davies equation.

Minimum highlight dot area at start-up is a critical measurement. Highlight dot gain is greatly affected by impression setting and is the most sensitive to adjustment.

Measure the control target periodically throughout the pressrun to verify consistency. If, after start-up, it is necessary to remove or hide the FIRST control target due to customer requirements, use the FIRST run target which is considerably reduced, providing less information but adequate to maintain a job throughout a pressrun. Educating customers on the importance of using control targets often results in willing cooperation. See Print Section 18.6 illustrations of FIRST control target and run target.

18.5.2.2.1 | Ink Viscosity Maintain ink viscosity within the range determined during optimization and characterization. Verify viscosity is correct before inking plates. Ink viscosity affects halftone dot reproduction and therefore print contrast. Control ink viscosity within a range of ±1 second for solvent inks and ±2 seconds for water based inks. This tolerance is established using a small aperture efflux cup such as a #2 Zahn. Once the correct viscosity is established, the ink supplier should be able to supply the same ink properties at the ideal viscosity for all subsequent orders. Remember that ink viscosity is dependent upon temperature and must be monitored and adjusted throughout the pressrun. Refer to Print Section 19.3.4.2.2 for viscosity testing information.

18.5.2.3 | Print Contrast The combination of low dot gain and high ink density creates a desirable print contrast between the midtone and shadow tone areas and strong solid colors. There are different opinions as to what tone ranges should be used to measure print contrast. Print contrast is described as the density difference between the 70% target on the control target and the solid. Being able to obtain a high print contrast between a 70% and a solid will open shadows and minimize the affect of subtle shifts in dot gain normally experienced throughout the duration of the printrun.

Print Contrast Formula:

$$PC\% = \left(\frac{D_S - D_T}{D_S} \right) \times 100$$

Where:

PC% = Print Contrast Percentage

D$_S$ = Density of Solid

D$_T$ = Density of 70% Tint

PROCESS COLOR PRINT CONTRAST	
CYAN	≥ 20%
MAGENTA	≥ 20%
YELLOW	≥ 20%
BLACK	≥ 15%

Achieve the following minimum print contrast percentages as starting points for process printing. Print contrast recommendations may vary according to the substrate, ink, press, operator skill, etc. The variation in print contrast of all process/screen colors should be balanced and be maintained within 5 percentage points of each other. Because yellow has a lower solid ink density, it is specified at a lower print contrast than the other three colors.

18.5.2.4 | Ink Trap The ability of one ink to lay smoothly over the next is referred to as ink trap. In process print, it is the ability of each process color to overprint the previous color. One source of poor ink trap comes from the first down color not drying before the next color is applied over it. This condition causes the second or third down color to mottle or bleed into the first down ink. The change in laydown results in a change in the color value and therefore affects image reproduction accuracy. Ink pigment characteristics may also affect trap. For example, certain yellow pigments do not allow over printed colors to lay smoothly.

The higher the number, the better the ink trap. If the current ink trap is less than 80%, check the dryers. If the dryers are properly performing within tolerance, check with the ink supplier for advice on reformulating the ink.

18.5.2.5 | Hue Error/Grayness Using a densitometer, hue error and grayness can be indicators of process ink purity. Hue error indicates a hue shift from an ideal process color while grayness characterizes the relative gray content of a process ink. Hue error/grayness should be measured prior to, and during, the production run to monitor the process ink colors for consistency and identify contamination if it occurs. Refer to Prepress Section 12.0 for additional information on color separations.

Although using hue error/grayness to measure and verify an ink color is better than a subjective opinion, it is not as accurate as when using a spectrophotometer. Refer to Prepress Section 13.0.

18.5.2.6 | Color Sequence Traditionally Y, M, C, K is the most commonly used flexographic color sequence for surface print. Some printers are finding benefits in reversing the traditional rotation to K, C, M, Y for certain applications. Printers should evaluate print sequence during print optimization trials to determine if this sequence affords improved print quality with the given substrate.

18.5.3 | Spectrophotometer – Measuring Line Colors
ISO 2846-5 (Graphic Technology – Colour & Transparency of Printing Ink Sets for 4-Colour Printing Part 5: Flexographic Printing) defines the standard spectrophotometric instrument settings.

ISO 2846-5 SPECTROPHOTOMETER SETTINGS	
GEOMETRY	0°/45° or 45°/0°
OBSERVER	2° standard observer
ILLUMINANT	D50 (5,000° Kelvin)

Colorimetric parameters shall be calculated using the equations of *CGATS.5; (1993 Graphic Technology—Spectral Measurement and Colorimetric Computation for Graphic Arts Images)* specific parameter calculation details may be found in that publication. In general, the most commonly used colorimetric parameters are CIE L^*, a^*, b^*, C^*ab, h^*ab.

- **L★** describes the lightness of a sample. Low values are perceived as darker; higher values are perceived as whiter.
- **a★** describes the red/green dimension of a sample. The more positive the a^* value, the more red the sample; the more negative the a^* value, the more green the sample.
- **b★** describes the yellow/blue dimension of a sample. The more positive the b^* value the more yellow the sample; the more negative the b^* value the more blue the sample.
- **C★ab** (Chroma) and **h★ab** (hue) are derived from a^* and b^* and are an alternative way of specifying the color of a sample.

A spectrophotometer provides the most accurate definition of a color (lightness, saturation, and hue). For line colors the spectrophotometer is used to measure the color's spectral reflectance and compare that measurement against an established color target or standard. Most spectrophotometers also have densitometric functions. For process inks it is recommended to match to the established densitometric specifications and then verify via the spectrophotometer (L, c, h, $L^*a^*b^*$ values). Refer to Prepress Section 13.3.2 CMS Calibration Intervals.

18.5.3.1 | Color Tolerancing Color measurement technology continues to evolve and improve. Newer methods employ better formulas for predicting visual color matches. While CMC (2:1) tolerancing has provided generally good predictions of a printed colors visual match to the intended target, CIE94 and CIE2000 (referred to in FIRST as CIE tolerancing) represent revised formulas with improved predictability. Each evolution in color tolerancing brings the human eye and the instrument closer together in the evaluation of color. As instrumentation is purchased, FIRST recommends buying equipment that utilizes the latest methods in color tolerancing and has a robust upgrade path.

If CIE tolerancing is not available, CMC tolerancing is also a FIRST recommended method for establishing a tolerance around a color target. The typical ratio of lightness to chromaticity is 2:1, although some colors, such as pastels, may require tighter tolerances. CMC automatically adjusts the tolerance for various color families. For example, the tolerance ellipse for a dark brown is larger than for a light tan.

Do not mix color tolerancing systems. All companies working on the same project should be using the same tolerancing system.

18.5.3.2 | **Ink Drawdown or Proofing**   The drawdown or bardown unit can be used to check line (and process) colors for color accuracy. The drawdown should be done on the same substrate as the job will be printed. For less variability and human error, an automatic unit is recommended rather than a hand proofer. Once proofed, the incoming ink can be compared to the customer-approved standard using a spectrophotometer prior to going to press. Refer to Print Section 19.3.1.2 on ink proofing.

18.5.4 | **Bar Code Verifier**

No material should be accepted for print unless it is accompanied by a bar code report scanned directly from the film supplied for plate making regardless of who makes the plates. When an assembled print-ready file is supplied for imaging to the printer or plate provider, it must be accompanied by a written report identifying the human readable number for the incorporated machine-readable code and the bar width adjustment applied. Incoming material must be checked to verify that the human readable number is correct and the proper BWR is applied.

A bar code verifier is used to confirm the bar code is printing within specifications. Most consumer product companies are requesting ANSI grading of bar codes. There is a wide range of devices available that rate bar codes according to ANSI standards. Some devices have a variety of diagnostic capabilities to help evaluate problems on printed symbols. Refer to Print Section 20.11 & 20.12 for additional information.

18.5.5 | **Magnifier**

10X and 30X magnifiers are used to examine printed dots for roundness, halo(s), donuts, slurring, color-to-color register, ink lay smoothness and sharpness.

18.5.5.1 | **Register**   Register marks belong on the left and right side of the image area. Registration targets are used for every color. When all marks are in register, the elements of the printed image should be in register as well.

18.5.5.2 | **Slur/Impression**   Slur targets indicate over impression and plate surface speed discrepancy. Slur is caused by the surface of the plate travelling at a different rate than the substrate or anilox roller. This surface speed differential shows as smearing, or slurring, of the halftone dots in the machine direction. The resulting oval shape of the dots causes excessive dot gain. Slur/impression targets quickly and easily indicate when the condition exists. Slur targets for each process color are included on the FIRST control target (Print Section 18.6).

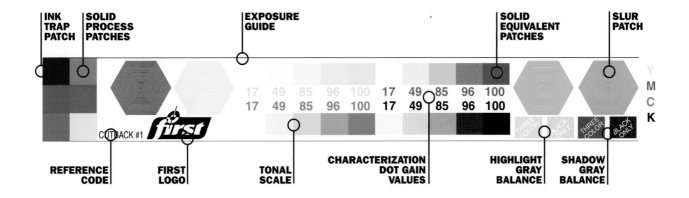

INK TRAP PATCH	SOLID PROCESS PATCHES	EXPOSURE GUIDE				SOLID EQUIVALENT PATCHES	SLUR PATCH

		17	49	85	96	100	17	49	85	96	100		Y
		17	49	85	96	100	17	49	85	96	100		M
													C
													K

CUTBACK #1 *first*

REFERENCE CODE	FIRST LOGO	TONAL SCALE	CHARACTERIZATION DOT GAIN VALUES	HIGHLIGHT GRAY BALANCE	SHADOW GRAY BALANCE

18.6 | Targets Required to Maintain the Job

18.6.1 | FIRST Control Target

All production images must include the control target generated as an integral part of the film negative (or plate file) and plate. Locate the targets in an area that is later die cut out or hidden from view after final assembly. Some packages require a reduced run target to be placed in the "live" area of the package. This target is necessary for measuring print characteristics during start-up and throughout the run. Compare and adjust the control target measurement data to the characterization data. Refer to Prepress Section 12.5 and Print Section 18.5 for more information on using the FIRST control target. The control target is provided on the FIRST CD that is included in this document.

18.6.2 | Run Targets

The FIRST run target is used when there is no room for the FIRST control target to remain on the job for the production run. The run target should be placed in the live area of the print, usually near the UPC symbol or nutrition label if no trim or glue flaps are available for placement. The FIRST run target is considerably reduced, providing less information but adequate to maintain a job through a pressrun. It consist of the minimum dot and solid (or image shadow value) patch for each process color

18.6.3 | Maintaining the Job

■ **Prior To The Pressrun:** A make-ready list should include: inspect doctor blades and check end seals, check air balance of the between deck dryers, clean ink filters and magnets, clean impression cylinder, chill rolls and nips. Complete job histories must be supplied with each production run. The job history should include: anilox roller configuration, ink viscosity, ink rotation, ink type, web tensions, dryer temperature and press speed. These are some of the most important factors that help to reduce set-up time. Anilox and ink identification and tracking systems should be in place so the correct anilox and ink is in the correct print deck, for a particular job. Anilox cleaning records, volume verification, TIR and hours of use should also be recorded.

■ **During The Pressrun:** The FIRST control target (or run target) should be just large enough to be read by instrumentation. Dot gain, density, line color matches and bar code scannability are monitored from the beginning of each job. Run charts with the documented measurements should be kept for each run and added to every time a job is rerun. This provides a history of the job to better define press capabilities and repeatability.

18.6.1 FIRST Control Targets The illustration above is a control target which incorporates all the necessary points of measurement required to be monitored by these specifications and is available from the FTA.

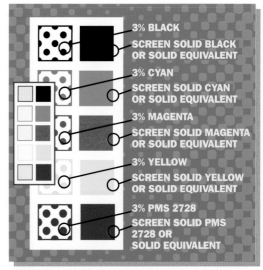

3% BLACK

SCREEN SOLID BLACK OR SOLID EQUIVALENT

3% CYAN

SCREEN SOLID CYAN OR SOLID EQUIVALENT

3% MAGENTA

SCREEN SOLID MAGENTA OR SOLID EQUIVALENT

3% YELLOW

SCREEN SOLID YELLOW OR SOLID EQUIVALENT

3% PMS 2728

SCREEN SOLID PMS 2728 OR SOLID EQUIVALENT

18.6.2 Run Target This target is necessary for measuring print characteristics during start-up and throughout the run. Compare and adjust the control target measurement data to the characterization data.

Print

In order to monitor dot gain and density, the control or run target must remain on the job throughout the printrun for measurement and consistency. All measurement tools must be maintained and calibrated according to the manufacturers' and FIRST specifications.

- **After The Pressrun:** A maintenance log should be kept at each press. The press crew should note on the maintenance log press deficiencies, problems or irregularities. The maintenance crew should review the log daily. Preventive maintenance programs must be in place and followed. Press shutdown should occur at regular intervals for maintenance inspections, cleaning and replacement of worn parts.

18.7 | The Numbers Match But the Image Doesn't

When a job is run on an optimized, characterized press and all print variables are printing to the results achieved during the print characterization, but the result does not match the contract proof, it is recommended that the following variables be evaluated:

- Verify incoming prepress materials were supplied in compliance with specifications. Refer to Prepress Section 14.0 Final Films.
- Verify the contract proof is within the tolerances for density, dot area, process ink colors, exposure and substrate. Refer to Prepress Section 15.0 Color Proofs.
- Verify the files/films were properly compensated based upon the characterization information. Refer to Prepress Section 13.0 Color Management.
- Verify the printing plates were made properly and within the same parameters as the characterization test plates—check the control target for proper exposure, relief, shoulder angle and dot structure of the plates. Refer to Prepress Section 16.10 Printing Plate Measurement.

Before choosing to deviate from the characterization parameters, it is extremely important to save single color progressives and full color printed samples. These samples should be returned to the prepress provider along with all job components including the original art, proofs, platemaking films and plates for review and correction.

If time does not permit review and rework, and a partial order must be run, it is important to document all deviations from specifications. When a job has been altered to best meet customer approval, document the changes and send the altered single color progressives and full color composite back to the prepress provider along with the samples requested above for review and correction.

A close match to the contract proof should be achieved on press if all parties closely monitor and adhere to FIRST specifications.

18.7 The Numbers Match But The Image Doesn't
Run charts with the documented measurements should be kept for each run and added to every time a job is rerun. This provides a history of the job to better define press capabilities and repeatability

19.0 Significant Print Variables

19.1 | Contract Proof

19.1.1 | Types of Proofs

The various proofs used in design, prepress and printing are defined below. The proof must be identified as one of the following to be compliant. Use the descriptions below and provide the specific information.

- **Concept Proof:** this proof is common in the early creative stages of the project. It is typically not color profiled and therefore, not used for matching color.

- **Color Target:** this proof is not profiled using the output source profile; however, it does represent the customer's color expectations for the final printed product.

- **Contract Analog Proof:** this proof uses film separations as an intermediate media to create an image. It is made to manufacturer's recommendations for exposing and processing (brand name of analog proofing system) and has been made according to FIRST specifications.

- **Contract Digital Proof:** this proof uses electronic files processed by a color-imaging device. It is profiled to (brand name of digital proofing system) and has been made according to FIRST specifications.

- **Profiled Contract Proof:** this proof represents the customer's complete content and color expectations for the final printed product and is the basis for negotiations on project performance. This proof is profiled using a color management system (CMS) and is prepared based upon profiles provided by the specific printer or prepress provider. It has been made according to FIRST specifications.

A contract proof illustrates how the printed image is expected to look when reproduced on press. It is an important quality control tool and communication device. The contract proof does not have to be a dot-for-dot reproduction, but it must be an overall visual simulation of the expected print results. Therefore, it must simulate the dot gain, color attributes, detail and contrast of the printed image.

Contract proofs represent an agreement between the printer, prepress provider, designer and the consumer product company regarding the expected appearance of the graphic reproduction on press. Following specifications, the contract proof should represent how the separations will reproduce when printed. Before a contract proof can be accurately used, the entire reproduction system must be characterized so that the proofing system is calibrated to match the printed result. Refer to Prepress Section 13.0 CIELab Color Management. Afterward, both press and proofing systems must be maintained for consistency and repeatability.

19.1.2 | Measurement of Contract Proofs & Printed Materials

Measurement of printed materials consistent with *ANSI/CGATS.4 (1993 Graphic Technology—Graphic Arts Reflection Densitometry Measurements—Terminology, Equations, Image Elements, and Procedures)* and *ANSI/CGATS.5 (1993 Graphic Technology—Spectral Measurement and Colorimetric Computation for Graphic Arts Image*s) are recommended. ANSI/CGATS.4 is the primary reference for evaluation of graphic arts materials using reflection densitometry. ANSI/CGATS.5 is the primary reference for evaluation of graphic arts materials by spectrophotometry.

There are numerous definitions, equations and guidelines in ANSI/CGATS.4 and CGATS.5. Some of these may be found in the Glossary of this document. Refer to Prepress Section 15.3 for detailed information on "Measurement of Contract Proofs & Printed Materials" including the following topics:

- 15.3.1, Reflection Densitometer Communications Specifications.
    - 15.3.1.1, Spectral Response.
    - 15.3.1.2, Printed Sheet Backing for Reading Densitometer Values.
- 15.3.2, Spectrophotometry Guidelines.
    - 15.3.2.1, Colorimetric Guidelines.
    - 15.3.2.2, Communicating Spectrophotometric Data.

19.1.2.1 | Solid Ink Density & Dot Area of Contract Proofs

Solid ink density values on dry proofs shall fall within ±0.07 for M, C and K and within ±0.05 for Y of the desired density values of the print segment for which the files/films are being prepared. The chart below identifies target density values by print segment.

SOLID INK DENSITY TARGETS				
WIDE WEB	CYAN	MAGENTA	YELLOW	BLACK
PAPER PRODUCTS	1.25	1.25	1.00	1.50
FILM PRODUCTS	1.25	1.20	1.00	1.40
NARROW WEB	CYAN	MAGENTA	YELLOW	BLACK
PAPER PRODUCTS	1.35	1.25	1.00	1.50
FILM PRODUCTS	1.25	1.20	1.00	1.40

The dot area on each of the colors containing a screen tint must be measured using the Murray-Davies equation for dot area measurement outlined in CGATS.4. The absolute value of apparent dot area must be consistent with the supplier's recommendations for the respective proofing system

19.1.3 | Proofing Pigments/Dyes

FIRST has identified process and line pigments by color index number. Proofing pigments need to match the spectral response of the inks being used. Using the pigment (referenced by the color index number) will prevent metamerism. If the proofing method employed does not utilize pigments, the C.I.# of the pigments being used by the printer will facilitate the identification of the best match available for the given proofing colorant. Refer to Print Section 19.3.2.2 & 19.3.3.1 for FIRST recommended pigments.

19.1.4 | Proofing Control Targets

Failure to monitor and maintain accuracy of the contract proof will result in inaccurate and inconsistent proofs, rendering them unusable for the printer and consumer product company to approve color.

The FIRST control and run targets (to be proofed and used for calibration purposes) must be imaged (and plated when providing press proofs) using the same devices and materials employed in live production. A variation in dot shape and material can significantly alter print results. The FIRST control and run targets must remain on the finished proof. The FIRST run target should be placed in the same location as it will be printed on the live job.

All proofs must be made to the manufacturer's specifications using their rec-

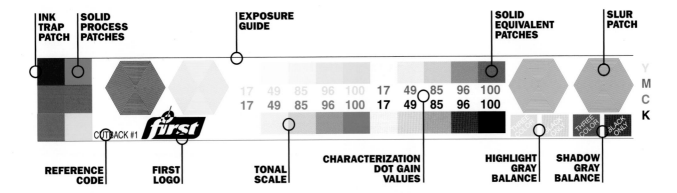

| INK TRAP PATCH | SOLID PROCESS PATCHES | EXPOSURE GUIDE | | | | | | SOLID EQUIVALENT PATCHES | | | SLUR PATCH |

CUTBACK #1

REFERENCE CODE FIRST LOGO TONAL SCALE CHARACTERIZATION DOT GAIN VALUES HIGHLIGHT GRAY BALANCE SHADOW GRAY BALANCE

ommended target for verification. The target should be outside the live image area of the graphics and must remain on the finished proof.

19.1.5 | Proof Compliance Cover Sheet/Label

A cover sheet or label should accompany the proof submitted for color match at press and approved by the customer. The cover sheet or label should state which proofing product or system was used, and the company supplying the proof (contact name, telephone and fax numbers).

If this proof is to be used for color approval as a contract proof, the cover sheet must also contain information required to verify the proof's compliance to the technical attributes required for that proofing type. Refer to Prepress Sections 15.3.1 & 15.3.2.2.

19.2 | Substrates

Table 19.2, Substrate Properties, provides an overview of substrate properties that affect print quality. It is divided into the four primary substrate categories used in flexography (film, corrugated, paper, paperboard). Specifications and tolerances vary widely since many are customer (buyer) driven. Additionally, there are wide differences within substrate groups, depending on gauge, basis weight, grade, supplier, etc. Specifications and tolerances for customer and supplier are to be mutually established, based on final print needs and process capabilities. The specifications listed in table 19.2 should be considered minimums. Tighter specifications for certain properties may be required for specific applications.

The customer is defined as the substrate buyer who has the responsibility to communicate the specifications and tolerances for both the printer and end user. Compliance is to be reported on a certificate of analysis (COA) or a certificate of compliance (COC) report.

The predominant substrate quality attribute required is uniformity (or consistency) within lots and between lots. Efforts continue to more precisely define print quality and establish methods to predict substrate performance for flexography prior to shipment from the substrate manufacturer to the printer.

Many testing procedures for substrates have been developed. The Technical Association of the Pulp and Paper Industry (TAPPI) has developed some of the most widely used paper and paperboard test methods. Several of these are referenced. See Appendix for TAPPI contact information. Refer to the Glossary for definitions of substrate properties.

19.1.4 Color Control Targets The illustration above is a control target which incorporates all the necessary points of measurement required to be monitored by these specifications and is available from the FTA.

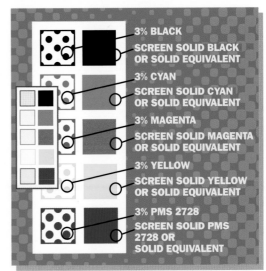

3% BLACK
SCREEN SOLID BLACK OR SOLID EQUIVALENT

3% CYAN
SCREEN SOLID CYAN OR SOLID EQUIVALENT

3% MAGENTA
SCREEN SOLID MAGENTA OR SOLID EQUIVALENT

3% YELLOW
SCREEN SOLID YELLOW OR SOLID EQUIVALENT

3% PMS 2728
SCREEN SOLID PMS 2728 OR SOLID EQUIVALENT

19.1.4 Run Target This target is necessary for measuring print characteristics during start-up and throughout the run. Compare and adjust the control target measurement data to the characterization data.

SUBSTRATE PROPERTIES

PROPERTY	FILM	CORRUGATED	PAPER	PAPERBOARD
AGING/FADE	Visual Customer	Visual Customer	Visual Customer T453- sp-97 T594 sp-97	Visual Customer T544- sp-97 T453- sp-97
BRIGHTNESS	±3% T452 om-98	±3% T452 om-98	±2% T452 om-98	±2% T452 om-98
CALIPER/ GAUGE/ THICKNESS	Micrometer ±10% T411 om-98	Micrometer ±0.005" T411 om-98 ISO 3034	Micrometer ±5% T411 om-89 ASTM D645	Micrometer ±0.001" T411 om-89 ASTM D645
CLARITY/ HAZE	Customer ±10%	Visual Customer	Visual Customer	Visual Customer
COLOR	Customer ΔE 4.00	Customer ΔE 4.00 T524 om-94	Customer ΔE 4.00 T524 om-94	Customer ΔE 4.00 T524 om-94
COEFFICIENT OF FRICTION	Visual Customer ±30% ASTM D1894-95	––	––	––
DIMENSIONAL STABILITY	Registration ±0.010" (0.25 mm)	Registration ±0.0625" (1.6 mm)	Registration ±0.005" (0.13 mm)	Registration ±0.005" (0.13 mm)
DIRT/GELS	Visual <2.0 mm^2/m^2	Visual Customer	Visual Customer T437 om-96	Visual Customer T437 om-96
FLATNESS	Go/No Go	Straight Edge <0.25" lin. ft.	Go/No Go	Go/No Go
FORMATION	––	Customer Visual Mottle	Customer Visual Mottle	Customer Visual Mottle
GLOSS	Customer ±5% @45°	Visual Customer ±5% @75° T480 om-92	Visual Customer ±3% @75° T480 om-92	Visual Customer ±5% @75° T480 om-92
INK ABSORBENCY	––	Spectrophotometer Customer ΔE 4.00	Spectrophotometer Customer ΔE 4.00	Spectrophotometer Customer ΔE 4.00
MOISTURE CONTENT	––	5.5%, ±2%	5.5%, ±1.5%	5.5%, ±1.5%
OPACITY	Customer ±5%	––	Customer ±2% T425 om-96	Customer ±2% T425 om-96
POROSITY	––	Customer Ink Color Match ±10%	Spectrophotometer Customer ±10% T460 om-96	Spectrophotometer Customer ±10%
SMOOTH-NESS	Embossed Smooth	Customer T538 om-96 ISO 8791/3	Customer T538 om-96 T555 pm-94 ISO 8791/3	Customer T538 om-96 T555 pm-94 ISO 8791/4
SURFACE STRENGTH/ PICK RESISTANCE	––	––	±2 T459 pm-93 T552 pm-92	Polylam=Customer ±2 T514 pm-92
SURFACE TENSION/ TREAT LEVEL	Visual Customer Dyne Indicator ±2 T552 pm-92	Visual Customer T552 pm-92	Visual Customer T453- sp-97 T453 sp-97	Visual Customer Polylam=Customer ±2T552 pm-92 T552 pm-92
WASH BOARDING	––	Visual Customer	––	––

19.3 | Ink

19.3.1 | Color Matching and Proofing

19.3.1.1 | Color Matching The color matching procedure for line inks requires that the following elements be in place:

- A dispenser color palette and pigments are recommended.
- A color measurement device such as a spectrophotometer is recommended.
- A numeric color target, and tolerancing—CMC 2:1 < 2.0DE and CIE<2.5DE are typical.
- A true visual color standard—correct substrate, ink, press.
- Proofing protocol correlated to the press.

Prepare a small lab batch (100 g) using these color matching guidelines:

- Use the fewest pigments possible for accurate color control.
- Use low cost combination of pigments.
- Be aware of special requirements such as lightfastness.

The batch making of an ink follows the workflow illustrated at right. The outcome is an approved formula that is used in the dispenser to produce the press ink.

19.3.1.2 | Ink Proofing The purpose of proofing is to generate accurate and repeatable color matches in the lab in order to minimize or eliminate color matching on press. The procedures developed must be:

- Accurate to the press.
- Operator independent.
- Reproducible over time.
- Based on durable, low cost mechanism.
- Easy to clean and maintain.

The mechanical drawdown coater such as the one below which uses wire wound rods is highly favored, widely used and meets the criteria identified above. The type and size of proofing rod being used should correlate to the anilox roller used to print the color on press.

19.3.1.2.1 | Proofing Equipment

- Flat-bed, mechanical proofer.
- Coating rod based on specific ink or coating used.
- Ink knives.
- Substrate.
- Heat gun.
- Signature Zahn cup #2 or equivalent efflux cup: Shell, Din, Ford, etc.

19.3.1.2.2 Proofing Procedure Example

- Cut a piece of substrate to the appropriate size for the proofer. (If using film check the dyne level of the film to confirm the proof is made on the treated side.)
- Reduce the ink sample to 35 seconds on a #2 Signature Zahn cup with appropriate solvent.
- Place the substrate and a #3 coating rod in the proofer.
- Place the ink sample on the substrate near the coating rod.
- Set the proofer to a speed of 7. Pull the proof by turning the proofer to the forward position.
- Dry the proof using a heat gun being careful not to distort the film.
- Examine the proof for defects.

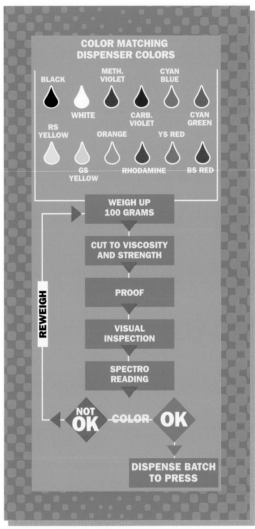

19.3.1.1 Color Matching The batch making of an ink follows this workflow, where the outcome is an approved formula that is used in the dispenser to produce the press ink.

19.3.1.2.2 Ink Proofing The purpose of proofing is to generate accurate and repeatable color matches in the lab in order to minimize or eliminate color matching on press.

19.3.2 | Process Ink Colors

19.3.2.1 | Pigment Selection Process These pigments have been selected for three purposes.

- To provide the largest color gamut of possible color matches available, on various substrates, with a minimum number of pigments.
- To obtain pigments that could be used across the flexographic industry in water, solvent and UV systems.
- To provide pigment selections that would render moderate to enhanced lightfast characteristics.

19.3.2.2 | FIRST Recommended Process Ink Pigments

FIRST PROCESS INK PIGMENTS

	WATER BASED		SOLVENT BASED		UV BASED	
	C.I. NAME	C.I #	C.I. NAME	C.I #	C.I. NAME	C.I #
YELLOW	Y14	21095	Y14	21095	Y13	21100
MAGENTA	R57:1	15850:1	R57:1	15850:1	R57:1	15850:1
	R52:1	15860:1	R52:1	15860:1	R52:1	15860:1
CYAN	B15:3	74160	B15:3	74160	B15:3	74160
	B15:4	74160	B15:4	74160	B15:4	74160
BLACK	K7	77266	K7	77266	K7	77266

19.3.2.3 | Process Inks Target and Tolerance In the second edition of FIRST, process inks were identified by color index name and number in an effort to improve consistency within a print facility and across print facilities. In the third edition of FIRST, the recommended pigments for process ink have expanded slightly to address specific printing needs. Using the recommended pigments (Print Section 19.3.2.2 & 19.3.2.4), in a global effort to identify flexographic process ink sets, multiple samples in triplicate, run at several concentration levels were proofed and measured by leading flexographic ink suppliers in compliance with *ISO 2846-5 (Graphic Technology – Colour & Transparency of Printing Ink Sets for 4-colour Printing – Flexographic Printing)*. The L*a*b values listed below are derived from the data generated. At this time there are not enough data points to arrive at reliable Delta E values. The L*a*b values provided are intended to be a starting point which will evolve as the data points increase. In future editions of FIRST, refined L*a*b values along with Delta E values will be provided.

FIRST PROCESS INKS L*a*b VALUES

		L	*a	*b
YELLOW	SOLVENT	90.42	−3.74	100.59
	WATER	91.72	−5.78	100.53
	UV	92.33	−4.94	82.72
MAGENTA	SOLVENT	45.59	71.69	8.5
	WATER	52.95	70.19	−4.0
	UV	50.22	76.12	−1.23
CYAN	SOLVENT	55.62	−40.54	−46.71
	WATER	59.4	−37.41	−45.23
	UV	55.6	−37.98	−45.28
BLACK	SOLVENT	21.46	1.35	3.04
	WATER	16.15	0.79	1.05
	UV	15.58	0.23	4.89

Color measurement technology continues to evolve and improve. Newer methods employ better formulas for predicting visual color matches. While CMC (2:1) tolerancing has provided generally good predictions of a printed colors visual match to the intended target, CIE94 and CIE2000 (referred to in FIRST as CIE tolerancing) represent revised formulas with improved predictability. Each evolution in color tolerancing brings the human eye and the instrument closer together in the evaluation of color. As instrumentation is purchased, FIRST recommends buying equipment that utilizes the latest methods in color tolerancing and has a robust upgrade path.

The tolerance of the established target values should be less than a Delta E of 2.0 using CMC tolerancing or a Delta E less than 2.5 using CIE tolerancing method. This is not a specification for the printrun but for the incoming ink and should be verified through internal audits.

19.3.2.4 | FIRST Alternative Process Pigments: Increased Fade Resistance

FIRST ALTERNATIVE PROCESS INK PIGMENTS: Increased Fade Resistance					
	WATER BASED INK		SOLVENT BASED INK		UV BASED INK	
	C.I. NAME	C.I #	C.I. NAME	C.I #	C.I. NAME	C.I #
YELLOW	Y74	11741	Y74	11741	Y74	11741
MAGENTA	Y184	12487	Y184	12487	Y184	12487

19.3.3 | Line Ink Colors

Use of the recommended dispenser pigments will result in improved consistency of flexographic print. The color gamut produced by this pigment palette can be fully quantified for use through the color management workflow. Refer to the following comments while working with these pigments:

- The pigment color index number represents a specific, unique chemical structure. Within a specific pigment color index number some variation in color can occur from vendor to vendor and from grade to grade from a specific vendor.
- Differences in manufacturing equipment and formula content from ink supplier to ink supplier may produce some color differences, even with identical pigments.
- Different ink chemistries (water base, UV or solvent base) can result in color shifts.

These differences are most often overcome using the recommended dispenser pigments by slight adjustments in ratios of pigment colors in the formulas for the line color match.

19.3.3.1 | FIRST Recommended Line Ink Dispenser Pigments The line ink dispenser colors are single pigment ink bases (system varnish is added to make the finished ink) or single pigment finished inks. These dispenser colors cover most flexographic printing applications with some exceptions as explained and noted in the following information.

FIRST LINE INK DISPENSER PIGMENTS

	COLOR INDEX NAME	COLOR INDEX #	FIRST PROCESS COLOR	COMMENT
LITHOL RUBINE	Red 57:1	15850:1	Yes	Blue shade red
YS NAPTHOL	Red 22	12315	No	Yellow shade red
YS RHODAMINE	Red 81	45160	No	Bright, very clean blue shade red
DIANISIDENE ORANGE	Orange 16	21160	No	Clean orange
AAOT YELLOW	Yellow 14	21095	Yes	Green shade yellow
HR YELLOW	Yellow 83	21108	––	Red shade yellow
PHTHALO GREEN	Green 7	74260	––	Blue shade green
PHTHALO BLUE	Blue15:3, 15:4	74160	Yes	Green shade blue
METHYL VIOLET	Violet 3	42535:2	––	Blue shade violet
CARBAZOLE VIOLET	Violet 23	51319	––	Red shade violet
TITANIUM WHITE	White 6	77891	––	Opaque white
CARBON BLACK	Black 7	77266	Yes	Untoned black

While these pigments probably represent less than 10% of all pigments currently available on the market, represent the majority of flexographic pigments used. They are proven for printability and capability of reproducing a majority of shades. These pigments were selected based on several key considerations.

- To provide the largest color gamut for possible color matches, using a minimum number of dispenser inks/bases.
- To provide reasonably priced bases—many on this list have more expensive counterparts that may have one or more distinct properties (cleaner, brighter, more lightfast, more resistant to special needs [oil, heat, etc.]).
- To be representative of products used in the flexographic industry, based on extensive data from the ink suppliers, pigment manufacturers, and printers.

19.3.3.1.1 | Pigment Properties: FIRST Line Ink Dispenser Pigments The pigment properties chart is a guide for linking pigment performance to end use requirements. It is important for the ink supplier to be included in the initial packaging design discussions so the pigment performance requirements can be matched to the actual use of the package.

FIRST LINE INK DISPENSER PIGMENT PROPERTIES

	COLOR INDEX NAME	INK SOLV	INK UV	WATER	LIGHTFAST	HEAT RESIST	BLEED RESIST	PMS BASE
LITHOL RUBINE	Red 57:1	Y	Y	Y	2.5	4	4	Rubine
YS NAPTHOL	Red 22	Y	Y	Y	3	4	5	
YS RHODAMINE	Red 81	Y	Y	Y	2	3	2	Rhodamine
DIANISIDENE ORANGE	Orange 16	Y	Y	Y	2.5	2	5	
AAOT YELLOW	Yellow 14	Y	Y	Y	2.5	4	4	
HR YELLOW	Yellow 83	Y	Y	Y	2.5	5	4	
PHTHALO GREEN	Green 7	Y	Y	Y	5	5	5	Green
PHTHALO BLUE	Blue 15:3	N	N	Y	5	5	5	Process Blue
PHTHALO BLUE	Blue 15:4	Y	Y	N	5	5	5	Process Blue
METHYL VIOLET	Violet 3	Y	N	Y	2	3	2	Violet
CARBAZOLE VIOLET	Violet 23	Y	Y	Y	5	4	5	
TITANIUM WHITE	White 6	Y	Y	Y	5	5	5	
CARBON BLACK	Black 7	Y	Y	Y	5	5	5	Black

RATINGS: 1 to 5, with 5 = best

LIGHTFASTNESS RATING:

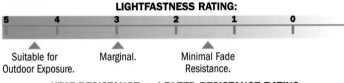

| 5 | 4 | 3 | 2 | 1 | 0 |

Suitable for Outdoor Exposure.   Marginal.   Minimal Fade Resistance.

HEAT RESISTANCE and BLEED RESISTANCE RATING:

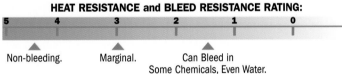

| 5 | 4 | 3 | 2 | 1 | 0 |

Non-bleeding.   Marginal.   Can Bleed in Some Chemicals, Even Water.

19.3.3.1.2 | Alternate Line Ink Pigments Alternate pigments are sometimes needed to achieve increased performance or color requirements. For example, if the packaging contains red line copy and is to be displayed outdoors, lightfast pigments are required. This requirement probably eliminates the use of Red 57:1, Red 22 and Red 81. A more expensive red pigment such as Red 184 is needed. Any decision relating to lightfastness, product and chemical resistance must be referenced to the ink supplier and be based on specific testing procedures. It should be remembered that substitute, non-standard pigments may result in conditional, metameric color matches.

19.3.3.2 | Line Ink Pigments: Color Gamut Illustrations

19.3.3.2.1 | General Concepts The exact color gamut of the dispenser inks will vary depending upon:

- Ink Chemistry: Water base, UV or solvent base.
  (**Note:** UV ink data is not provided at this time.)
- Ink Formulation: Lamination or surface print.
- Pigment Concentration. The inks for the example gamuts were made with a 5 – 10% pigment weight. The inks were proofed with a mechanical proofer equipped with a number 3 bar to represent a broad range of flexographic printing conditions. Actual press inks may contain more pigment, but are metered at lower film thicknesses.
- Substrate: Paper or film.
- Instrumentation geometry and measurement procedure used.

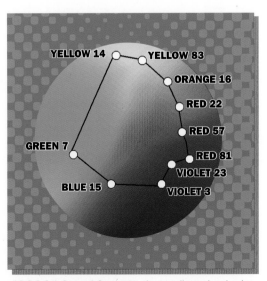

19.3.3.2.1 General Concepts the two-dimensional color gamut is an approximation of color and the following gamuts, on the next page, are not in any way absolute.

19.3.3.2.3 Water Ink Color Gamut

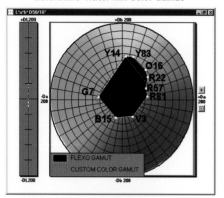

A) Leneta Stock—7.5% Pigment Levels
(acrylic water base ink)

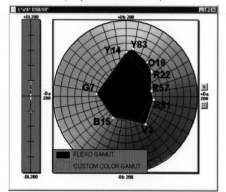

B) Coated Stock—7.5% Pigment Levels
(acrylic water base ink)

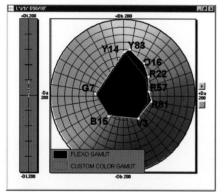

C) Coated Stock—5% Pigment Levels
(acrylic water base ink)

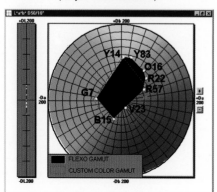

D) Leneta Stock—7.5% Pigment Levels
(acrylic water base ink) Restricted Gamut

The illustrations on this page are a relative gamut that represents a two-dimensional model plotting "chroma" and "hue" color values of each pigment in CIEL*a*b color space. Joining the points produces a color gamut of achievable color matches using the FIRST recommended pigments. The addition of "L" values would produce a three dimensional model.

The following color gamuts illustrate the critical role substrate and ink strength play in determining the available color gamut—even after pigment selection has been standardized. Standardizing pigments represents a major step forward in achieving consistent color matches; however, failure to consider substrate and ink formulation will lead to disappointment. Consumer product companies and design firms should consult with the printer(s) and ink supplier(s) involved to determine if a particular color is achievable given the chosen substrate or lamination structure. It should be noted that the two-dimensional color gamut is an approximation of color and the following gamuts are not absolute.

19.3.3.2.2 | Color Measurement Procedure Used All of the readings for this data were taken using a calibrated X-Rite 938 spectrophotometer (0/45 geometry) with a 4mm aperture. Measuring procedures were in compliance with *CGATS .5 (1993 Graphic Technology Spectral Measurement and Colorimetric Computation for Graphic Arts Images)*. The data is graphed in L*a*b* color space using a 5,000° Kelvin (D50) light source. All measurements were taken using a Leneta card as a standardized backing. Three measurements were taken across the sample and then averaged to create the final pigment color values. All samples were measured using the absolute values against neutral gray standard and plotted onto the L*a*b color gamut using X-Rite QA Master Software.

Note: The above equipment manufacturer was reported as a basis of the information outlined. FIRST is not recommending X-Rite or any other manufacturer as a preferred instrument manufacturer and encourages the reader to explore all available technologies and brands.

19.3.3.2.3 | Water Ink Color Gamuts All of the following gamuts are shown and compared against a widely used lithographic color matching system (Pantone Matching System). Many pigments used in offset inks are not soluble in water based flexographic ink systems; therefore, it is not possible to use all of the same pigments.

A Leneta Stock – 7.5% pigment load, acrylic water base ink. It is apparent the flexographic water based gamut is restricted in the blue/green region and extended in the yellow/red region compared to the offset color gamut. (Color gamut illustrated in graph 19.3.3.2.3-a).

B Coated Stock – 7.5% pigment load, acrylic water base ink. In this example FIRST recommended pigments provide a wider gamut than that represented by the basic offset system. (Color gamut illustrated in graph 19.3.3.2.3-b).

C Coated Stock – 5% pigment load, acrylic water base ink. The flexographic gamut, at 5% pigment level, is larger than the standard offset gamut, but appreciably smaller than the flexographic gamut at 7.5% pigment. (Color gamut illustrated in graph 19.3.3.2.3-c).

D Leneta Stock – 7.5% pigment load, acrylic water base ink, restricted gamut. In this example two "risky" pigments have been eliminated from the list to meet specific end use requirements. The pigments eliminated are rhodamine and methyl violet, both of which can be unstable in some packaging applications. The restricted color gamut is apparent and must be communicated to all involved in the color management workflow. Color gamut illustrated in graph 19.3.3.2.3-d

19.3.3.2.4 | Solvent Ink Color Gamuts

A Leneta Stock – 7.5% pigment load, nitro/polyamide solvent base ink. This color gamut is slightly restricted in the green/yellow region. (Color gamut illustrated in graph 19.3.3.2.4-a).

B Coated Stock – 7.5% pigment load, nitro/polyamide solvent base ink. (Color gamut illustrated in graph 19.3.3.2.4-b).

C White Opaque Poly – 7.5% pigment load, nitro/polyamide solvent base ink. This gamut is slightly restricted in the green/yellow region and somewhat fuller in the red/blue region. (Color gamut illustrated in graph 19.3.3.2.4-c).

19.3.3.2.5 | Pantone Custom Color Gamut Because custom lithographic-printed colors (Pantone) are so prevalent as targets within the printing industry, it is important to plot the base colors within the custom color book (PMS book) on the same color space model for comparison with the FIRST recommended flexographic gamuts. Pantone, PMS and the Pantone Matching System are trademarks of Pantone, Inc.

The following table lists the Pantone Custom Color pigments with a cross-reference to FIRST line pigments.

PANTONE CUSTOM COLOR CHART

PANTONE BASE	PIGMENT COLOR INDEX NAME	FIRST RECOMMENDED BASE PIGMENT
BASIC YELLOW	Yellow 12	No
BASIC WARM RED	Red 53:1	No
BASIC RUBINE RED	Red 57:1	Yes
BASIC RHODAMINERED	Red 81	Yes
BASIC PURPLE	Violet 1 + Red 81	No
BASIC VIOLET	Violet 3	Yes
BASIC REFLEX BLUE	Blue 61	No
BASIC PROCESS BLUE	Blue 15:3	Yes
BASIC GREEN	Green 7	Yes
YELLOW 012	Yellow 13	No
ORANGE 021	Orange 34	No
RED 032	Red 112	No
BLUE 072	Blue 1:2	No

19.3.3.2.6 | Other Substrates It is recognized that kraft paper and board are widely used in the flexographic industry. The variability in color of these substrates affects the color gamut achievable from the recommended dispenser pigments, which will vary accordingly. Foil and metallized films may present unique color measurement challenges. Consult with the substrate supplier and color measurement instrumentation supplier to determine the best method to measure difficult substrates.

19.3.3.2.4 Solvent Ink Color Gamuts

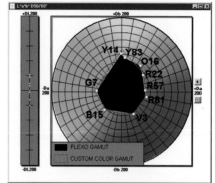

A) Leneta Stock—7.5% Pigment Levels (nitro/polyamide solvent base ink)

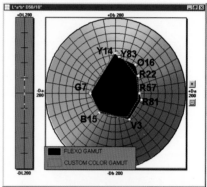

B) Coated Stock—7.5% Pigment Levels (acrylic water base ink)

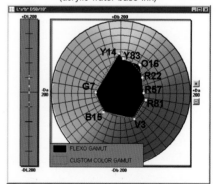

C) White Opaque Poly—7.5% Pigment Levels (nitro/polyamide solvent base ink)

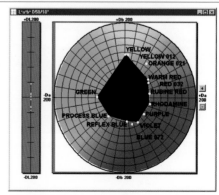

19.3.3.2.5 Pantone Color Gamut it is important to plot the base colors within the color book on the same color space model for comparison with the flexo gamuts.

BLOCK/SET-OFF RESISTANCE TEST

HEAT RESISTANCE TEST

WATER RESISTANCE TEST

19.3.4 Ink Functionality These are the most common ink resistance tests performed.

19.3.4 | Ink Functionality

19.3.4.1 | **Functional Properties** The functional properties of flexographic printing inks are divided into two distinctively different categories: physical virgin ink properties and printed ink properties.

A large number of functional ink properties have some degree of impact on the performance of flexographic ink. The properties addressed here have a significant impact on the printability and finished properties of the ink. Test methods, specifications and tolerances are also described.

A variety of procedures may be used for any given test. Where possible, ASTM or industry standard methods have been adopted for these tests. See Appendix for information on how to obtain ASTM and TAPPI standard test methods.

"Core" physical virgin ink properties include:

1. Fineness of Grind.
2. Viscosity.
3. Specific Gravity.
4. pH (for water inks only).
5. Color (this involves proofing to check reproducibility and not correlation to press performance).
6. Foam.
7. Solids.
8. Drying Rate.

"Core" printed ink properties include:

1. Adhesion to Nonporous Substrates.
2. Color Correlation to Press Results.
3. Gloss on Surface Printed Product.
4. Block/Set-off Resistance for all Printed Substrates.
5. Rub/Abrasion for all Printed Substrates.
6. Opacity/Transparency for all Printed Substrates.

Critical performance tests for packaging applications include:

1. Coefficient of Friction.
2. Heat Resistance.
3. Crinkle Resistance/Flexibility.
4. Odor and Taint.
5. Lamination Bond Strength.
6. Water Resistance.
7. Chemical or Product Resistance.
8. Lightfastness.

19.3.4.2 | "Core" Physical Virgin Ink Properties

19.3.4.2.1 | Fineness of Grind

PROCEDURE	ASTM D1316—*(Fineness of grind of printing inks by the NPIRI grindometer)*
IMPORTANCE	Grind is a determinant factor for color strength, opacity/transparency, gloss and abrasion characteristics. In general, finer grind implies higher transparency, stronger color, higher gloss and less abrasion.
SPECIFICATION	Based on production specification with a NPIRI grind measuring from 0 – 10 microns.
TOLERANCE	**For Dispersions:** 0 – 1 microns maximum for all pigments. Pigment "White 6" may be coarser for desired opacity. **For Finished Inks:** Additives used to provide functional properties (such as wax) may lead to false readings. Even with additives, maximum grind should not exceed 3 microns.

19.3.4.2.2 | Viscosity

PROCEDURE	ASTM D1200—*(Test Method for Viscosity of Paints, Varnishes, and Lacquers)* ASTM D4212—*(Test Method for Viscosity by Dip Type Viscosity Cup)* ASTM 2196—*(Test Method for Rheological Properties of Non-Newtonian Materials by Rotational (Brookfield) Viscometer)*
IMPORTANCE	Viscosity is a measure of resistance to flow at a specified temperature and plays a vital role in determining print quality of the ink. Controlling viscosity on press is necessary to maintain color (hue, strength), print quality (ink flow out, dot gain, trapping) and performance properties (coating weight, drying speed, solvent retention).
TEST METHOD	The flexographic industry commonly utilizes gravimetric or dip type cups. The accuracy of these cups vary with design, manufacturer, condition and operator. Zahn cups are the most widely used in the flexographic packaging industry due to their ease of use. RIT Laboratory studies have shown Shell Cups to provide overall greater precision.
TOLERANCE	Dip Cups: Zahn = ±3 seconds; Shell = ±2 seconds; Brookfield viscometer = ±10% centipoise.

19.3.4.2.3 | Specific Gravity

PROCEDURE	ASTM D 1475—*(Standard Test Method for Density of Paint, Varnish, Lacquer, and Related Products)*
IMPORTANCE	The specific gravity (or density) of an ink is indicative of ink mileage, as well as the solids (volatile) content of an ink or coating.
TEST METHOD	Specific gravity is a weight of a unit volume of the material at 25° C. In the printing industry, it is typically expressed in pounds/gallon or grams/milliliter. When expressed as specific gravity, it is the ratio of the density of the product tested to the density of water at 25° C and therefore is not expressed in any units. Specific gravity is normally measured on the virgin ink prior to extending or reducing.
TOLERANCE	The allowable tolerance for density is ±5%.

19.3.4.2.4 | pH for Water Inks

PROCEDURE	ASTM E70—(97 *Standard Test Method for pH of Aqueous Solutions with the Glass Electrode*)
IMPORTANCE	pH is a measure of the acidity or alkalinity of a water based ink. Water based inks rely on good pH control to maintain resin solubility, which in turn directly impacts printability, drying speed and viscosity. This test applies only to water based ink systems. Optimal pH ranges for water based inks vary, depending on the chemistry of the ink and the end-use application. The typical pH range for the majority of water based inks (anionic) is 7.5 – 9.5 (>7.0 = alkaline). There are a limited number of chemistries that are pH neutral (7) or acidic (cationic). The ink supplier should recommend the optimal pH range for peak performance of a particular system and the preferred method to maintain the pH level.
TOLERANCE	±0.3 pH units.

19.3.4.2.5 | Color (Ink Batch Reproducibility, not Press Correlation)

PROCEDURE	Reference ASTM D1729 (Visual) and D2244 (Instrumental). Identically prepared drawdowns are compared visually and instrumentally. The preferred instrument is a spectrophotometer conforming to ISO 2846-5.
IMPORTANCE	Color is what the consumer sees when viewing a package. It identifies the product and, if not consistent from package to package, results in the perception of poor quality.
TEST METHOD	A wet ink sample, at a pre-determined viscosity, is printed on a controlled substrate with a mechanical proofer using a standard wire wound rod to achieve equal film thickness. This is compared to a print of the accepted standard that was produced identically. The color standard should also be stored as a digital file for long-term reference and to prevent color drift. In the case of reverse printed laminations, it is sometimes necessary to view the color in the finished lamination structure. It is of extreme importance to make every effort to make the lamination exactly as the laminated control. Refer to Print Section 21.2 Laminating Print: Color Matching for more information. Color comparisons should first be made visually, and if necessary, adjusted until acceptable by eye. Following this, an instrumental measurement should be made, and also compared to the accepted standard. The measurement is reported as a difference between the new batch and the accepted standard. This is recorded as a difference (ΔD) in lightness (L^*), saturation or chroma (c^*), hue (h^*), and total color (E).
TOLERANCES	The allowable tolerance for virgin ink is $DL^* = \leq 1.0$ $Dc^* = \leq 1.0$ $Dh^* = \leq 1.0$ $DE = \leq 2.0$
CONDITION OF TOLERANCE	**Instrument:** 0°/45° or 45°/0° geometry and 2° standard observer. **Aperture:** Either 30 mm (fixed) or 10 mm (portable). **Illuminant:** D50. **Color Space:** $LCh°$. **Tolerancing:** CIE or CMC (2:1).

19.3.4.2.6 | Foaming

PROCEDURE	ASTM D3519—(*88: Standard Test Method for Foam in Aqueous Media*)
IMPORTANCE	The occurrence of excessive foaming in ink, which is caused by air entrapment, leads to handling and print problems such as pinholing or ink starvation. Although typically associated with water based inks, problems arise infrequently with both solvent and energy-cured (UV) systems. The test method described here is a useful guide to determine the tendency of a non-flammable ink or coating to produce foam under high shear conditions by measuring the volume of an ink or coating before and after subjecting it to high shear forces.
TEST METHOD	The foaming observed, after the test, is recorded as an increase in height from the original liquid level in the graduated cylinder. The foam height should be quoted in millimeters (mm).
TOLERANCE	Allowable tolerance limit ≤5% of the original ink volume.

19.3.4.2.7 | Ink Solids (Non-volatile Content)

PROCEDURE	ASTM D4713—(*Standard Method for Non-volatile Content in Printing Inks, Resin Solutions and Vehicles*)
IMPORTANCE	Solids content is a measure of the percentage of non-volatile matter of which a compound or mixture is composed, based on the entire weight of the mixture.
TOLERANCE	Allowable tolerance is ±2.0%.

19.3.4.2.8 | Drying and Curing Rates

PROCEDURE	ASTM D1640—(*Standard Test Method for Drying, Curing or Film Formation*)
TEST METHOD	**For solvent and water inks**—On a clean NPIRI grind gauge, place a small amount of the test product at the top on the right hand side and a similar amount of the standard at the top on the left-hand side. Hold the cursor blade vertically with both hands and draw the inks down the full length of the gauge scale while applying even pressure. The comparative drying rate can be observed and confirmed by drawing a finger across both samples at various points starting from the bottom of the scale and working up. Once dry, the ink film will not be smudged by the finger. This is a very subjective test. **For UV inks**—The drying or cure rate of UV inks and/or coatings can be readily measured: ■ MEK rub resistance (used for inks and coatings). ■ Stain test using potassium permanganate ($KMNO_4$) (only for clear coatings). A wet-ink sample and a wet ink standard are printed on a controlled substrate with a mechanical proofer then cured under stated conditions (lamp power, speed). **MEK resistance.** A cotton swab soaked in MEK is rubbed (light pressure) in a single motion across the print. This is repeated as per the specification set by the printer/converter. The print is examined for deterioration of the ink/coating. The swab should be examined for color transfer. **KmnO4 test.** One drop of a 10% solution of potassium permanganate is placed on the surface of the cured coating. The solution is allowed to sit for 30 seconds. It is wiped off with a clean towel. The discolored area is measured for color density (K). The level of discoloration is proportional to the degree of cure.
IMPORTANCE	This is a very useful QC test to determine if drying rates of subsequent batches of inks and coatings are equal. This test can also be used to isolate and identify drying problems while on press.
TOLERANCE	The standard and test sample should dry at equivalent rates. For UV inks/coatings both the standard and batch samples should attain a similar level of cure as judged by MEK resistance. For the stain test, the density of the test areas should not vary by more than ±10%.

19.3.4.3 | **"Core" Printed Ink Properties** For the "core" printed ink properties and specific application properties listed below, the printer/customer determines the specification based upon the end-use application of the printed material.

19.3.4.3.1 | **Adhesion to Nonporous Substrates**

PROCEDURE	ASTM D3359—(*Test Method for Measuring Adhesion by Tape*)
IMPORTANCE	Ink provides both functional and decorative properties. In order to meet most of the functional needs (flexibility, chemical resistance) it is vital the ink adheres to the primary substrate.
TEST METHOD	The adhesion strength of an ink or coating to a substrate is frequently determined by a tape test. The most common version for water and solvent inks uses 3M 610 tape. For UV ink, 3M 810 tape is preferred. Determining the results is subjective and based upon the level of ink removal from the test sample.
TOLERANCE	For the majority of inks, less than 15% ink removal from the test sample is acceptable.

19.3.4.3.2 | **Color (Proofing for Ink Approval)**

PROCEDURE	Reference ASTM D1729 (Visual) and D2244 (Instrumental)
IMPORTANCE	Ink color consistency on press from run to run is vital in maintaining the consumer's perception of product quality. Color adjustment on press can be a lengthy and costly process. Predictive color proofing methods are critical for this method.
TEST METHOD	A print produced under standard running conditions is compared visually and instrumentally against a hard copy and digital file of the customer approved standard. The preferred instrument is a spectrophotometer. The measurement is reported as a difference between the new batch and the accepted standard. This is recorded as a difference (ΔD) in lightness (L^*), saturation (or chroma) (c^*), hue (h^*), and total color (E).
SPECIFICATION	Customer-based specification.
TOLERANCE	The allowable tolerance for ink supplied to press is: $DL^* \leq 1.0$ $Dc^* \leq 2.0$ $Dh^* \leq 1.0$ $DE \leq 2.0$
CONDITION OF TOLERANCE	**Instrument:** 0°/45° or 45°/0° geometry and 2° standard observer. **Aperture:** Either 30 mm (fixed) or 10 mm (portable) aperture . **Illuminant:** D50. **Color Space:** LCh°. **Tolerancing:** CIE or CMC (2:1).

19.3.4.3.3 | **Gloss of Surface Printed Product**

PROCEDURE	ASTM D523—(*Standard Test Method for Specular Gloss*); ASTM E97— (*Standard Test Method for 0 degrees/45 degrees—Direction Reflectance of Opaque Specimens*)
IMPORTANCE	Gloss level is a critical decorative property of a finished print. It is often associated with the perception of product quality.
TEST METHOD	Gloss is a measurement of the ratio of the reflectance of the print to the reflectance of a "standard surface" under the same measurement conditions. The "standard surface" is polished glass. Reflectance measurements are made with 20°, 60°, or 85° geometry. For most printing applications the 60° geometry is used. 20° is normally used if the specimens measured at 60° have a gloss reading higher than 70, and 85° is used when 60° readings are below 10.
TOLERANCE	The allowable tolerance for gloss is ±5%.

19.3.4.3.4 | Blocking or Set-Off

PROCEDURE	ASTM D2793—*(Standard Test Method for Block Testing)*
IMPORTANCE	Blocking resistance measures the ability of a printed substrate to withstand heat and pressure without sticking or transferring ink. This is extremely critical in roll-to-roll or stacked print operations.
TEST METHOD	This test utilizes a Koehler IC block tester, which uses calibrated springs to exert pressure.
TOLERANCE	Based on customer specification. Pressure, time, and temperature must be specified. Usually no visible ink transfer or significant cling allowed.

19.3.4.3.5 | Rub/Abrasion Resistance for All Printed Substrates

PROCEDURE	ASTM D5264/92—*(Standard Test Method for Sutherland Rub Test)*
IMPORTANCE	Printed packaging materials are subject to many abrasive forces during printing, conversion, shipping and end use. Rub or abrasion resistance from the ink and or coating is important to the aesthetics of the final package. Printers use different terms such as scuffing, marring, blotching, rub off, and scratching to describe abrasion.
EQUIPMENT	Sutherland Rub Tester is most commonly used. Less commonly used alternatives to the Sutherland Rub Tester are the Taber Abraser and the Gavarti CAT tester.
SPECIFICATION	(Industry Expectations) **Paper and Board Substrate:** ■ Corrugated Postprint: 40 rub cycles, 4-lb. block, print to board. ■ Preprint 40 rub cycles, 4-lb. block, 400° F. **Print-to-Heat Platen:** ■ Multiwall Bags: 100 rub cycles, 4-lb. block, print to paper. ■ Folding Carton: 200 rub cycles, 4-lb. block, print to board. **Film Substrates:** ■ Surface 100 rub cycles, 4-lb. block, print to film.
TOLERANCE	No observable transfers of ink or coating to the rubbing sheet or visible damage to the test print surface under the specified testing conditions.

19.3.4.3.6 | Opacity/Transparency

PROCEDURE	TAPPI T425 (Opacity) ASTM D2085
IMPORTANCE	The level of transparency or opacity (hiding power) of an ink governs the quality of the printed image. For example, process inks require high transparency to provide good graphic reproduction while high opacity for whites and/or colors may be important.
TEST METHOD	A visual comparison of the relative opacity of the test sample against an accepted standard can be made as follows: the inks (standard and batch) are proofed side by side, at a pre-determined viscosity, with a mechanical proofer using a standard wire wound rod to achieve equal film thickness. For visual tests it is recommended that a controlled substrate featuring a pre-printed black bar, for example a Leneta card, be used. The opacity of a print, produced either in the laboratory or on press, can be measured and compared against a known print standard (produced under identical conditions) using a spectrophotometer and black trap. The relative transparency of an ink can be gauged from a measurement of the contrast ratio where an ink is compared spectrophotometrically over white and black.
TOLERANCE	■ **Visual:** The test samples should not exhibit any major visual difference in opacity or transparency. ■ **Instrumental:** Opacity (Black Trap Method) allowable tolerance: ±5%; Contrast ratio allowable tolerance: ±10%.

19.3.4.4 | Critical Performance Tests

19.3.4.4.1 | COF/Slide Angle

PROCEDURE	ASTM D 1894/95—(*Standard Test method for Static and Kinetic Coefficients of Friction of Plastic Films and Sheeting*). ASTM D4518—(*Standard Test Methods for Measuring Static Friction of Coating Surfaces*)
IMPORTANCE	Friction is the force that opposes the motion of two surfaces in contact. In packaging terms, it provides an indication of the level of slip or lubricity of the surfaces. Low COF denotes high slip and high COF denotes low slip. Coefficient of friction is a measure of relative difficulty with which one material will slide over an adjoining surface of itself, or another material. It is the ratio of the frictional force to the gravitational force acting perpendicular to the two surfaces in contact. Flat-bed testing equipment provides direct COF data. Two measurements typically quoted are static COF and kinetic COF. Static COF is a measure of the force required to begin movement of the surfaces relative to each other. Kinetic COF is a measure of the force required to sustain this movement.
TEST METHOD	There are two common measuring methods using either an inclined plane or flat bed equipment. The inclined plane provides results as a slide angle. Slide angle and static COF can be related as follows: static COF = 1/tan (slide angle).
TOLERANCE	**Slide Angle:** $\pm2°$ on the third reading. **Static & Kinetic CoF:** $\pm10\%$ of specification.

19.3.4.4.2 | Heat Resistance

PROCEDURE	No known ASTM/TAPPI Standard
IMPORTANCE	Ink and/or coating resistance is vitally important to maintain the functional and aesthetic quality of various types of packaging that may be heat-sealed or subjected to heat during the life of the package.
TEST METHOD	Generally, heat resistance is determined and tested using a heat seal testing machine. These test machines have either one or two jaws, which can maintain a constant set temperature. The pressure with which the jaws come together and the duration of the test are also controllable. Testing temperatures, pressures and dwell times are specified by the printer or converter depending on the processing or packaging equipment used. Printed samples may be tested: ■ Face to face. ■ Face to back. ■ Face to specified substrate.
TOLERANCE	There should be no visible transfer of ink from one test surface to another. The level of cling between two test samples should be less than 15 g per linear inch if measured on a tensile tester.

19.3.4.4.3 | Crinkle or Flexibility

PROCEDURE	No known ASTM/TAPPI Standard
IMPORTANCE	The crinkle test indicates the flexibility of an ink and the level of ink adhesion after subjecting the print to mechanical forces.
TEST METHOD	Crinkle test is performed by firmly grasping a piece of the printed substrate between the two thumbs/forefingers. Place hands approximately 2" apart and rotate rapidly in a circular motion (similar to bicycling motion) for ten cycles. The print is observed for cracking, crazing, flaking or ink removal. This test cannot be used on rigid or heavy gauge substrates. Caution should also be exercised in interpreting results when the test is performed on coated substrates or materials subject to high levels of extensibility.
TOLERANCE	This test is subjective. Ink removal from cracking, crazing or flaking should not exceed 5% of the crinkle test area.

19.3.4.4.4 | Odor and Taint

PROCEDURE	ASTM E-462—(*Odor Panel*)
IMPORTANCE	Many materials (e.g., solvents, monomers, oligomers) commonly used in solvent, water and UV inks have characteristic odors. Residual levels of such materials when retained within the printed film can affect the odor or taste of the product to be packaged. Low odor/taint levels are necessary for food packing application.
TEST METHOD	Many of the materials that cause odor are volatile and can be quantitatively determined by gas chromatography. Unfortunately the accuracy of such tests is entirely dependent on the test protocol followed. Odor levels can also be determined subjectively by an odor panel.
SPECIFICATION	Customer-based specification. Acceptable rating 2 or below. **Gas chromatography:** for food packaging the total level of all retained solvents should not exceed 7,500 mg per ream. Levels for individual solvents should never exceed 25% of this limit.
TOLERANCE	Experienced odor panels rate samples 0 (no odor/taint) to a 6 (strong odor/taint).

19.3.4.4.5 | Lamination Bond Strength

PROCEDURE	No known ASTM standard.
IMPORTANCE	A wide variety of packaging relies on multilayered structures bonded together to provide the necessary performance properties. Package integrity and performance relies on maintenance of this bond.
TEST METHOD	Cut laminated print into one inch strips. Carefully separate lead edge. If difficulty is encountered, the edge can be immersed in solvent (THF, MEK, Toluene, Ethyl Acetate) or add slip sheets during the lamination. Measure the bond value using a tensile strength tester. Bond values are quoted as grams per linear inch. If the substrates tear before getting a good bond reading, it is sometimes necessary to back the sample with tape. Note on results if tape backed.
SPECIFICATION	Customer-based specification. As a general guideline: **Extrusion:** 50 g per linear inch—minimum. **Adhesive:** 100 g per linear inch to film destruction.
TOLERANCE	Customer-defined tolerance is normally quoted as a minimum requirement. The mode of failure should be noted, ink split is generally most desirable.

19.3.4.4.6 | Water Resistance

This section explains three tests for water resistance commonly used:

- Resistance to bleeding in water at room temperature.
- Adhesion/flexibility when subjected to ice water or to freezing and thawing
- Resistance to boiling water

PROCEDURE	No known ASTM standard.
IMPORTANCE	Water resistance is a critical property required for all packages that are subject to water contact in some manner. Some examples of such packages include frozen food packaging, boil-in-bags and microwaveable food packages.
TEST METHOD	To test for bleeding in water at room temperature, place the printed film in contact with a damp filter paper or towel for 1–5 hours and note any bleed onto the paper. Also check the print for color fastness. The freeze-thaw test involves immersing the printed film in ice water for a specified time and examining the loss of adhesion and/or flexibility, or freezing the film for a specified time and then testing adhesion and/or flexibility upon thawing. To examine resistance to boiling, place the printed sample in boiling water for the specified time. Remove and inspect the print for ink adhesion.
TOLERANCE	**For water bleed**: No color bleed or transfer onto the towel or filter paper should be observed. **For ice water & freeze/thaw resistance**: Allowable tolerance is less than 5% loss of tape adhesion or crinkle (See previous tests). **For boiling water**: Tolerance is less than 5% removal of ink.

19.3.4.4.7 | Chemical or Product Resistance (Spot Test)

PROCEDURE	ASTM D1647 and ASTM D2248
IMPORTANCE	The ink on a printed package must be able to resist the product being packaged, especially when chemicals are being packaged. While most chemical packaging has barriers to prevent migration of the material through the substrate, the chemical can still get on the outside of the package during filling.
TEST METHOD	Several drops of the specified chemical or product are placed on a flat, printed portion of the package. The chemical or product is left on the print, under ambient or otherwise specified conditions.
TOLERANCE	Any visible deterioration of the print or rub off of color onto the swab could be cause for failure.

19.3.4.4.8 | Lightfastness

PROCEDURE	ASTM D3424—(*Lightfastness of Printed Matter*) Other references ASTM D4459, G23, G26.
IMPORTANCE	Resistance to fading or discoloration is important if an ink is to be used on a printed piece that will be exposed to light for extended periods (wallcoverings, labels, window displays). Some pigments have much greater resistance to fading or discoloration than others. The primary pigments specified are designed for general use. Higher performance pigments are available.
TEST METHODS	Fade tests typically utilize equipment with a Xenon light source. The test sample is only partially exposed to the light source in order for a visual (subjective) or instrumental (objective) comparison to be made. Lightfastness can be measured and specified either as a time period (hours) or on a scale (blue/gray wool scale). A spectrophotometer can be used to measure the difference in color between the sample exposed to light and the control sample.
TOLERANCE	**Visual:** No visible difference after the stated test time. **Instrumental:** Customer based tolerance.

19.3.5 | Ink Control

19.3.5.1 | Efflux Cup and Stopwatch The efflux cup (Zahn, Shell, Din, Ford, etc.) is a vessel with a hole in the bottom, which is submerged in an ink and then removed. The time required for the ink to drain from the cup (measured in seconds using a stopwatch) relates to ink viscosity. A larger aperture cup is preferred for water base inks; a smaller aperture cup is preferred for most flexographic solvent inks. To ensure accuracy, efflux cups must be kept clean and periodically checked to a "standard" liquid. Recommended viscosity should be maintained at ±1 second for solvent inks and ±2 seconds for water based inks using a small aperture efflux cup such as a #2 Zahn. Refer to Print Section 18.5.2.2.1 and 19.3.4.2.2 for additional information.

19.3.5.2 | Automatic Viscosity Controllers An electronic tool, installed on the press, automatically measures and adjusts ink viscosity. Some units also monitor ink temperature. Automatic viscosity controllers should maintain viscosity within ±1 second.

19.3.5.3 | pH Meter pH meters are used to check acidity or alkalinity levels of water based inks. During a pressrun, water based inks are checked frequently to maintain a tolerance of ±0.3 units.

19.3.5.4 | Ink Temperature A thermometer for measuring the temperature of an ink in the pumps should be available. Ink suppliers can recommend the temperature range for optimum ink performance.

19.3.5.5 | Pyrometer/Infrared Thermometer The pyrometer is used to measure the actual surface temperature of the central impression drum (CID) or web. Analog and digital models are available which measure a surface temperature by either a probe or infrared beam. Uneven CID temperature can result in high/low spots and poor ink transfer from the plate to the substrate. Additionally, in web printing, the substrate temperature can be measured as it exits the dryer section of the press.

19.4 | Plate Mounting

19.4.1 | Mounting Materials

The materials used to adhere plates to the print cylinder or carrier sheet have inherent gauge variation that can significantly affect print quality. Similarly, the individual characteristics of the mounting material can change the overall hardness of the plate mount combination and this can also significantly affect plate performance. Mounting variables include:

- **Stickyback or mounting tape.** The definition varies by industry segment. Carrier sheet printers use very thin double-sided tape having less impact on image quality.

  In segments using the thicker tapes to attach plates directly to the cylinder, there is significant influence on print reproduction. Plate performance is linked to the specific properties of mounting tape. Critical properties include density, thickness and resiliency. Although different brands claim similar properties, differences in the printed image are measurable.

- **Compressible backings** cushion the impression of the plate to the anilox and substrate. This cushioning effect reduces dot gain by compensating for imperfections in plates and cylinder TIR. It also cushions (like a shock absorber) any mechanical bounce created by certain image designs or press components.

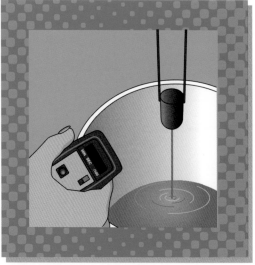

19.3.5.1 Efflux Cup and Stopwatch The efflux cup (Zahn, Shell, Din, Ford, etc.) is a vessel with a hole in the bottom, which is submerged in the ink and then removed. The time it takes for the ink to drain from the cup (measured in seconds by using a stopwatch) relates to ink viscosity.

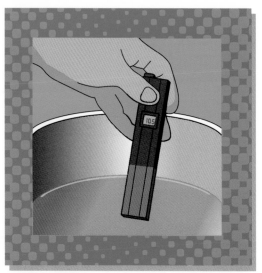

19.3.5.3 pH Meter During a pressrun water based inks are checked frequently to maintain a tolerance of ±0.3 units.

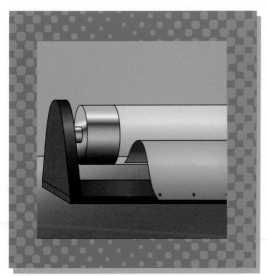

19.4 Plate Mounting The materials used to adhere plates to the print cylinder or carrier sheet have inherent gauge variation and can potentially create caliper deviations that can significantly affect print quality

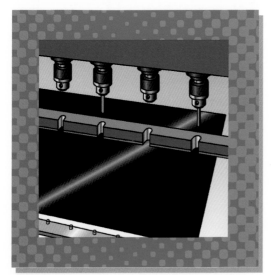

19.4.2.2 Pin Register This photomechanical method of attaching the plates to the cylinder requires pinholes which are either drilled or punched in the negatives and in the raw plate material to ensure accurate register.

Consider the following properties of compressible backing:

19.4.1.1 | **Thickness** The thicker the cushion backing, the more "give" it has on press. Thicker tapes have greater variances in caliper because they are made of a foam material. Thinner tapes have less cushioning effect and less caliper variance.

19.4.1.2 | **Density** Tapes are generally listed as high, medium and low density. Medium density cushions the plate less than low. Although low-density tapes normally produce less dot gain, they may also cause pinholing in the solid areas or on the line portion of a combination plate. Medium density tapes print solids smoother but create more dot gain. High-density tapes are most appropriate for large solids. The plate choice also influences which density of tape performs best.

19.4.1.3 | **Resiliency** Foam tapes can have either a closed cell or open cell design. Closed cell generally has a better memory or ability to rebound after the impression pressure is relieved. This helps the tape last longer on long production runs, therefore it has greater resistancy.

Use of sleeves, their type, material and hardness may affect the print results. Some sleeves are specifically designed to influence ink transfer all sleeves must therefore be part of the optimization/characterization process. Refer to Print Section 19.5 Sleeve Systems.

19.4.2 | **Mounting Equipment**

19.4.2.1 | **Optical** Optical mounters, the oldest of the three types of mounting equipment, operate on the principle of mirrors that reflect a proofed image from the impression drum onto the plate cylinder. It is critical when using this type of mounter to verify that the mirror alignment is accurate and the cylinders are parallel before beginning to mount a job. This method of mounting is the only one that allows visual inspection within the total image that is critical when mounting rubber plates that do not have a stable backing. It is possible to achieve specifications for mounting using an optical mounter, however, since it is so dependent on operator judgment, it is important to pull a mounter proof to verify the concentricity and fit of the mounted plates before going to press.

19.4.2.2 | **Pin Register** This is a photomechanical method of attaching the plate to the cylinder. Pinholes are either drilled or punched in the negatives and in the raw plate material to ensure accurate register. Finished plates are then mechanically attached to a pin bar or table which allows the plate to be applied squarely to the plate cylinder. This equipment can only be used with stable backed plates such as photopolymer or rubber with a stable backing. With this type of mounting, each color is mounted as a single plate; therefore, stepped negatives of multiple images can be mounted. The accuracy of this mounting technique is dependent upon the ability to accurately place the pinholes in the plate material. It is also critical to verify the parallelism of the mounting pin bar to the plate cylinder at the point of contact to ensure accurate register color to color. The speed and repeatability of mounting is usually an improvement over optical mounting, however, the degree of accuracy is not always consistent.

19.4.2.3 | **Video** The newest approach to mounting, this equipment can only be used with stable-backed plates. Registration is achieved through the use of microdots (ten thousandths of an inch) that are accurately imaged in the film and remain permanently on the printing plate. Mounting is done by aligning video cameras into datum positions based on the location of the dots and their position on the web. Magnification of the dots in the video monitor varies by manufacturer. Typical magnifications range from 40X to 140X. Such high levels of magnification ensure superior accuracy in mounting registration and repeatability color to color. Dot-to-dot registration can be achieved within ±0.001" (0.025 mm). In narrow web applications, registration cross hairs are used instead of microdots. Typically, the crosshairs are located in the matrix and are 0.0625" (1.6 mm) tall.

19.4.3 | Mounting for Accurate Impression

Before printing plates are mounted, they should be inspected for defects and measured with a micrometer to ensure that gauge tolerances are within specifications. Refer to Prepress Section 16.10 for Printing Plate Measurement and Control. It is helpful to mark the gauge readings on the plates for review by the mounter while laying out the work.

Since flexography is so dependent upon even impression for quality print, it is important to evaluate each process that contributes to the total gauge variation of the mounted printing plate cylinder. The bare cylinder face and journals should be measured for total indicated runout (TIR) as well as consistent diameter before the mounting procedure begins. When sleeves are used it is critical to measure the TIR and diameter of the sleeve after it has been applied to the base mandrel. It is wise to mark the position of the sleeves on the plate mandrel if a demounted sleeve is to be re-used for multiple runs. Although it is not currently possible to accurately measure stickyback for gauge, foam density, and consistency, inspection for visible defects is critical.

19.4.4 | Mounting for Accurate Register

The mounting process must minimize its contribution to registration inaccuracies. The registration tolerance built into the artwork is intended to allow for variation occurring during the printing process. The maximum allowable mounting registration tolerance is less than half the dimension built into the art for trap.

19.4.5 | Photopolymer Plate Mounting

On critically registered jobs, internal quality specifications may be required to verify the pitch diameter of each mounted print cylinder. Pitch diameter must match, for each color, within the allowable tolerance. Differences in each material's height around the cylinder, from color to color, will cause registration issues.

19.4.6 | Mounter's Proof

Ultimately, it is the responsibility of the printer to print within specifications. The mounter's proof verifies that plate cylinder TIR, concentricity and fit have been achieved prior to going to press. The mounter's proof is not necessarily accurate for color, but rather it proves that all contributing elements have been manufactured and used in accordance with specifications in order to achieve the registration quality expected on press. In narrow web, typically the press serves as the proofing press. In wide web, a mounter's proof is often used.

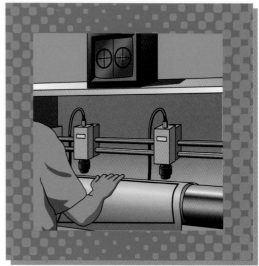

19.4.2.3 Video Mounting The newest approach to mounting, this equipment can only be used with stable backed plates. Registration is achieved through the use of microdots (ten thousandths of an inch) that are accurately imaged in the film and remain permanently on the printing plate.

19.5 | Sleeve Systems

19.5.1 | Sleeve Materials

- **Nickel Sleeve**: A thin seamless metal tube made to varying diameters, lengths and thickness'. The nickel sleeve is the thinnest sleeve available permitting the printer to become a sleeve user with minimum modifications to existing equipment. The only modifications required are:
  - Air holes drilled in plate cylinder
  - Thinner stickyback or plate used to compensate for the sleeve thickness.

NICKEL SLEEVE SPECIFICATIONS	
SURFACE HARDNESS	40 Rockwell C
TENSILE STRENGTH	200,000 psi (13,790 bars)
DIAMETER	3" – 24" (76.2mm – 609.6 mm)
LENGTH	Up to 145" (3,683 mm)
THICKNESS RANGE	0.003" – 0.015" (0.08 mm – 0.38 mm)
STANDARD THICKNESS	0.005" (0.13 mm)
SURFACE FINISH	≥ 2 Ra

- **Composite Sleeve**: A polymer (plastic), which is reinforced with a fiber such as fiberglass or carbon fiber. Various polymers and fibers are combined to obtain specific characteristics and properties.
  - **Fiber**: Fiberglass is the most widely used fiber, primarily because of its low cost. Additionally, tensile strength and strain to failure, heat and fire resistance, chemical resistance, moisture resistance, thermal and electrical properties are also advantages of fiberglass.
  - **Polymer**: Epoxies, Polyesters and Vinyl Ester are the most widely used polymers. Polymers are used as the matrices to bind together the reinforcement material (fiber) in composites.

19.5.2 | Sleeve Design

- **Parallel/Cylindrical Sleeves** have constant and parallel inner and outer diameters and are designed to mount on existing plate cylinders.
- **Tapered/Conical Sleeves** have a tapered inner diameter and constant outer diameter and are designed to mount on matched, tapered mandrels or print cylinders. Advantages include:
  - Greater sleeve locking force.
  - Ease of mounting.

The increased locking force is estimated to be as much as eight times that of parallel sleeves and is created by the counter-acting angles found in the mandrel and the sleeve. These counter-angles also allow for as much as half the length of the sleeve to be slid onto the mandrel before the introduction of air is required. This ease of mounting advantage is both safer for operators and less potentially damaging to the mandrel and sleeves.

19.5.3 | Mandrel & Print Cylinder Specifications

AIR-ACTUATED SLEEVE MOUNTING MANDREL & CYLINDER SPECIFICATIONS	
MANDREL/PRINT CYLINDER	Seamless tubing preferred
HEADER JOURNAL	Either machined from solid round stock or welded plate configuration
BCD (BARE CYLINDER DIAMETER)	±0.0005" (0.013 mm)
TIR (TOTAL INDICATED RUNOUT)	0.0005" (0.013 mm)
CYLINDER DIMENSIONAL STABILITY	Thermally stress relieved
AIR HOLES	**Cylinder Repeat <18":** 6 holes @ 0.156" (3.96 mm) diameter spaced circumferentially **Cylinder Repeat >18":** 8 holes @ 0.156" (3.96 mm) diameter spaced circumferentially **Distance from Leading Edge :** 0.625" (15.9 mm)
LEADING EDGE	0.25" (6.4 mm) bevel, 20°
AIR INLET	0.25" (6.4 mm) NPT 1 hole either through journal or header
AIR PRESSURE	Minimum 80 psig (5.5 bars); 100 psig (6.9 bars) preferred
CHROME-PLATED CYLINDERS	Minimum 0.0005" (0.013 mm) chrome
CHAMPFER	5°; Length: 0.157" (4 mm) from mandrel end
INTERNALLY PIPED CYLINDERS	Optional

REGISTER PIN STANDARDS: SLEEVE PREPOSITIONING	
MANDREL LOCATION	Gear/drive end
PIN	**Diameter:** 0.236" (6 mm)
	Location: 0.276" (7 mm) from gear/drive end
	Height: 0.787" (20 mm)

19.5.4 | Laser-engraved Rubber-covered Sleeves

- **Material:** Rubber can be vulcanized onto a nickel sleeve and then laser engraved (Prepress Section 16.5) to create a continuous printing design roll. Rubber can be bonded onto some composite sleeves. Composite sleeves can be provided with two different finishes. One finish is smooth for plate-mounting applications and the other finish rough for the vulcanization process. Polyester sleeves are not suitable for the vulcanization process because most polymers cannot be exposed to the high temperatures required to vulcanize rubber.

- **Cleaning of Laser Engraved Sleeves:** Clean the surface of the sleeve using a horsehair brush and a solvent recommended by the ink supplier for the proper breakdown of the ink. Clean the entire sleeve of all ink and let it dry completely before storing. Do not clean sleeves with rags, nylon, cheesecloth, etc. as these products will wear edges of plates and destroy process or screened plate dots.

19.5.5 | Sleeve Mounting & Demounting

Typically, sleeves are mounted/demounted onto mandrels or print cylinders using air. The inside diameter of the sleeve is slightly smaller than the outside diameter of the plate cylinder/mandrel. Compressed air is used to expand the sleeve in order to slide it onto the mandrel/print cylinder. Once in position, the air is disconnected and the sleeve clamps tightly into place.

It is necessary to conform to the air pressure and volume requirements as described by each sleeve manufacturer. The recommended ranges in pressure and volume required for the safe and proper mounting and demounting of the different sleeve materials available is as varied as the range in sleeve thicknesses available.

19.5.6 | Sleeve Storage Considerations

■ Vertical storage of sleeves is recommended. Sleeves ranging from 3" (7.62 cm) diameter to 9.5" (24.13 cm) diameter can be stored horizontally but should be supported internally. Due to the weight, sleeves over 9.5" (24 cm) diameter should be stored in the vertical position. If stored in the horizontal position, the core will start to egg-shape over time.

■ If sleeves are to be stored in a horizontal position, the maximum height of storage should be restricted to a height at which the temperature does not exceed 75° F (24° C). Refer to supplier recommendations.

■ If sleeves are stored in lighted areas, they should be wrapped with a barrier such as cardboard, so that oxidation is minimized.

■ Sleeves should be stored under normal room temperatures. Sleeves that have been exposed to excessive cold or heat should be allowed to return to room temperature prior to mounting or digitally imaging.

19.6 | Anilox Rollers

19.6.1 | Anilox Roller Selection

The engraving of an anilox roller consists of cell volume (the size of each cell), cell/screen count (number of cells per linear inch) and the angle the cells are engraved. The table on the following page identifies the most common volumes and cell counts used by printers today. The specific combination of anilox count/volume will vary based on substrate and ink properties and therefore should be discussed with the anilox supplier.

COMMON ANILOX CELL COUNT & VOLUME RANGES

		ENGLISH MEASURMENT		METRIC MEASUREMENT	
		CELL COUNT LPI	CELL VOLUME BCM/in²	CELL COUNT LPCM	CELL VOLUME cm³/cm²
FLEXIBLE PACKAGING	150 – 175 lpi Process	800 - 900	1.4 - 2.0	315 - 355	2.2 - 3.1
	120 – 133 lpi Process	650 - 750	1.8 - 2.5	255 - 295	2.8 - 3.9
	85 – 110 lpi Process	500 - 600	2.2 - 2.9	195 - 235	3.4 - 4.5
	Screen Text	360 - 440	3.2 - 4.2	140 - 175	5.0 - 6.5
	Line Text	300 - 360	4.2 - 5.5	120 - 140	6.5 - 8.5
	Line Solids	250 - 330	6.0 - 7.0	100 - 130	9.3 - 10.9
	Solids	200 - 300	7.3 - 8.0	80 - 120	11.3 - 12.4
	Heavy Solids/ Opaque White	180 - 220	9.9 - 10.0	70 - 90	15.3 - 15.5
TAG & LABEL	150 – 200 lpi Process	800 - 900	1.4 - 2.0	315 - 375	2.2 - 3.1
	120 – 133 lpi Process	600 - 800	1.5 - 2.0	235 - 315	2.3 - 3.1
	100 – 110 lpi Process	500 - 600	2.0 - 3.0	195 - 235	3.1 - 4.7
	Screen Text	500 - 600	2.5 - 3.5	195 - 235	3.9 - 5.4
	Line Text	360 - 440	3.5 - 4.5	140 - 175	5.4 - 7.0
	Line Solids	300 - 400	4.5 - 7.5	120 - 160	7.0 - 11.6
	Solids	300 - 360	5.0 - 6.5	120 - 140	7.8 - 10.1
	Heavy Solids/ Varnish	200 - 250	7.2 - 8.7	80 - 100	11.2 - 13.5
DIRECT-PRINT CORRUGATED	110 – 120 lpi Process	440 - 550	2.0 - 3.5	175 - 220	3.1 - 5.4
	85 lpi Process	360 - 440	3.0 - 3.5	140 - 175	4.7 - 5.4
	Line Work (2 Roll)	250 - 330	5.5 - 6.0	100 - 130	8.5 - 9.3
	Line Work (Doctor Blade)	250 - 300	6.5 - 7.8	100 - 120	10.1 - 12.1
	Solids (2 roll)	200 - 250	6.5 - 7.8	80 - 100	10.1 - 12.1
	Solids (Doctor Blade)	200 - 250	8.0 - 9.0	80 - 100	12.4 - 14.0
	Varnish	200 - 250	7.8 - 12.0	80 - 100	12.1 - 18.6
MULTIWALL BAGS	100 – 120 lpi Process	440 - 550	2.0 - 3.5	175 - 220	3.1 - 5.4
	85 lpi Process	360 - 440	2.5 - 3.5	140 - 175	3.9 - 5.4
	Line Work (2 Roll)	250 - 330	4.5 - 6.0	100 - 130	7.0 - 9.3
	Line Work (Doctor Blade)	250 - 300	4.5 - 9.0	100 - 120	7.0 - 14.0
	Solids (2 roll)	200 - 250	4.5 - 8.0	80 - 100	7.0 - 12.4
	Solids (Doctor Blade)	200 - 250	4.5 - 9.0	80 - 100	7.0 - 14.0
	Varnish	200 - 250	6.5 - 12.0	80 - 100	10.1 - 18.6

19.6.2 | Cell Volume

The cell volume of an anilox roller is responsible for the amount of ink supplied to the printing plate and the resulting density. An anilox roller's volume is measured in cubic billion microns per square inch (BCM/in²) or cubic centimeters per square meter (cm³/m²). The conversion of anilox volume between BCM/in² to metric cm³/m²:

$$\frac{BCM}{in^2} \times 1.55 = \frac{cm^3}{m^2} \quad OR \quad \frac{cm^3}{m^2} \times 0.645 = \frac{BCM}{in^2}$$

19.6.2.1 | Cell Volume Measurement   There are three common methods to determine the volume of the cells on an anilox roller. It is important to note that volume measurements often do not agree between measurement methods. Therefore, it is recommended that the printer select one method to identify cell volume in order to avoid confusion at press. The three methods for determining volume are:

- Calculating the volume based on the depth of the engraved cells.
- Measuring the volume using a liquid measurement system.
- Scanning interferometry.

19.6.2.1.1 | Liquid Volume Measurement Procedure

- Draw an exact amount of a liquid, typically 10 to 25 microliters (one microliter equals 1 billion cubic microns or BCM), into a micro-pipette.
- Dispense the liquid on the surface of the anilox roller.
- Spread the liquid across the anilox roller using some type of metering device. This is commonly done with a "tractor" or some other device where a "metering blade" can be held stationary and drawn down the surface of the roll. This causes the ink to fill the cells and spread across the surface of the roll.
- Transfer a "blot" of the area filled with the liquid to a piece of paper.
- The outline of the blot is traced with a planimeter that measures the perimeter of the blot and automatically calculates the area of the blot. The area measured is then divided into the amount of fluid used. This yields the cell volume in BCM/in².

The most important aspect in liquid volume measurement is consistency. Typically these types of systems can be as loose as ±10% although consistency of ±3% to 5% should be expected from a properly trained operator using properly calibrated equipment. The liquid volume measurement method will usually measure the cell volume based on the cells in an area of 2 to 3 square inches.

19.6.2.1.2 | Scanning Interferometry Measurement   The most recent method for analyzing anilox engravings is the scanning interferometer microscope. Used by most anilox roller suppliers for the last several years, this system can determine

- Volume of the measured cells.
- Cell depth.
- Depth-to-opening ratio (DTO) of the cells.
- Percent of cell opening.
- Cell/screen count.
- Screen angle.

Additionally, scanning interferometry can produce a three-dimensional view of the cell.

The major disadvantage of this system, for the converter, is the cost. Another concern to the scanning interferometer microscope is the small number of cells analyzed in each reading, typically 30 to 300 cells per reading, dependent upon screen count.

Because of the cost, very few printers have invested in a scanning interferometer microscope system. An alternative is to use a very thin metal foil strip to make an impression of an area of cells on the anilox roller. This strip can be sent to the anilox roller supplier and analyzed using scanning interferometry.

19.6.2.2 | Cell Volume Tolerance There are various methods used to measure the cell volume of an anilox roller. The printer and anilox roller supplier must agree upon the method used. Once this method is identified, all newly manufactured rolls should be supplied with a COA (Certificate of Analysis) confirming the roll meets specifications. Manufacturer tolerance on cell volume, regardless of BCM, is ±5%.

19.6.3 | Cell Count

Generally, the cell (screen) count chosen should be the highest possible that will accommodate the cell volume necessary to provide the required ink volume and that can be properly maintained during operation. When screen or process work is being printed, the industry standard is to select an anilox cell count that is, at a minimum, four times (4X) the value of the plate screen.

For example, printing a process job with a plate screen of 120 lines per inch (lpi) would require an anilox roller with a minimum cell count of 480 lpi. A printer may choose a 550 lpi or even a 650 lpi anilox roller when using a 120-line plate, depending upon the volume requirement. In some instances, a printer may select even higher cell counts, for instance, 700 or 800 lpi, on the theory that the finer the cell count, the better the print quality. Higher cell counts have lower volumes; in order to achieve desired densities (or color matches) the ink formulation must be adjusted.

Work being printed today using high cell count (700 –1,000 lpi) / low volume (1.8 – 1.2 BCM) anilox rollers requires high-strength inks. There is a limit to how much pigment an ink chemistry can hold in suspension and still achieve the necessary performance properties (such as rub resistance). An additional challenge of very low volume rolls is getting the "pigment particle size" of the ink small enough to fit within the cells. Ink dry-rate is another variable to consider with very low volume rolls. If the transition to low volume rolls is to be successful within a plant, the anilox and ink supplier must work closely with each other and the printer. The inks must be formulated for the desired anilox count/volume combination.

To convert between LPI (lines per inch) and the metric LPCM (lines per centimeter), use the following equations:

$$LPCM = \frac{LPI}{2.54} \quad OR \quad LPI = LPCM \times 2.54$$

19.6.4 | Engraving Angle

Theoretically, any angle between 0° and 90° can be produced, but the most common screen angles are 30°, 45° and 60°. The most prevalent engraving angle used today is 60° whether for solids and type or screen and process work. Both the 30° and 60° engravings have 15% more cells per unit of area than does the 45° engraving. The higher the number of cells per area, the more uniform the dispersion of ink across the anilox will be and the better the print quality.

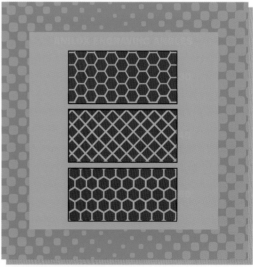

19.6.4 Engraving Angle The higher the number of cells per area, the more uniform the dispersion of ink across the anilox and the higher the print quality. Therefore, for this reason alone, it is almost always a better choice to select the 30° or 60° engraving.

For some of the higher viscosity radiation cured inks, the 30° or 30° channeled engraving appears to be a better choice than the 60° engraving, as it reduces pinholing and striations when printing solids. When working with radiation-cured inks, it is always best to discuss the anilox requirements with the anilox supplier and the ink supplier, as well as the press manufacturer.

19.6.5 | Inspection of Incoming Anilox Rollers

The anilox roller supplier will issue a certificate of analysis (COA) with each roll. The certification includes the actual engraving specifications and the roll dimensional specifications. Often, the COA replaces a full dimensional and engraving inspection of the incoming anilox by the printer.

If the printer performs an incoming dimensional and engraving inspection, it should be completed as soon as possible after the roll is received and before it is used. An inspection table for general visual inspection and to check TIR is required. A microscope with a minimum 10X eyepiece and objectives of at least 20X, 40X and 80X is also needed to inspect the overall appearance of the engraving.

19.6.5.1 | Anilox Inspection Procedures

First, check the roll for any damage that may have occurred in shipping by looking at the face of the roll and the shafts. Next, check the TIR of the roll face and journals and compare to the blueprint requirements.

Using a microscope, inspect the engraving for general quality. Look for excess land area between the cells, cell shape and for unspecified channeling. An excessive amount of channeling or excessive channel depth can indicate a poor engraving.

Measure the roll volume using a volume measurement system (Print Section 19.6.2.1). Usually three readings across the roll face are sufficient to determine the average volume of the roll. Photograph the engraving or request that the anilox roller supplier provide a photograph of the engraving on the anilox roller.

All anilox roller information, both COA's and in-house inspections, should be maintained for reference purposes.

19.6.5.1.2 | Total Indicated Runout (TIR)

TIR measures the centricity of the anilox roller. Rollers that are out of round will have a negative impact on the consistency of the ink lay down.

TOTAL INDICATED RUNOUT (TIR)		
CERAMIC ROLLERS <65" WIDE	±0.0005"	0.013 mm
CERAMIC ROLLERS >65" WIDE	±0.001"	0.025 mm

19.6.6 | Anilox Roller Maintenance

To maximize the life of an anilox roller, regular maintenance and inspection procedures should be implemented. Keeping the anilox clean will help maintain the print density and extend the life of the anilox roller. To minimize score lines, run proper doctor blade pressures and install/maintain magnets and filters in the ink-delivery system.

Anilox rollers should be checked on a regular basis to monitor the cleanliness and wear of the engraving. Wear and ink dried in the cells reduces the effective volume of the roller. If a decrease in density occurs when printing with a clean roller, the roller should be analyzed to verify the current cell volume compared

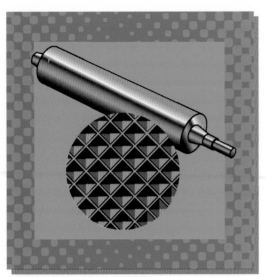

19.6.5 Anilox Rollers An inspection table for general inspection and to check runout is required for inspection. A microscope (having at a minimum a 10X eyepiece and objectives of at least 20X, 40X and 80X) is also needed to inspect the overall appearance of the engraving.

to the actual cell volume when the roll was new. Anilox suppliers can assist in implementing a monitoring program.

19.7 | Doctor Blades

19.7.1 | Doctor Blade Materials

Doctor blades are manufactured in steel, plastic and composites. Regardless of the material used, the doctor blade must be flat and straight (chamber) with a controlled thickness and the surface finished in order to provide clean, uniform metering of the anilox roller.

- **Steel blades** are all made of high purity ores to provide consistent metering and minimize damage to the anilox roller. Steel blades provide the cleanest wipe of the anilox surface. Carbon steel, either bright or blue, is the most common blade material. Stainless steel is often used in water-based applications where corrosion is a concern. Tool steel is used when long life is needed or abrasive inks are a problem.

- **Plastic blades** provide long life and corrosion resistance. They are safer to use because they do not sharpen like steel or composite blades. Since they are thicker to provide the necessary support, the wipe of the anilox surface is not as clean and surface ink will be present. The corrugated print segment often uses plastic blades. Containment blades in a chambered doctor blade assembly are often polyester to reduce anilox wear and scoring.

- **Composite blades** provide long life and corrosion resistance. While sharper than plastic blades, they are not as sharp as steel blades. Because of the thinner edge, they provide a cleaner wipe than plastic with only a small amount of surface ink. Composite blades are typically run in corrugated and flexographic newspaper print applications.

TYPICAL DOCTOR BLADE THICKNESSES		
STEEL	0.006" | 0.15 mm 0.008" | 0.20 mm	0.010" | 0.25 mm
PLASTIC	0.020" – 0.125" | 0.51 mm – 3.18 mm	
COMPOSITE	0.015" – 0.025" | 0.38" mm – 0.64" mm	

19.7.2 | Doctor Blade Edge Profiles

There are three types of edge profiles available for reverse angle doctoring.

- Beveled edges are available from 2° to 45°. When installing a beveled blade, the bevel should be installed away from the anilox roller so that the small tip is in contact with the roll.

- Lamella or stepped edge maintains a constant tip thickness as it wears.

- Round or radius edge, designed for flexographic printing, provides a faster run-in on press.

UPC-A

6 12345 00000 5

UPC-E

0 123456 5

EAN-8

1234 5670

EAN-13

1 234560 000005

20.1 Bar Codes Bar codes are used in many different ways or "applications". For example, one application is bar coding products for retail checkout lanes, while another is bar coding shipments for conveyor lane routing in distribution centers. The specifications for the bar codes in these two application areas are different because the conditions for scanning the bar codes are very different.

20.0 Printing Bar Codes

20.1 | Bar Code Specifications

Bar code print specifications are produced by combining three types of related specifications:

■ **Application Standards** are published by accredited standards organizations. Before explaining what application standards specify, it might be useful to know more about what they are. Simply put, bar codes are used in many different ways or "applications". For example, one bar code application is bar coding products for retail checkout lanes and another application is bar coding shipments for conveyor lane routing in distribution centers. The specifications for the bar codes in these two application areas are different because the conditions for scanning the bar codes are very different. Accredited standards organizations (see Appendix) provide specifications in the form of guidelines and standards to assist in answering:

■ What bar code type should be used?

■ How to structure the data inside the bar code?

■ How to print human-readable information that is inside the bar code?

■ What bar code size ranges are acceptable?

■ Where the bar code should be placed on the package or container?

■ What are the minimum print quality requirements?

■ **Print Specifications** prescribe a minimal level of capability for all printers. All specifications will fall within the acceptable specification limits of the appropriate application standard for the bar code being printed. Print specifications will assist in answering:

■ What is the minimum size for a bar code depending on selected printing press type and substrate?

■ How should the bar code be oriented given the direction the web will travel?

■ **Job Specifications** should be published within the job specification for film or plate output. This type of specification should answer:

■ What output resolution was selected for film or plate production?

■ What BWR was used in film or plate production?

Because scanners read bar code graphics, they must be produced according to the specifications appropriate to the application standard, printing press type, substrate type, and film/plate output conditions. There are many considerations that apply when producing any bar code; this section is a guide through the significant issues pertaining to printing.

20.2 | Bar Code Data

A good manufacturing practice for each phase of the production process is to confirm that the information printed below the bar code matches the information encoded within the symbol. It is the responsibility of the supplier providing final films or digital files for platemaking to verify that the bar code is properly encoded. However, it is in the printer's best interest to check the encoding for accuracy. The UCC has provided a spreadsheet for calculating check digits to the FTA and can be found in the Appendix and on the CD in this book.

20.3 | Substrate Considerations

20.3.1 | Substrate Texture/Porosity

Bars and spaces are most accurately reproduced on smooth substrates with high ink holdout characteristics. The rougher, more textured and more porous a substrate, the greater the potential for printing bars with voids and ink in the spaces, either of which can reduce scanning rates. Textured and more porous stocks also tend to increase bar edge roughness, bar growth and bleeding. Any of these characteristics can reduce scanning rates.

20.3.2 | Substrate Color/Transparency

Bar codes scan most successfully with an opaque white background that provides white spaces and quiet zones with the maximum reflectance possible. When printing on a transparent or colored substrate, a solid, light-colored (white is optimum) background, with maximum opacity, is recommended in the area where the bar code is to be located. Special considerations for the background ink formulation and press set-up (anilox, double bumps of background color and mounting material selection, etc.) may be necessary in order to achieve maximum opacity.

20.3.3 | Printer Responsibility

Printers are responsible for reviewing the proposed substrate and design to determine the impact on bar-code scanning (e.g., symbol contrast, size, need for second print deck). Printers are also responsible for inspecting incoming materials to verify they meet predetermined specifications (e.g., reflectance on corrugated).

20.4 | Bar Code Colors

20.4.1 | Printing Ink Colors and Symbol Contrast (SC)

The colors specified for the symbol background and bars have different reflectance values. It is important to remember that colors with acceptable ANSI Symbol Contrast (SC) grades on opaque substrates may be completely unacceptable on translucent or transparent substrates. In order to obtain an accurate prediction of a bar code's SC it is mandatory that both the bar color and background color reflectance are measured. Translucent or transparent substrates must be measured against a background that is representative of the final, filled package contents.

Symbol contrast is a mathematical expression for the difference in reflectivity between the symbol's dark bars and light background. It is based on scan reflectance profiles specified by *ANSI X3.182-(1990 Bar Code Print Quality Guideline)*. The minimum SC specified varies depending on the bar code symbol selected and where it is used. For example, the EAN/UPC symbol used in retail point-of-sale applications, requires a minimum 40% SC on the final filled product according to *ANSI/UCC5—(Quality Specification for the U.P.C. Printed Symbol)*. To meet this 40% specification, it is recommended to target achieving a SC minimum of 55% for the U.P.C. at the print stage (before the packaging process).

Bar-code scanners typically use red light; therefore, red, and orange inks with a high percentage of red pigments should be avoided when printing the bars in a bar code, but may be used for the symbol background. The optimum combination is opaque black ink for the bars and opaque white ink for the symbol background. Bars printed in black, dark blue or dark green and backgrounds

20.4.1 Printing Ink Colors and Symbol Contrast (SC)
It is important to remember that colors with acceptable ANSI Symbol Contrast (SC) grades on opaque substrates may be completely unacceptable on translucent or transparent substrates.

Print

(spaces and quiet zones) printed in yellow, orange, pink, peach and red generally scan successfully.

Ink color specifications should be evaluated individually for particular substrates. No matter what color is specified, it is strongly recommended that SC is monitored closely, and ink densities controlled carefully. A relatively small change in density, on a marginal bar/space combination, can result in an unacceptable SC. Bar codes require bars with sharp edges in order for the scanner to correctly read the code. The bars comprising a bar code must be printed on a single print station.

20.4.2 | Predicting Adequate Symbol Contrast

Some commercially available ANSI-based verification devices have a mode that allows the user to make static or spot reflectance readings of sample ink and substrate combinations (called a "reflectometer" mode). Two reflectance readings, one of a substrate or background color (known as RL) and one of an ink sample for the bars on the substrate (known as RD) may be used to estimate whether the sample color combination will, when used to print a bar code, ensure an adequate symbol contrast (SC) for the bar code.

20.5 | Bar Code Orientation

The bar code should be oriented in the direction of the web going though the press. Printers need to advise designers of their requirements regarding the bar code's orientation based on the printed web direction. If the printed symbol must be printed with its bars perpendicular to the direction the web is moving, the printer should provide the designer with the minimum size symbol they can print and continue to meet the minimum print quality specifications within the appropriate application standards.

20.6 | Press Characterization Procedure For Bar Codes—Symbol Matrix

Press characterization is a prerequisite for printing quality bar code symbols and should provide the printer with two vital pieces of information:

■ The minimum symbol size that can be consistently and accurately reproduced.
■ The proper BWR (also called cut back) to be applied in the design stage.

The symbol matrix procedure specifies a method for selecting the optimum magnification and BWR to use in the prepress design of UPC-A (U.P.C. Version A) symbols for a given production process. It shows how to select the magnification and BWR that will provide the best results for the range of impressions encountered on press using verifiers based on *ANSI X3.182-(1990 Bar Code Print Quality Guideline) and ISO 15416:2000 – (Information technology – Automatic identification and data capture technique – Print Quality Test Specification – Linear symbols)*. This methodology, while focused on UPC-A symbols, is appropriate for use with any bar code symbol.

20.6.1 | Magnification and Bar Width Reduction for the Symbol Matrix

The press characterization method instructs that a matrix of UPC-A symbols are printed with various magnification and BWR combinations. For example, a matrix of symbols for a particular printing process might test UPC-A magnifications of 90%, 100%, 110%, and 120% and BWRs of 2, 3, 4, 5, and 6 mils. The following page shows an example of this symbol matrix.

ANSI MATRIX
SYMBOL CHARACTERIZATION TEST PLATE

Flexographic Image Reproduction Specifications & Tolerances

0 01827 72815 3 (each)

SIZE: 90% SYMBOL	BWR: -0.002
SIZE: 100% SYMBOL	BWR: -0.002
SIZE: 110% SYMBOL	BWR: -0.002
SIZE: 120% SYMBOL	BWR: -0.002

0 31827 72815 0 (each)

SIZE: 90% / 100% / 110% / 120% SYMBOL — BWR: -0.003

0 41827 72815 9 (each)

SIZE: 90% / 100% / 110% / 120% SYMBOL — BWR: -0.004

0 51827 72819 6 (each)

SIZE: 90% / 100% / 110% / 120% SYMBOL — BWR: -0.005

0 61827 72814 0 (each)

SIZE: 90% / 100% / 110% / 120% SYMBOL — BWR: -0.006

RUN DATE _____ PLATE MATERIAL _____ PRESS _____
OUTPUT DEVICE _____ MOUNTING TAPE _____ ANILOX ROLL SPECS _____
OUTPUT RESOLUTION _____ INK TYPE _____ MACHINE DIRECTION

20.6.1 Range of Magnification and Bar-Width Reduction for the Symbol Matrix The press characterization method instructs that a matrix of UPC-A symbols are printed with various magnification and BWR combinations.

Print

Experienced UPC-A symbols printers can test using a narrower range of magnification and BWR combinations. For example, the magnification and BWR combinations tested might begin with current design parameters and test lower magnifications only. Those using the symbol matrix method in an unknown situation (e.g., new press, substrate, or anilox cell count) might begin by testing a wide range of magnification and BWR combinations and then use the findings to conduct subsequent tests with a narrower range.

The exact numbers encoded (used) in the symbols of the "example test plate" should be used when creating the matrix to ensure optimal tests of UPC-A symbol decodability. There are slight differences in the numbers encoded for each BWR row, to make the process of compiling data easier. Be sure to make dimensional corrections for the addressable output resolution.

20.6.2 | Create and Mount Symbol Matrix Printing Plate

Once the magnification and BWR combinations in the matrix for the test plate are determined, it is important to produce and mount the plate using the standard processes (e.g., software, output device, and output resolution) for generating UPC-A symbol artwork, films, and plates.

20.6.3 | Begin Sampling at Kiss and Maximum Impressions

1. Bring the press to "kiss" impression and begin sampling at this impression level for verification.

2. Bring the press to maximum impression and begin sampling at this impression level for ANSI based verification.

When sampling at the maximum impression, take into account maximum tolerances for a high spot on any part of a plate. For example, if the TIR tolerance is 1 mil and the normal maximum impression is 3 mil, bring the press to 4 mil for the purpose of this "maximum impression" test. This will simulate the worst case maximum impression for UPC-A symbols mounted on a high spot.

20.6.4 | Selecting the Optimum Magnification and Bar-width Reduction Combination

For each magnification and BWR combination, the average ANSI decodability for "kiss" and maximum impression should be recorded in a table similar to the following example.

RECORDING SYMBOL MATRIX
PRESS CHARACTERIZATION RESULTS

INDIVIDUAL MAG/BWR COMBINATIIONS		AVERAGE DECODABILITY FOR MAG/BWR COMBINATION @KISS IMPRESSION	AVERAGE DECODABILITY FOR MAG/BWR COMBINATION @MAXIMUM IMPRESSION		MINIMUM DECODABILITY FOR EACH MAG/BWR COMBINATON
90%	−0.002"	55%	57%	➡	55%
90%	**−0.003"**	**67%**	**59%**	➡	**59%**
90%	−0.004"	64%	53%	➡	53%
90%	−0.005"	56%	56%	➡	56%
90%	−0.006"	43%	43%	➡	43%
100%	−0.002"	56%	58%	➡	56%
100%	**−0.003"**	**68%**	**58%**	➡	**58%**
100%	−0.004"	65%	56%	➡	56%
100%	−0.005"	57%	58%	➡	57%
100%	−0.006"	44%	47%	➡	44%
110%	−0.002"	57%	59%	➡	57%
110%	**−0.003"**	**68%**	**62%**	➡	**62%**
110%	−0.004"	66%	54%	➡	54%
110%	−0.005"	57%	58%	➡	57%
110%	−0.006"	45%	41%	➡	41%
120%	−0.002"	57%	59%	➡	57%
120%	**−0.003"**	**69%**	**65%**	➡	**65%**
120%	−0.004"	66%	59%	➡	59%
120%	−0.005"	58%	61%	➡	58%
120%	−0.006"	49%	53%	➡	49%

To determine the optimum magnification and BWR combination for each symbol matrix test:

1. Record the minimum decodability percentage for each magnification and BWR combination row in the column labeled "minimum decodability for each MAG/BWR". Find the highest percentage in the column labeled "minimum decodability for each MAG/BWR" and highlight that row (in bold type).

2. The optimum magnification and BWR combination used in this test corresponds to 120% magnification with a 0.003" BWR. However, if the desired symbol size is 100%, the selected BWR would be 0.003" based on 58% "minimum decodability for each MAG/BWR".

20.7 | Bar Code Size

20.7.1 | Minimum Bar-code Size Specifications

Bar code symbol sizes are specified in an acceptable range for the optics found in the scanning system. A printer may also determine a minimum size symbol that can be printed repeatedly while meeting minimum print quality specifications. Printing a bar code below the minimum size specified by the applicable symbol specification is not supported by FIRST. Compliant printers will be able to meet the minimum bar-code size specifications in the table at right while meeting the minimum print quality specifications found within appropriate application section standards. This chart is only applicable to symbols that are printed with the bars running in the machine direction.

MINIMUM BAR CODE MAGNIFICATION		
WIDE WEB		**MACHINE DIRECTION**
PREPRINT LINER	SBS Board	100%
COMBINED CORRUGATED Flute Dependant	All	UPC: 110%–200% ITF-14: 100%
FOLDING CARTON	SBS Board	100%
	CRB Board	100%
MULTIWALL BAG	Coated Paper	115%
	Uncoated Paper	115%
FILM PRODUCTS	Polyester	100%
	Polypropylene Clear	100%
	Polypropylene Opaque White	100%
	Polyethylene Clear	100%
	Polyethylene Opaque White	100%
	Metallized	100%
NARROW WEB		**MACHINE DIRECTION**
PAPER PRODUCTS	Coated Paper	80%
FILM PRODUCTS	All	100%

20.7.1.1 | Combined Corrugated: Bar-code Size Specifications

- **U.P.C. Symbol:** A 200% symbol is the maximum size specified by the UCC. Generally, this represents the minimum size recommended for direct printing on combined corrugated. However, many printers with newer presses, thinner printing plates, smaller flutes, and improved white substrates are successfully printing in the 110–160% range. A minimum magnification of 150% is specified by the UCC for all containers that will be scanned on automated conveyor lines during the distribution stage.

- **ITF-14 Symbol:** The nominal size specified by the UCC for ITF-14 symbols carrying the SCC-14 number is based on an X-dimension (narrow bar width) of 0.040" (1.0 mm) and a height of 1.250" (31.8 mm). Generally, the 100% specification is recommended as a minimum size for direct printing on combined corrugated. If the carton size prohibits the 1.250" (31.8 mm) height, (e.g. the height restrictions of a tray) it may be preferable to print a slightly truncated symbol while leaving the X-dimension at 0.040" (1.0 mm).

The current magnification range for ITF-14 symbols has a UCC specification between a minimum of 70% and a maximum of 120%. These specifications are changing in two ways:

1. If the container is large enough to be scanned on an automated conveyor line scanner during distribution, then the minimum height is fixed at 1.25" (31.8 mm) regardless of the X-dimension used for the symbol.
2. To improve scanning efficiency, packages marked with ITF-14 symbols

that are scanned in a conveyor-based environment should have a maximum X-dimension of 0.040" (1.0 mm) not 0.048" (1.2 mm). While current packages marked with ITF-14 symbols with X-dimensions between 0.040" (1.0 mm) and 0.048" (1.2 mm) remain acceptable based on historical UCC specifications, new packages should begin using 0.040" (1.0 mm) X-dimensions as the maximum.

20.7.2 | Bar-code Truncation

Certain symbols have a fixed relationship between height and width, while others have minimum heights specified. Bar code truncation is a reduction of a symbol's height below the application standard or symbol specification and is not acceptable.

20.8 | Quiet Zones

The quiet zone is the area, free of printing, that precedes the left bar and follows the right bar in a bar code symbol. The quiet zones allow scanners to detect when a bar code starts and stops. Quiet zones are based on multiples of the symbol's narrowest element width (X-dimension). Minimum quiet zone specifications depend on the symbol specified.

Example: the UPC-A symbol requires a quiet zone of 9X on each side, while an ITF-14 symbol (Interleaved 2-of-5 with the UCC's UCC/EAN-14 number in it) requires a 10X quiet zone on each side. Bar-code specifications where the quiet zone is omitted, obstructed or too small are not acceptable.

20.9 | Bar-width Reduction

Bar widths increase in flexographic printing in a manner similar to dot gain. As the bar widths increase, the corresponding space widths between the bars decrease. Just as a dot gain curve is typically applied to a process image to account for expected dot gain on press, a BWR is typically applied to a bar code prior to film/plate output to account for the bar growth expected on the press. Printers are required to specify the amount of BWR appropriate to the anticipated printing conditions (e.g. press type, plate material, mounting material, substrate, and anilox roller). The specified amount of BWR should be corrected at the symbol design stage for digital bar codes files (see Design Section 4.4). Bar code design specifications outside the BWR specified by the printer are not acceptable.

20.10 | Distortion

Printers must specify a distortion factor (or plate-roll circumference) to prepress providers for any bar code whose bars are printed perpendicular to the direction the web will travel. Printing symbols in the cross-direction is not recommended.

20.11 | Bar Code Quality Assessment

ANSI X3.182-(1990 Bar Code Print Quality Guideline) and ISO 15416:2000 – (Information technology – Automatic identification and data capture technique – Print Quality Test Specification – Linear symbols) describe a standard method for measuring bar-code symbol quality. This method is designed to assess a symbol's quality after it is printed and does not replace the bar-width tolerance measurements taken in the pressroom for process control. This method specifies the use of an ANSI/ISO-based verifier that can be used by the printer and

20.8 Quiet Zones The quiet zone is the area, free of printing, that precedes the left bar and follows the right bar in a bar code symbol. The quiet zones allow scanners to detect when a bar code starts and stops. Minimum quiet zone specifications depend on the symbol specified.

20.9 Bar-Width Reduction Printers are required to specify the amount of BWR appropriate to the anticipated printing conditions (e.g. press type, plate material, mounting material, substrate, and anilox roller). The specified amount of BWR should be corrected at the symbol design stage for digital bar codes files.

the printer's customer to assess the quality of the printed symbol and facilitate communication about the results between all parties. The minimum symbol grade required, as well as the verifier's measuring aperture and peak wavelength of light, are determined by industry application standards or symbol specifications depending on the symbol being analyzed and where it will ultimately be scanned. For example, EAN/UPC symbols are measured based on *ANSI/UCC5—(Quality Specification for the U.P.C. Printed Symbol)* and ISO *15420:2000 –(Information technology – Automatic identification and data capture technique – Symbology Specification – EAN/UPC)*, which applies the ANSI/ISO method to the EAN/UPC symbol-scanning environment. Minimum bar code print quality specifications outside of those determined by the accredited standards organizations are not acceptable.

For more information on determining formal symbol grades and the parameters that are measured see:

- *ANSI/UCC5 (Quality Specification for the U.P.C. Printed Symbol).*
- The UCC's Guideline for Producing Quality Symbols.
- The UCC's Technical Bulletin #1: "Understanding UCC Specified Methods for Assessing EAN/UPC Symbol Quality".

For a summary of what can happen in design, prepress, and on press to reduce the grade attained for specific ANSI/ISO parameters (assuming proper use of the measuring instruments), refer to the table on the following page.

20.12 | Bar-code Verification: Conformance and Training

Many verifier/reflectometer instruments are available from different manufacturers. To maintain accuracy, some require the user to periodically calibrate by using the patch that accompanies the instrument, while others may rely on periodic manufacturer participation in the maintenance process. In addition to proper maintenance and use of the equipment, experience has taught the bar code industry that reliable measurement and communication of ANSI-based bar code grades between trading partners mandates the availability of some universally available reference point of comparison of the results.

The bar-code industry has agreed that an ANSI/ISO-based bar-code verifier (including its user), as with any instrument designed to precisely measure, evaluate and communicate results, must be validated by determining how well it agrees with some universally accepted and traceable "judge" or conformance standard. To satisfy this need for a common reference point, the UCC offers the Calibrated Conformance Standard, (Test Card for EAN/UPC Symbol Verifiers). All bar-code verifier users should leverage this widely recognized tool, traceable to NIST (National Institute of Standards and Technology, formerly the National Bureau of Standards) to confirm the accuracy and repeatability of both the instrument and its user. Refer to the Appendix for ordering information.

VARIABLES FOR REDUCING ANSI/ISO GRADES FOR BAR CODE QUALITY

ANSI/ISO PARAMETER	POTENTIAL PROBLEM AREA
SYMBOL CONTRAST	■ Specify adequate colors for bar code and monitor color throughout pressrun. ■ Monitor ink "application": density, quality, ink receptivity. ■ Monitor the substrate qualities as they relate to overall reflectance of the bars and spaces (reflectance uniformity and properties of printed substrates). ■ Insufficient reflectance of substrate (translucency). ■ To simulate the best & worst case filled package make measurements against an opaque white and opaque black background.
EDGE CONTRAST	■ Monitor anything that would reduce the symbol's edge acuity or "print sharpness". ■ Uneven impression or over impression (halos). ■ Ink density and application quality (feathering or improper adhesion). ■ Plate problems (cylinders out of round, low & high spots, or nicks in the plate).
MINIMUM REFLECTANCE	■ See Symbol Contrast.
EDGE DETERMINATION	■ Monitor anything that could cause an additional bar to appear or space to disappear. ■ Verify match between bar-code size and the specified imaging resolution (bars or spaces may be "rounded" in or out of a symbol). ■ Monitor conformance to "predicted" bar-width growth in prepress (allocated BWR) and on press (running within press characterization range). ■ Significant designer manipulation of the symbol (resizing, ungrouping). ■ Damaged plate cylinder, plate or impression cylinder. ■ Substantial ink bridging/ink feathering.
MODULATION	■ Monitor bar-width growth. ■ Insufficient BWR (bar-width reduction) for print conditions. ■ Insufficient BWR specified based upon the print conditions. ■ Excessive impression (narrow spaces). ■ Ink spread (ink bridging / ink feathering into substrate).
DEFECTS	■ Monitor any variable that can cause "spots" in spaces or "voids" in bars. ■ Process: bar code design, bar code negatives, plate cylinder, plate wear. ■ Ink: metering (pooling, absorption, splatter, "ghosting"). ■ Substrate: surface texture, dirt, recycled content, absorption/rejection.
DECODABILITY	■ Monitor conditions that cause element-width variations within individual elements. ■ Verify match between bar-code size and the specified imaging output resolution to avoid individual element (bar or space) widths to be "rounded" up or down. ■ Monitor conditions that can result in incorrect positioning of an individual element (defective plate cylinder, printing plate defects or improper mounting). ■ Distortion for plate circumference (if bars are printed in the transverse direction).
QUIET ZONES	■ Not enough room reserved for the quiet zones. ■ Debris (ink spots) in the quiet zones. ■ Symbol is partially located underneath a fold, flap, die-cut, emboss or laminate in the final, filled package.

21.0 Specialty Print Applications

21.2 | Laminating Print: Color Matching

Color matching on press when printing a design that will be laminated in a downstream operation is particularly challenging. A reverse-printed web that is part of a lamination will have very different color off press (pre-lamination) then it will after final lamination. There are a couple of ways to simulate the final lamination in order to achieve the desired color match on press:

1. Laminate the reverse-printed web to a similar secondary substrate press-side using a tabletop laminator (designed to laminate paper documents and posters).

Procedure:

- Cut the image to be laminated from the press tear sheet.
- Place the image on a non-sealable carrier sheet ink side up (paper will work as a carrier in most cases).
- Cut a piece of secondary substrate (simulate lamination) and place it on top of the printed sample.
- Cover with a non-sealable carrier sheet and run it through the heated lamination device.

With proper selection of the secondary substrate, press-side lamination should be a close match to the final product and can be used for color matching procedures.

2. Laminate the printed press characterization target on production equipment. By measuring the printed characterization target both laminated and unlaminated the resulting color shift can be quantified and predicted. The data from the laminated press characterization can then be used to show the expected color shift on a digital proof.

Dark, wet products, such as soups or meats, can dramatically affect the appearance of the graphics compared to the graphics mounted as a sample on white board stock.

Glossary of Terms, Acronyms and Equations

absolute humidity A measure of the total amount of water vapor in the atmosphere or material such as paper; also known as moisture content. It is determined by the weight difference of a sample before and after oven drying to "bone dry" or by measuring with various handheld moisture sensing equipment (hygrometer). Excessive atmospheric relative humidity changes may affect a paper's structural properties resulting in print misregister, wrinkles and other converting problems. See "relative humidity."

acid Any chemical that undergoes dissociation in water with the formation of hydrogen ions. Acids have a pH less than 7.0; lower numbers indicate greater acidity. Among its properties is a corrosive action on many materials and sour in taste. Will turn litmus paper red.

addressable output resolution Maximum number of image positions along a straight line one inch in length that can be addressed by a bar code designer. This resolution would exclude further resolution enhancing techniques performed by the imaging device or software that are beyond the control of the designer.

American National Standards Institute (ANSI) The USA member of the International Standards Organization (ISO) that develops voluntary standards for business and industry. See *Appendix* for contact information

aging/fade resistance Ability of a paper and/or ink to resist changes in its optical, chemical or structural properties over time. Accelerated aging, yellowing, brightness loss and fading upon exposure to ultraviolet light and humidity can be determined with instruments such as a fadeometer or weatherometer. Also known as permanence, colorfastness and lightfastness.

anilox roll Engraved ink metering roll used in flexographic presses to provide a controlled film of ink to the printing plates, which print onto the substrate.

ANSI See **American National Standards Institute.**

apparent trap (Preucil) Ratio of the difference between the density of the overprint and the density of the first down ink to the density of the second down ink; all densities are measured with the complementary color (major) filter of the second down ink. For example, in measuring red created by overprinting yellow over magenta, one would use the densitometer blue filter, complement of yellow.

$$\% \text{ Apparent Trap} = 100 \times \frac{D_{op} - D_1}{D_2}$$

Where (using the major filter of the second down color)
D_{op} is the density of overprint minus paper density;
D_1 is the density of first-down ink minus paper density;
D_2 is the density of second-down ink minus paper density.

archival Pertaining to the long-term storage of data.

ASCII American Standard Code for Information Interchange. A 7-bit standard code adopted to facilitate the interchange of data among various types of data processing and data communications equipment

bar-width reduction (BWR) A prepress decrease in bar-code image width to compensate for normal image growth as predetermined by press fingerprinting and production monitoring.

ASCII file A digital file encoded in the industry-standard ASCII representation for text. An ASCII file contains only plain text and basic text-formatting characters such as spaces and carriage returns, but no graphics or special character formatting.

backup copy A copy of a file or data set that is kept for reference in case the original file or data set is destroyed.

base alignment On a typesetter or printer, a mode specifying that the lower reference edge of all letters in a line of mixed sizes or styles should be horizontally even; also called baseline alignment.

basis weight Paper weight in pounds per ream of a given grade, sheet size and number of sheets (usually 500) in North America. Reported in lbs./ream using TAPPI Method T410. Common ream sizes and grades include the following.

PAPER GRADE	SHEET SIZE/QUANTITY	SQ. FT. AREA/REAM
BOND, COMPUTER, COPIER	17" x 22"/500	1,300 (Actual 1,298.6)
BOOK, OFFSET, TEXT	25" x 38"/500	3,300 (Actual 3,298.6)
BRISTOL, TAG	22.5" x 28.5"/500	2,700 (Actual 2,226.6)
COVER	20" x 26"/500	1,806 (Actual 1,805.6)
INDEX	25.5" x 30.5"/500	2,700 (Actual 2,700.5)
LINERBOARD	1,000 sq. ft.	1,000
BAG PAPER, NEWSPRINT, PAPER-BOARD, TISSUE, WRAPPING	24" x 36"/500	3,000
PRINTING, WRITING	17" x 22"/500	1,300 (Actual 1,298.6)

International operations report basis weight in grams per square meter.

Conversion formula:

$$\text{Basis Weight (lbs..)} \times \frac{1406.5}{\text{square inches in basic size}} = \text{grams per square meter}$$

bcm Abbreviation for billion cubic microns; a measurement of the average volume per square inch of engraved ink-carrying cells on an anilox. 1 bcm = 1 microliter.

binary A coding or counting system with only two symbols or conditions, such as on/off or zero/one; the format for storing data in computers.

black and white Original art or proof in single color (black image on a white background), as distinguished from multicolor.

bleed Image or color that extends beyond the trim edge of the finished printed piece.

blocking 1. An undesired adhesion between touching layers of materials such as might occur under moderate pressure and/or temperature in storage or use; **2.** The extent to which damage to at least one surface is visible upon their separation.

blueline A blue image photoprint (such as Dylux) made from film negatives or positives. Blueline proofs can be used to check position of image elements and to show color breaks by varying exposure time to produce light and dark blue images but cannot show process color.

brightness A measure of reflectance in the blue region of the visible light spectrum, specifically at a wavelength of 457 nm, as specified by TAPPI Method T452 using directional 45°/0° geometry. This method is an industry standard for the determination of the brightness of white, near-white, and naturally colored paper and paperboard. The non-USA standard for paper brightness is measured with diffuse illumination and diffuse reading using spherical geometry. Higher numbers on a 0 – 100 scale indicate brighter surfaces that increase the perception of print contrast, brilliance and paper quality, especially when viewed under blue-white illumination common with fluorescent lighting. High brightness papers can improve bar code contrast and scannability.

bump curve Highlight compensation applied to avoid imaging dots in the mask, which are too small to allow full dot formation on the plate during UV exposure. A bump curve can also be referred to as a tonal value increase of any portion of or the entire curve to calibrate the proofing process with the printing process.

BWR See *bar width reduction.*

caliper Thickness measurement of a single sheet of paper as defined by TAPPI Method T411 and reported in mils or thousandths of an inch (1 mil. = 0.001"). Multiply inches by 25.4 micrometers and round to the nearest whole number to find metric thickness expressed in microns (μ) or micrometers. Also used to identify thickness of other printing materials such as plates, mounting tape, etc. See **gauge** for flexible film substrate thickness and **point** for paperboard thickness.

camera ready Copy and/or artwork that is ready for the photography step to make a film negative for platemaking in the printing process.

C1S coated, one side.

CCN See **clay coated news**.

CEPS See **color electronic prepress system**.

CGATS See **Committee for Graphic Arts Technologies Standards**.

character count The number of characters included in a block of text. In graphic arts, spaces are counted but other nonprinting characters usually are not. In information processing, both printing and nonprinting characters are usually included.

character set The entire set of characters that can be either shown on a monitor or used to code computer instructions. In a digital printer, the entire set of characters that the printer is capable of printing.

CIE See **Commission Internationale de l'Eclairage**.

CIE standard illuminants Common lighting conditions used to evaluate color as defined by the CIE in terms of relative spectral power distributions, or color temperature. Lower numbers are warmer/redder, higher numbers are colder/bluer.

ILLUMINANT	DESCRIPTION
ILLUMINANT A	Incandescent lighting at a color temperature of about 2,856° Kelvin.
ILLUMINANT B	Direct sunlight at about 4,874° Kelvin.
ILLUMINANT C	Tungsten illumination simulating daylight at about 6,774° Kelvin.·
ILLUMINANT D50	Graphic arts standard viewing condition at about 5,000° Kelvin.
ILLUMINANT D65	Used by textile, paint and ink industries at about 6,500° Kelvin.
ILLUMINANT F2	Cool white fluorescent lamp at about 4,200° Kelvin.
ILLUMINANT F7	Broadband daylight fluorescent lamp at about 6,500° Kelvin.
ILLUMINANT F11	Narrow band white fluorescent lamp at about 4,000° Kelvin

CIE standard observer A hypothetical average human observer who sees color at a 2° viewing angle as defined in a 1931 CIE study. A supplementary observer for a larger viewing angle of 10° was adopted in 1964. The 2° standard observer should be assumed if not otherwise specified. If the field of view is larger than 4°, the 10° standard observer should be used.

clarity/haze Material characteristics permitting distinct images to be observed through it; typically a visual comparison to a standard clear transparent material. Poor formation and other related properties could negatively affect clarity and apparent print quality.

clay coated news (CCN) Paperboard made from recycled newsprint base fiber with a clay coated surface to improve printability.

CMYK Cyan, magenta, yellow, black; the four process color printing inks.

CNK See **coated natural Kraft**.

Coated Natural Kraft (CNK) Unbleached paperboard, usually clay coated on the side to be printed for folding cartons.

coated recycled board (CRB) Paperboard made from recycled fiber (newspapers, office waste paper, old corrugated cartons, etc.), clay coated on one or both sides, and printed as folding cartons.

coefficient of friction Measure of static and/or kinetic slip resistance of one material against another. COF has limited effect on printability, but it is critical in converting and bag filling operations as well as end use applications.

COEX Co-extruded. A multi-layer film or coating in which each distinct layer is formed by a simultaneous extrusion of hot polymers through a single die.

color A visual sensation produced in the brain when the eye views various wavelengths of light. Light is transmitted, reflected and/or absorbed. For example, if a printed sheet of paper is sufficiently thick, all light will be either absorbed or diffusely reflected; there should be no significant amount of light transmitted. Color viewing is a highly subjective experience that varies from individual to individual. Lighting and viewing standards help ensure the accuracy of color reproduction in the graphic arts industry. A number of objective color measurement systems have been developed. In the Hunter L, a, b system, for example, "L" represents the "lightness" of the sheet and varies from 100 for a perfect white to 0 for absolute black; "+ a" indicates redness; "– a" indicates greenness; "+ b" indicates yellowness; and "– b" indicates blueness. TAPPI methods T524 and T515 are common sources of paper color measurement protocol. Instruments for measuring color include spectrophotometers, colorimeters and, for printed process colors YMCK, densitometers.

color break Designation of ink colors to be used for specific image areas.

color correction Any method (masking, dot-etching, screening, scanning, etc.) used to change reproduction of the color original (photograph, transparency, chrome, 35mm slide, digital photo, painting, etc.).

color difference Can be expressed mathematically in many ways such as $LCh°$ or $L^*a^*b^*$ values calculating Delta Error (ΔE) in the following equation where higher ΔE indicates greater color differences.

$$\Delta E^*{}_{ab} = \sqrt{\Delta L^{*2} + \Delta a^{*2} + \Delta b^{*2}}$$

$$\textit{Where:}$$
$$\Delta L^* = L^*{}_1 - L^*{}_2$$
$$\Delta a^* = a^*{}_1 - a^*{}_2$$
$$\Delta b^* = b^*{}_1 - b^*{}_2$$

Sample 1 measurements are noted with the subscript 1;
Sample 2 measurements with subscript 2.

color electronic prepress system (CEPS) A high-quality, proprietary computer-based system that may include equipment for page make-up, scanning color separations and making color corrections. PC-based color scanning and manipulation systems, often referred to as desktop publishing systems, usually lack the capabilities and sophistication of CEPS.

colorimeter An optical measurement instrument that responds to color in a manner similar to the human eye by filtering reflected light into its dominant regions of red, green and blue. A color's numeric value is then determined by using the CIE XYZ color space or one of its derivatives such as CIE $L^*a^*b^*$ or CIE $L^*u^*v^*$.

color key An overlay proof made of layers of acetate or polyester attached in register to a backing substrate. Each overlay film carries the colored image from a film negative. Color breaks and traps can be judged, but exact color match to the final printed product cannot be made.

color monitor An RGB or composite monitor that uses separate video signals of red, green, and blue, the three primary additive colors. It uses these signals to display almost any number of hues, depending upon the computer software and calibration. This type of monitor usually produces clearer, sharper colors and images than can be reproduced by printing CMYK process inks. Composite monitors use one signal that combines the three primary colors.

color resolution The number of different colors or gray-scale values a system can work with or present. The value is usually given in bits; each added bit doubles the number of available colors. For example, 8-bit color displays show 256 colors (or shades of gray).

color saturation A measure of the amount of white light in a hue. High saturation means there is no white-light component and that the color is intense or of good quality.

color separation The process of exposing an original color image through RGB filters to produce complementary images that will be printed with CMYK inks. The final digital file includes masking (color modification) for specific inks and substrates, as well as halftone screening to enable printing a uniform tone scale with proper gray balance from extreme highlights through midtones and shadows to maximum solid color. This can be accomplished through the use of a digital camera, digital or analog scanner, or photographically.

color target A proof that is not profiled using the output source profile; however it represents the customer's color expectations.

combination plate In flexographic, printing halftones or screen tints and solid line or text copy using the same plate; may require print quality compromises because halftone dots require minimum impression and ink film thickness whereas solids need maximum impression and ink film thickness for optimum printability; often can be avoided with advance planning. In offset litho, ganging several designs on the same plate with no concern about mixing halftone and line copy.

combination run A common image remains throughout a pressrun; plate or color changes are made for different design elements such as weight marks, UPC codes, ingredients, nutritional labeling, etc.

Committee for Graphic Arts Technologies Standards (CGATS) Formed in 1987, this group reports to ANSI and is charged with the overall coordination of graphic arts standard activities and the development of graphic arts standards where no applicable standards developer is available. The IT8 Committee, developer of digital data exchange standards, was merged under CGATS in 1994. Information about existing and pending CGATS activities is available , see *Appendix*.

comprehensive layout, comp A mock-up of a printed piece showing all type and pictures in rough form but in the right size and in the correct position; used for evaluating a design before final type and artwork are produced.

concept proof A proof that is not profiled and is not to be used for matching color.

continuous tone An image containing a range of color tones from light to dark. Appear as pixels on a color monitor or silver/pigment particles on a photograph. Must be converted to halftone dots in order to be printed. See *CT*.

contract analog proof This proof is made to manufacturer's recommendations for exposing and processing by (brand name of analog proofing system) and has been profiled according to FIRST specifications.

contract digital proof This proof is profiled to a specific brand of digital proofing system and has been made according to FIRST specifications.

contrast The difference between extreme highlight and shadow areas of a continuous tone original or halftone reproduction. Image contrast usually is compressed to bring an original's density range to what can be reproduced on a printing press.

cross direction The direction at right angle to the paper grain or flow of material through a machine (paper machine, extruder, printing press, etc.). See **machine direction**.

CT Continuous tone A picture file; conveying the concept that halftone screening can be performed on this file upon output, as when screening CTs at a specific size and screen ruling on an image setter. CT files are created by either scanning a picture into the system or by generating a CT image internally.

CT merge The function of combining two CT files in such a manner that they appear to vignette together smoothly without a noticeable break between images.

cut-back curves Data that indicates the halftone dot areas needed to compensate for normal dot gain throughout the entire tone scale during the printing process. This data is specific to particular printing materials and process conditions.

DDCP See **direct digital color proof.**

DDES See **Digital Data Exchange Standards**.

densitometer A photoelectric instrument that measures the optical density of images or colors. A reflection densitometer measures the amount of incident light that is reflected from the surface of a substrate, such as ink on paper or film. A transmission densitometer measures the amount of light that is transmitted through film from a measured light source.

density, absolute Optical density referenced to a perfect reflecting diffuser through calibration procedures; typically referred to as "density with paper/film included."

density, optical (reflection density) The light absorbing property of a material, expressed as the logarithm of the reciprocal of the reflectance factor (i.e., higher density indicates more light is absorbed or a darker surface). Also called print density.

$$\text{Reflection Density} = \log_{10}\left(\frac{1}{R}\right)$$

Reflectance

100%	=	0.0
10%	=	1.0
1%	=	2.0
0.1%	=	3.0
0.01%	=	4.0

density, optical (transmission) The light absorbing property of a material, expressed as the logarithm of the reciprocal of transmittance (i.e., higher density indicates more light is absorbed).

$$\text{Transmission Density} = \log\left(\frac{1}{T}\right)$$

Where:

T = Transmittance

density, relative The absolute (optical) density of the sample minus the absolute (optical) density of the substrate; typically referred to as **density minus paper**.

densitometer response (spectral response) Spectral response is the product of the spectral power distribution of the lamp, attenuation of the optics and filters, and the spectral response of the detector used. The aim responses (spectral products) for densitometers are contained in *ISO 5-3:1995, Photography—Density measurements—Part 3: Spectral conditions*. The status responses of interest to the graphic arts are Status E, Status I, and Status T.

digital bar code file A bar code symbol that is designed and stored in a digitized format.

D-max The highest measured density on a sample. This is not to be confused with the maximum density achievable by the material.

D-min The lowest measured density on the clear/non-image area of a sample. This is not to be confused with the minimum density achievable by the material.

Digital Data Exchange Standards (DDES) A body of standards developed for the graphic arts industry by the ANSI accredited Image Technology Committee (i.e., ANSI IT8) and the ISO accredited graphics technology committee (i.e., ISO TC130). DDES provides standardized exchange formats for the digital information developed and used in printing design and production.

dimensional stability Ability of a substrate (paper, board, corrugated, film) to retain its dimensions and its shape despite changes in its moisture or mechanical stressing. Moisture changes are caused by differences in ambient relative humidity from the internal relative humidity of the substrate. Converting, printing and ink drying processes may apply mechanical stresses (roll build, baggy/slack edges, etc. Changes in surface moisture and relative humidity tend to cause curl, wavy edges, frame shrinkage, etc. These can degrade print registration.

Direct Digital Color Proof (DDCP) Prepress color proof that is imaged directly from digital data without the intermediate steps of film and contact exposure.

dirt/gels Apparent dirt area on a substrate affecting its aesthetic appearance and possibly resulting in print defects/voids. Size, frequency, color and location are typical criteria for measuring dirt/gels visually against a standard agreed upon between the customer and the supplier.

dispersion A uniform distribution of solid particles in a vehicle by mixing or milling.

display type In composition, type set larger than the main reading body text. Used to attract attention; for example, a headline.

distortion The amount art is reduced to compensate for cylinder wrap—not stretch of plate material due to the instability of the plate.

distortion factor A multiplier that compensates for normal flexographic image shrinkage with rubber plates and image stretch when any type of flexographic plate is made flat and mounted around a cylinder for printing.

dot area (%), apparent (tone value in ISO documentation) The dot area of a printed halftone element that is computed from reflection densities of the printed element and area of solid, continuous coverage. The computation of apparent dot area makes use of the Murray-Davies equation. It accounts for the physical area covered by the dot pattern plus optical effects that cause the dots to appear larger in size (optical gain). This approximates the visual impression of the printed area.

dot area (%), film printing (tone value in ISO documentation) The area that will print as the final dot on the substrate. For making calculations, the following applies:

- The film printing dot area for positive separations is that value measured as the opaque dot on the input film.
- The film printing dot area for negative separations is that value measured as the opaque dot in the input film subtracted from 100.

dot gain (apparent, equivalent or total) The difference in dot area between the digital data/film dot area and the apparent dot area measured on the printed sheet. The computed value includes both physical changes in dot size and optical effects which increase the apparent size of the printed dot (e.g., a 72% apparent printed dot area from a 50% input film dot area is reported as 22% total dot gain).

dot gain A physical and/or optical measurement and theoretical calculation of the apparent increase in dot area from one medium to another. Normally expressed as the difference between a midtone (nominal 50%) dot area on a film negative and the printed dot area; for example, a 50% film dot area which prints as a 78% dot has a 28% dot gain. Dot gain (and loss) is normal and must be controlled throughout the prepress and printing process.

dot-gain curve Graphic illustration of dot gain data throughout the entire highlight (non-image) to extreme shadow (solid image) tone scale.

double bump Application of two layers of ink to achieve greater opacity or more intense color.

dpi Dots per inch.

Dylux See **blueline**.

EAN/UPC Symbols A family of bar-code symbols using UPC Version A, UPC Version E, EAN-8, and EAN-13.

Encapsulated PostScript (EPS) A file format that carries both a description of an image in the PostScript page-description language and an optional bitmap equivalent for screen display. Commonly used for image interchange on the Macintosh.

EPS See **Encapsulated PostScript**.

fade See **vignette** and **aging/fade resistance**.

FFTA See **Foundation of Flexographic Technical Association**.

flatness Departure of a substrate from a flat plane to the extent that contributes to misregistration or other print/converting quality degradation.

Flexographic Technical Association (FTA) Member supported nonprofit organization that promotes, develops and maintains the advancement of flexographic processing and/or printing. For contact information, see *Appendix*.

fluorescence The ability of a substrate and/or ink to absorb ultraviolet light waves and reflect them as visible light.

font A complete set of characters in one design, size, and style. In traditional typography usage, font may be restricted to a particular size and style or may comprise multiple sizes, or multiple sizes and styles, of a typeface design.

Foundation of Flexographic Technical Association (FFTA) Organization exclusively for educational purposes benefiting members of the Flexographic Technical Association and the flexographic industry.

formation Distribution of fibers in paper. Excessive non-uniform distribution or flocking of fibers can contribute to print mottle. Although instruments exist to measure paper formation and print mottle, these characteristics are typically measured visually against a standard agreed upon between the customer and the supplier.

FPO (For Position Only) The image that will be replaced in production (usually on the film image setter) with a high-resolution image.

frequency modulation (FM) screening See **stochastic screening**.

FTA See **Flexographic Technical Association**.

gamut The total range of colors that can be displayed.

GATF See **Graphic Arts Technical Foundation**.

gauge Thickness of flexible packaging film substrates (100 ga. = 0.001"). Also a measurement used to identify thickness of printing materials such as plates, mounting tape, etc.

GCR See **gray component replacement**.

gels See **dirt/gels**.

General Requirements for Applications in Commercial Offset Lithography (GRACoL) Guidelines for sheetfed offset litho prepress, press and binding/finishing operations, were introduced in 1996 with the third edition in 1999. Available from Graphic Communications Association; for contact information, see *Appendix*.

gloss Specular reflection of light from a surface, measured by a variety of instruments and reflection angles, reported as percentage with higher values indicating higher gloss. Film gloss is often specified at 45°; most paper is manufactured to specifications of 75°; print gloss is commonly measured at 60°; and very high gloss is commonly measured at 20° to correlate with visual perception.

GRACoL See **General Requirements for Applications in Offset Lithography**.

grade Paper classification based primarily upon end use and brightness.

Graphic Arts Technical Foundation/Printing Industries of America (GATF/PIA) A member-supported, nonprofit, scientific, technical, and educational organization serving the international graphic communications industries; for contact information, see *Appendix*.

gray component replacement (GCR) System to reduce overprinted halftone dot sizes of C, M or Y when it acts as a graying component by increasing the appropriate black halftone dot sizes to achieve a color parity with less process ink and improved printing conditions.

ghosting Presence of a faint image of a design in areas that are not intended to receive that portion of the image. Usually a repeat pattern in the press machine direction.

gray balance The proper combination of cyan, magenta, and yellow ink dot area, hue/density, trap, transparency, and register on a specific substrate under normal printing conditions which reproduce as a neutral gray.

halftone A pictorial that has been converted from a continuous tone original image, such as a photograph, into dots of appropriate size which, when printed, give the visual illusion closely resembling the original over a gradation range from highlight to shadow.

halftone tint An area of approximately equal sized halftone dots producing a uniform optical density.

haze A milky discoloration of a transparent film or liquid solution such as ink or overprint coating in any printing process. Reflection haze is scattering of reflected light in directions near that of specular reflection by a specimen having a glossy surface thereby masking print quality. Transmission haze is scattering of light within or at the surface of a nearly clear specimen causing a cloudy appearance when viewed by transmission typically negatively affecting the quality of reverse printed or laminated items. See **clarity/haze**. Also a gravure defect characterized by printing in non-image areas caused by incomplete ink removal from the gravure cylinder surface by the doctor blade.

HDPE See **high density polyethylene**.

high-density polyethylene (HDPE) Film that has excellent moisture barrier and stiffness so it is used in applications such as cereal and cracker packaging. It is frequently co-extruded with heat-seal layers such as Surlyn to make a finished packaging material. Blown HDPE film has better stiffness and moisture barrier than cast HDPE, but is hazier. Extrusion coated HDPE resins are generally used to improve grease resistance.

highlight The lightest or whitest parts in a photograph represented in a halftone reproduction by the smallest dots or no dots.

hue Color, which can be further described by saturation, intensity and lightness.

ink absorbency Ability of an ink to penetrate a substrate surface to a desired level promoting adhesion, high density, high gloss and ink lay uniformity.

ink trap percent A measure of how well one ink prints over another, calculated from print densities measured using the filter for the second ink printed to form the overprint. Higher numbers are desirable indicating the ability of an ink to transfer equally to an unprinted substrate and to a previously printed ink film. "Perfect" 100% trap is rarely achieved due to the inherent measuring geometry and data additive failure. Calculated as follows from print densities taken using the complementary filter for the second ink printed.

$$\% \text{ Ink Trap} = \frac{\text{Overprint Ink} - \text{First Ink Printed}}{\text{Second Ink Printed}} \times 100$$

International Standards Organization (ISO) A worldwide group from 100 countries with a mission to promote the development of international standards for intellectual, scientific, technological and economic activity. The ISO Technical Committee for graphic arts is TC 130. See *Appendix* for address.

ISO See **International Standards Organization**.

kerning Modifying the normal space between letters during typesetting; can be plus or minus letter spacing in computerized typesetting; traditionally involved reducing space between only selected characters, such as the L and Y in ONLY, to be more readable or pleasing to the eye; see letter spacing.

keyline An outline on finished art indicating the exact shape, position, and size for elements such as halftones, line art, UPC symbols, etc.

kiss impression The minimum pressure at which proper ink transfer is possible.

letter spacing Adding space between characters and spaces during typesetting; also known as "tracking" in some typesetting software; see kerning.

LDPE See **low density polyethylene**.

linear low density polyethylene (LLDPE) Film having the same features as LDPE but is stronger with better hot tack strength. Film resins are more expensive than LDPE, and extrusion coating grades are even more expensive.

linear medium density polyethylene (LMDPE) Film is similar to LLDPE but provides improved stiffness, gloss, and reduced flavor adsorption.

line copy, line art, line drawing, line film, line work Any image suitable for reproduction without using a halftone screen.

lines per inch (lpi) The number of dots per linear inch in a halftone. Dot size varies from very small highlight dots to large shadow dots. More lines per inch increases resolution detail and dot gain. Lines per centimeter are specified outside the USA. Also used to define the screen line count in anilox rolls.

LIVE Indicates a scan or illustration in an electronic document that is ready for production of the platemaking film negative.

LLDPE See **linear low density polyethylene**.

LMDPE Linear medium density polyethylene. Film is similar to LLDPE but provides improved stiffness, gloss, and reduced flavor adsorption.

loose color proof Process color proof with no line copy or special ink colors (e.g.. PMS®).

low density polyethylene (LDPE) Low-cost resin LDPE film has good moisture barrier, heat sealability, and strength. Extrusion LDPE has an excellent bond to paper and varying bonds to other substrates.

lpi See **lines per inch**.

machine direction (MD) Flow or movement of material through a machine. Cellulose paper fibers are oriented somewhat parallel to the direction of flow through a papermaking machine. Also see **cross direction**.

mask 1. Outline of an image on original art; **2.** Opaque material used to protect open or selected areas of a printing plate during exposure.

MB See **megabyte**.

MD See **machine direction**.

MDPE See **medium density polyethylene**.

mechanical Camera-ready paste-up of artwork including type, photos, line art, etc., on a piece of artboard.

medium density polyethylene (MDPE) This film provides better barrier and chemical resistance than LDPE.

megabyte (MB) A unit of measure equal to 1,048,576 bytes, or 1,024 kilobytes; commonly used to specify the capacity of computer memory.

moiré An optical interference pattern caused when two screened images are superimposed at inappropriate angles. It is possible for an anilox roll screen pattern to be one of the sources of screen interference.

moisture content See **absolute humidity and relative humidity**.

mottle Non-uniform ink lay; also known as orange peel, pigment flocculation, striations, etc.

Murray-Davies (M-D) equation This measurement approximates the total of physical dot size plus optical dot gain due to insufficient light absorption of the ink and extra light absorption of the substrate, thus the term "apparent dot area." Under visual examination with a 10X magnifying glass, the printed dot would appear smaller than the calculated apparent dot area, which correlates well with visual perception when holding the printed piece at normal viewing distance. The equation shown is for the case of D-max greater than 3.0 with the densitometer zeroed on clear film.

For reflection:

$$\text{Optical Dot Area (ODA)} = \frac{1 - 10^{-(D_T)}}{1 - 10^{-(D_S)}}$$

Where

D_S = the Density of Solid Ink/Printed Solid;
D_T = the Density of the Halftone Tint.

$$\% \text{ Optical Dot Area} = \text{ODA} \times 100$$

opacity Comparison of the percentage of light reflected by a sheet of paper with a black backing compared to the light reflected with a white backing. Higher values indicate higher opacity (less undesirable show-through of an image printed on the opposite side of a sheet).

OPP See **oriented polypropylene**.

optical disk A high density storage device that uses a laser to burn a pattern of holes into a tellurium film on the disk surface. A single optical disk can hold billions of bytes of data.

optical scanner A device that analyzes the light reflected from or transmitted through copy, art, or film and produces an electronic signal proportional to the intensity of the light or color.

oriented polypropylene (OPP) A clear, stiff film with good heat resistance and good moisture barrier. Coated grades also have good oxygen barrier or good heat sealability.

ortho response Specified as Type 2 in ISO 5-3:1995: Photography—Density measurements—Part 3: Spectral conditions. This is generally used for measuring densities when printing to orthochromatic (blue/green sensitive) materials with sensitivities of 350 nm to 520 nm with a peak at approximately 435 nm.

output Information that comes from a computer as a result of its processing.

Pantone Matching System® (PMS) The company/brand name of a system for specifying colors, a standard in the printing industry.

Parker Print-surf An instrument that uses an air leak principle to estimate substrate surface micro roughness by the average mean pore depth in microns using TAPPI method T555. Higher numbers indicate a rougher surface.

PE, poly See **polyethylene, HDPE, LDPE, LLDPE, LMDPE, MDPE**.

PET Polyester (polyethylene terepthalate) Oriented PET film has excellent stiffness, clarity, heat resistance and dimensional stability, good oxygen barrier, and some moisture barrier.

pica Unit of measurement principally used in typesetting. One pica equals 12 points or approximately $\frac{1}{6}$ of an inch.

pinholing Failure of a printed ink to form a completely continuous film. This condition appears in the form of small holes or voids in the printed area.

picking Rupture of the surface being printed that occurs when the force necessary to split (transfer) an ink film is greater than the surface strength of the substrate being printed. Contaminated printing results.

pick resistance A balance of substrate surface cohesive strength being higher than the force necessary to split a wet ink film.

pixel Picture element, or the smallest unit (cell, dot, square) on a color monitor display screen grid that can be displayed, stored, or addressed. A picture is typically composed of a rectangular array of pixels.

phthalocyanine Official name for phthalic acid commonly referred to as "Phthalo Blue" or "Phthalo Green". A bright greenish blue crystalline compound $C_{32}H_{18}N_8$; metal derivatives that are brilliant fast blue to green dyes or pigments.

plate break Non-print area where the two ends of a flexographic plate butt together after being wrapped around the plate cylinder on the printing press.

PMS See **Pantone Matching System®**.

point **1.** A typesetting measurement indicating type size. One point equals 0.01383"; **2.** Paperboard thickness measurement (20 pts. = 0.020").

polyethylene (PE, poly) A polymerized ethylene resin used for packaging films or molded for a wide variety of containers, kitchenware and tubing; see **HDPE, LDPE, LLDPE, LMDPE, MDPE**.

poly See **polyethylene**.

polypropylene (PP, polyprop) Film has the highest melting point of the economical polyolefin family. It has excellent optics, high stiffness, and good moisture barrier. Copolymer polypropylenes give improved low temperature impact resistance and sealability. PP can be oriented (OPP) to make films with improved stiffness, barrier and optics.

polyvinylidene chloride (PVDC) Film has excellent water, oxygen and flavor barriers. In emulsion form, it can be used as a barrier coating.

porosity The resistance of paper to the passage of air, oil or water; it can affect ink absorbency, drying and adhesion. Measured with a densitometer, such as Gurley, that determines the time (seconds) for 100 cc of air at a constant pressure to pass through a given area of sample. The higher the time, the lower the air porosity of the paper.

PostScript Adobe® Systems' trademarked page description language.

PP See **polypropylene**.

print contrast A ratio of the difference between the printed solid area density and a printed shadow tint area (traditionally 75% as measured on the platemaking file or film negative for offset lithography; 70% for flexography) to the density of the solid, expressed as a percentage. This indicates the printing system's capability to hold image detail in the upper tone region. Most desirable (highest) print contrast occurs with the simultaneous highest solid print density and the lowest dot gain.

$$\text{Print Contrast} = \frac{D_S - D_T}{D_S}$$

Where:

D_S = is Density of Solid Ink/Printed Solid;

D_T = is Density of the Halftone Tint.

Note: Solid and tint must be the same color.

% Print Contrast = Print Contrast $\times$ 100

process colors Cyan, magenta, yellow, and black; inks used in four-color process printing; hue may be modified to meet specific needs. Incorporated in this edition of FIRST, process colors have been specified and are mono-pigmented.

process black One of the four ink colors used in four-color process printing. Like all process inks, this ink must be a transparent. This will allow for the blending of varying amounts of each of the process colors to achieve the visual appearance of the many thousands of shades capable of being printed by flexography. In this edition of FIRST a single pigmented ink is specified for process black.

process cyan One of the four ink colors used in four-color process printing. Like all process inks, this ink must be a transparent. This will allow for the blending of varying amounts of each of the process colors to achieve the visual appearance of the many thousands of shades capable of being printed by flexography. In this edition of FIRST a single pigmented ink is specified for process cyan.

process magenta One of the four ink colors used in four-color process printing. Like all process inks, this ink must be a transparent. This will allow for the blending of varying amounts of each of the process colors to achieve the visual appearance of the many thousands of shades capable of being printed by flexography. In this edition of FIRST a single pigmented ink is specified for process magenta.

process yellow One of the four ink colors used in four-color process printing. Like all process inks, this ink must be a transparent. This will allow for the blending of varying amounts of each of the process colors to achieve the visual appearance of the many thousands of shades capable of being printed by flexography. In this edition of FIRST a single pigmented ink is specified for process yellow.

profiled contract proof This proof is profiled using a color management system (name CMS) and is prepared based upon profiles provided by (brand name of proofing system) on (date proof is generated). It is to be used as a contract proof.

PVDC or **PVdC** See **polyvinylidene chloride**.

quiet zones Areas free of printing that precede the leftmost bar and follow the rightmost bar in a bar-code symbol.

raster display A video display that sweeps a beam through a fixed pattern building an image with a matrix of points.

raster graphics Manner of storing and displaying data as horizontal rows of uniform grid or picture cells (pixels). Raster scan devices recreate or refresh a display screen 30 to 60 times a second in order to provide a clear image for viewing. Raster display devices are generally faster and less expensive than vector tubes and are therefore gaining popularity for use with graphics systems.

raster image file format (RIFF) A file format for paint-style graphics, developed by Letraset® USA. RIFF is an expanded version of the TIFF format used by many scanner makers.

raster image processor (RIP) A computer device or program that translates digital information in page description language to the pattern of dots to be delivered by the output unit of the system.

raster scan The generation of an image on a display screen made by refreshing the display area line by line.

reflection densitometry The practice of characterizing the amount of light absorption of materials by measuring reflectance and calculating and reporting optical density.

register (registration) Proper alignment or positioning of two or more images with each other.

relative humidity A percentage of the amount of water vapor the air or a material such as paper can hold at a given atmospheric temperature and pressure. Most paper is made to be dimensionally stable in equilibrium with the atmosphere at 35% to 50% relative humidity. Excessive variation from this general range can result in non-flat paper, print misregister and other converting complications.

resolution A measure of image sharpness, usually expressed in lines or dots per inch or millimeter. On a prepress visual display terminal, the number of pixels per unit of linear measure, e.g., 12 pixels per millimeter is a RES 12. Normally, the resolution of a file is the same vertically and horizontally, thus a square millimeter contains $12 \times 12 = 144$ pixels for a RES 12 file. The higher the RES, the better the image detail; but the file will be larger and will require longer processing time.

reverse To change the tonal orientation of an image, making the darker elements lighter and the lighter darker. **Note** that to physically reverse the spatial orientation of an image is known as "flopping" the image.

reverse (knock-out) The process of dropping a surprinted image out of the background color so type, for example, will appear white with a color surround.

reverse print 1. Printing wrong-reading on the underside of transparent film which, when laminated to another substrate with the ink in the middle of the "sandwich," causes the image to become right-reading when viewed through the sheet it was printed upon. See surface print; **2.** Design in which the "copy" is "dropped out" and the background is printed.

RGB Red, green, and blue primary additive colors, which are the backbone of computer color visual display monitors and prepress color separation. They also are the complementary or secondary subtractive ink colors which produce red by overprinting magenta and yellow, green by trapping cyan and yellow, and blue by overprinting cyan and magenta.

RIFF See **raster image file format**.

RIP See **raster image processor (processing)**.

rheology 1. The science of dealing with the deformation and flow of matter; **2.** The ability to flow or be deformed.

rollout Fluid ink print on a substrate using a Meyer rod applicator.

rounding errors (bar codes) The process of allocating imaging device dots to bar or space modules in an uneven manner.

sans serif Without serifs, which are the fine lines that finish off the main strokes of a letter, like the type face you are reading. This is a sans serif typeface.

SBS See **solid bleached sulfate**.

screen tint See **halftone tint**.

Sheffield smoothness Macro smoothness of a substrate surface (typically uncoated paper, corrugated, etc.) measuring the rate of surface air flow as specified by TAPPI T538 using a Sheffield instrument. Reported as Sheffield units, values are inversely related to smoothness; the higher the value, the rougher the surface.

SKU See **stock-keeping unit**.

solid bleached sulfate (SBS) Paperboard made from bleached wood pulp, usually clay coated on one or both sides to improve printability.

solvent A substance that is liquid at standard conditions and is used to dissolve or dilute another substance; this term includes, but is not limited to, organic materials used as dissolvers, viscosity reducers, degreasers or cleaning agents. Water is considered the universal solvent.

smoothness Arguably the most important substrate surface uniformity requirement for high quality flexographic printability that affects ink lay and ink transfer. Measured mostly by a variety of air-leak instruments and profilometers. See **Parker Print-surf**, **Sheffield**.

specific gravity The ratio of the weight of a body to the weight of an equal volume of water at the same specified temperature.

Specifications for Web Offset Publications (SWOP) A set of production specifications developed for those involved in heatset web offset litho magazine publication printing. First published in 1975, the eighth edition became effective in 1997, and is available from SWOP Incorporated; see *Appendix* for contact information.

spectrophotometer A device to measure three-dimensional color space.

spots (bar codes) Undesirable presence of ink or dirt within the space of a bar code symbol.

standard reference material A physical sample with characteristics traceable to an accepted primary standard or set of standards. It is commonly used for densitometer calibration or calibration verification. One standard reference material of interest is the SWOP Hi-Lo Color and Single Color References. These references may be obtained from the International Prepress Association; see *Appendix* for contact information.

stat A thermal proof or copy of final art before making platemaking film.

stochastic screening (frequency modulation, FM) An alternative to conventional halftone screening by placing same-size microdots (typically 12 to 30 microns diameter) in a computer-controlled random order within a given area.

stock-keeping unit (SKU) An assortment or variety of wholesale items shipped in one physical case.

striations A printing defect characterized by light and dark streaks parallel to the direction through the press.

substrate Material that is printed upon, i.e., film, paper, paperboard.

surface print Conventional flexographic printing resulting with a right-reading image on the top surface of the web. See **reverse print**.

surface strength See **pick resistance**.

surface tension Measurement of surface energy that affects ink transfer and adhesion to a substrate. Commonly measured with a dyne indicator solution applied to a film substrate surface. Substrates typically should be 8 to 10 dynes/cm higher then the ink.

surprint Overprint. In photomechanics, exposure from a second negative or flat superimposed on an exposed image of a previous negative or flat. Often used to superimpose type over a light screen tint to print from the same plate.

SWOP See **Specifications for Web Offset Publications**.

TC 130 See **International Organization for Standardization**.

TIFF (tagged image file format) A file format for graphics developed by Aldus, Adobe, and Apple that is particularly suited for representing scanned images and other large bitmaps. The original TIFF saved only black-and-white images in uncompressed forms. New versions support color and compression.

tint See **halftone tint**.

TIR See **total indicated runout**.

total indicated runout (TIR) A measure of the out-of-roundness of a printing press roller or cylinder. The difference in the lengths of a roller's radius as measured from the center to the outside surface. A perfectly round roller would have zero TIR.

transmission densitometry The practice of characterizing the light absorption of materials by measuring transmittance, and calculating and reporting optical density.

trapping (image) To allow for registration variation, two adjacent colors butting each other must be compensated allowing normal registration tolerances to exist without degrading the design. This is accomplished by spreading or enlarging the lighter of the two adjacent colors under the dominant color.

trapping (ink) Overprinting and adhering one ink over another to enable producing desired secondary and tertiary colors required in process printing;

tristimulus The magnitudes of three standard stimuli needed to match a given sample of light. A method for communicating or generating a color using three stimuli (colorants such as RGB or CMY) or three attributes (such as lightness, chroma and hue).

truncated Shortened. Decreasing the height of the bars in an UPC bar code symbol below the normal specification decreases the symbol's ability to be read omni directionally and should be avoided.

undercolor addition (UCA) A prepress means of intensifying dark neutral gray areas in process color reproduction by selectively increasing cyan, magenta and yellow dot areas.

undercolor removal (UCR) A prepress process color separation technique used to reduce cyan, magenta and yellow in dark neutral gray areas and replace them with appropriate increased black dot area.

Universal Product Code (UPC) A 12- or 8-digit code number that identifies a wide range of products; printed on packages as the UPC bar code symbol which can be read electronically by a scanner at retail store checkout counters.

Uniform Code Council (UCC) An organization responsible for overseeing and administering the Universal Product Code.

UV (Ultraviolet) response Refers to that response specified as Type 1 in ISO 5/3. This is generally used for measuring densities when printing to UV/blue sensitive materials. Type 1 (UV) printing density was standardized to provide printing density values for use when exposing diazo and vesicular films normally sensitive in a narrow band of the blue and ultraviolet region of the spectrum, between 380 nm and 420 nm with a peak at 400 nm.

varnish The binder component of an ink; also resin.

vehicle The liquid components of printing ink.

vector A line between two points. Vectors are created and displayed on the screen with drawing software. Vector drawings can be processed as a series of points and connections that are compact for a computer to store and manipulate.

vector display A cathode ray tube that moves the electron beam randomly to trace figures on the color monitor screen, as compared with raster display.

Velox A black and white photographic paper print (proof) made from a negative film; originally an Eastman Kodak Company chloride printing paper and today used erroneously generically for similar proofs.

vignette A halftone image in which the background gradually fades away until it blends into the unprinted substrate or a solid print. Also called "fade". Term is occasionally used to indicate a conventional halftone.

viscosity A measure of a fluid's (ink, coating) resistance to flow, which influences the amount of ink (color) printed.

voids (bar codes) The undesirable absence of ink or presence of dirt within a bar of a bar code symbol.

washboarding Print defect of combined board in which the linerboard is depressed between flutes, giving the appearance of a washboard; typically measured visually against a standard agreed upon between the customer and the supplier.

white opaque polyethylene (WhOPE, WOPE) Film frequently used to package frozen foods.

WhOPE, WOPE See **white opaque polyethylene**.

X-dimension The specified width of the narrow element in a bar code symbol.

Yule-Nielsen equation Used to calculate the physical dot area or actual dot size, usually for analytical purposes. It eliminates the optical dot gain with an "n" factor.

$$\text{Physical Dot Area (PDA)} = \frac{1 - 10^{-\left(\frac{D_T}{n}\right)}}{1 - 10^{-\left(\frac{D_s}{n}\right)}}$$

Where:

D_s = the Density of the Solid Ink/Printed Solid;

D_T = the Density of the Halftone;

n = the Yule-Nielsen compensation factor for optical gain from the internal light scattering of the substrate.

% Physical Dot Area = PDA $\times$ 100

Typical "**n**" values for various conditions:

1.65 = Coated Paper
2.70 = Uncoated Paper
2.60 = Cromalin
4.00 = Color Key

Appendix A: Contact List

AIM-USA
(Automatic Identification Manufacturers)
634 Alpha Drive, Pittsburgh, PA 15238-2802
T: 412-963-8588 **F:** 412-963-8753
EM: info@aimglobal.org **www.**aimusa.org

- ANSI/AIM Bar Code Specifications
- *"Layman's Guide to ANSI Print Quality"*

THE AMERICAN ASSOCIATION OF TEXTILE CHEMISTS & COLORISTS
1 Davis Drive, P.O. Box 12215,
Research Triangle Park, NC 27709-2215
T: 919-549-8141 **F:** 919-549-8933
www.aatcc.org

- *"Colour Index International Pigments & Solvent Dyes"* Reference Book (purchase)

ANSI
(American National Standards Institute)
25 West 43rd Street, New York, NY 10036
T: 212-642-4900 **F:** 212-302-0023
EM: info@ansi.org **www.**ansi.org

- ANSI & CGATS standards

APPLIED IMAGE
653 East Main Street, Rochester, NY 14609
T: 716-482-0300 **F:** 716-288-5989
www.appliedimage.com

- Calibrated Conformance Standard Test Cards for Code 39 & Code 128 Symbol Verifiers

ASTM
(American Society for Testing & Materials)
100 Barr Harbor Drive,
West Conshohocken, PA 19428-2959
T: 610-832-9585 **F:** 610-832-9555
EM: service@astm.org **www.**astm.com

- ASTM standards & test methods

CIE
(Commission Internationale de l'Eclairage)
United State National Committee of CIE
c/o TLA-Lighting Consultants, Inc.
7 Pond Street, Salem, MA 01970-4819
T: 978-745-6870 **F:** 978-741-4420
EM: tmcattla@aol.com (USA)
www.cie.co.at/cia (international)
www.cie-usnc.org (USA)

- CIE Illuminant D50 & CIE 1931 Standard Colorimetric Observer
- *"Colorimetry, 2nd Edition"* Publication CIE 15.2–1986

FTA
(Flexographic Technical Association)
900 Marconi Avenue, Ronkonkoma, NY 11779-7212
T: 631-737-6020 **F:** 631-737-6813
EM: membership@flexography.org **www.**flexography.org

- Technical Trade Association
- Environmental and Safety Programs
- FlexSys Press Simulation Tool
- FLIPSS - Flexographic Integrated Process Support System

FFTA
(Foundation of the Flexographic Technical Association)
900 Marconi Avenue, Ronkonkoma, NY 11779-7212
T: 631-737-6020 **F:** 631-737-6813
EM: expert@flexography.org **www.**flexography.org

- Flexographic Printing Certification Programs, Levels I, II, II and IV.
- *FP&P–Flexography Principles and Practices* (product code TX-001)
- *Beginner Flexographer* Series (product code TX-007 through TX-016)
- Interactive Training CDs; Press Characterization (product code SET-PC)
- *Flexographic Inks* (product code CD-005)
- *Flexo Print Station, Operation and Functionality* (product code CD-006)

Appendix A: Contact List

GCA
(Graphic Communications Association)
IDEAlliance
100 Daingerfield Road, Alexandria, VA 22314-2888
T: 703-837-1070 **F:** 703-837-1072
EM: pubs@idealliance.org (for T-ref card)
www.idealliance.org

■ T-Ref Calibration Standard
■ *"Introduction to Densitometry –*
Users Guide to Print Production
Measurement Using
Densitometry"

NAPIM
(National Association of Printing Ink Manufacturers)
581 Main Street, Woodbridge, NJ 07095-1104
T: 732-855-1525 **F:** 732-855-1838
EM: napim@napim.org   **www.**napim.org

■ *"NPIRI Raw Materials Data*
Handbook, Volume 4 Pigments"
(purchase)

NPES
(The Association of Suppliers of Printing,
Publishing & Converting Technologies)
1899 Preston White Drive, Reston, VA 20191-4367
T: 703-264-7200 **F:** 703-620-0994
EM: npes@npes.org   **www.**npes.org/standards

■ ISO standards

RAD-TECH INTERNATIONAL
6935 Wisconsin Avenue, Chevy Chase, MD 20815
T: 240-497-1242 **F:** 240-209-2337
EM: uveb@radtech.org   **www.**.radtech.org

■ Technical Trade Association

THE SOCIETY OF DYERS AND COLOURISTS
P.O. Box 244, Perkin House
82 Grattan Road, Bradford, BD1 2JB UK
T: 01274-725138 **F:** 01274-392888
EM: sales@sdc.org.uk   **www.**sdc.org.uk

■ *"Colour Index International*
Pigments & Solvent Dyes"
(producer)

TAPPI
(Technical Association of the Pulp and Paper Industry)
P.O. Box 105112, Atlanta, GA 30348-5113
T: 770-446-1400 **F:** 770-446-6947
EM: cbohanan@tappi.org   **www.**tappi.org

■ TAPPI standards &
test methods

TLMI
(Tag and Label Manufacturers Inst., Inc.)
40 Shuman Boulevard, Naperville, IL 60563
T: 630-357-9222 **F:** 630-357-0192
EM: office@tlmi.com   **www.**tlmi.com

■ Trade Association

UCC (Uniform Code Council)
7887 Washington Village Drive, Suite 300,
Dayton, OH 45459
T: 937-435-3870 **F:** 937-435-7317
EM: info@uc-council.org   **www.**uc-council.org

■ ANSI/UCC Bar Code standards

USPS (United States Post Office)
www.usps.com/customerguide
www.usps.com/directmail
www.usps.com/businessmail101

■ Bulk Mailing Guidelines

Appendix B:
Referenced Standards/Specifications/Publications

Adobe STANDARDS/SPECIFICATIONS/PUBLICATIONS

- **Adobe PDF Reference Manual**, version 1.3, second edition;
  and **Adobe Technical Note #5413**.

AIM-USA STANDARDS/SPECIFICATIONS/PUBLICATIONS

- **ANSI/AIM BC1-1995**, Uniform Symbology Specification, Code 39
- **ANSI/AIM BC2-1995**, Uniform Symbology Specification, Interleaved 2-of-5
- **ANSI/AIM BC4-1995**, Uniform Symbology Specification, Code 128
- *"Layman's Guide to ANSI Print Quality"*

American Assoc. of Textile Chemists & Colorists STANDARDS/SPECIFICATIONS/PUBLICATIONS

- *"Colour Index International Pigments and Solvent Dyes"* Reference Manual

ANSI STANDARDS/SPECIFICATIONS/PUBLICATIONS

- **IT8.7/4 Characterization Target** Proposed CGATS target
- **ANSI 2.30 1989**
- **ANSI PH2.30-1989** (Graphic Arts & Photography - Color Prints, Transparencies and Photomechanical Reproductions - Viewing Conditions)
- **ANSI X3.182-1990** Bar Code Print Quality Guideline
- **ANSI/CGATS.4** (1993 Graphic Technology—Graphic Arts Reflection Densitometry Measurements—Terminology, Equations, Image Elements, and Procedures)
- **ANSI/CGATS.5** (1993 Graphic Technology—Spectral Measurement and Colorimetric Computation for Graphic Arts Images)
- **ANSI/CGATS.9** (1994 Graphic Technology—Graphic Arts Transmission Densitometry Measurements—Terminology, Equations, Image Elements and Procedures)
- **ANSI/UCC5** Quality Specification for the U.P.C. Printed Symbol
- **CGATS TR-011** (2002 Graphic Technology – Package Development Workflow – Design Concept Through Approved Production File)
- **CGATS TR-012** (2003 Graphic Technology – Color Reproduction and Process Control for Package Printing)

Applied Image STANDARDS/SPECIFICATIONS/PUBLICATIONS

- **Calibrated Conformance Standard**, Test Cards for Code 39 and Code 128 Symbol Verifiers

ASTM STANDARDS/SPECIFICATIONS/PUBLICATIONS

- **ASTM 2196**—Test Method for Rheological Properties of Non-Newtonian Materials by Rotational (Brookfield) Viscometer
- **ASTM D 1475**—Standard Test Method for Density of Paint, Varnish, Lacquer, and Related Products
- **ASTM D1200**—Test Method for Viscosity of Paints, Varnishes, and Lacquers
- **ASTM D1316**—Fineness of Grind of Printing Inks by the NPIRI Grindometer
- **ASTM D1640**—Standard Test Method for Drying, Curing or Film Formation
- **ASTM D1647**
- **ASTM D1729**
- **ASTM D1894-95**—Standard Test Method for Static and Kinetic Coefficients of Friction of Plastic Films and Sheeting
- **ASTM D2085**
- **ASTM D2244**
- **ASTM D2248**
- **ASTM D2793**—Standard Test Method for Block Testing
- **ASTM D3359**—Test Method for Measuring Adhesion by Tape

- **ASTM D3424**—Lightfastness of Printed Matter
- **ASTM D3519 88**—Standard Test Method for Foam in Aqueous Media
- **ASTM D4212**—Test Method for Viscosity by Dip Type Viscosity Cup
- **ASTM D4459, G23, G26**
- **ASTM D4518**—Standard Test Methods for Measuring Static Friction of Coating Surfaces
- **ASTM D4713**—Standard Method for Non-volatile Content in Printing Inks, Resin Solutions and Vehicles.
- **ASTM D523**—Standard Test Method for Specular Gloss
- **ASTM D5264/92**—Standard Test Method for Sutherland Rub Test
- **ASTM D645**—Caliper/Gauge/Thickness – Paper & Paperboard
- **ASTM E-462**—Odor Panel
- **ASTM E70-97**—Standard Test Method for pH of Aqueous Solutions with the Glass Electrode
- **ASTM E97**—Standard Test Method for 0 degrees/45 degrees.

CIE STANDARDS/SPECIFICATIONS/PUBLICATIONS

- **CIE Illuminant D50** & **CIE 1931 Standard Colorimetric Observer**
- **CIE 15.2-1986** (Colorimetry, 2nd Edition)

FFTA STANDARDS/SPECIFICATIONS/PUBLICATIONS

- **Flexographic Printing Certification Program**
- **FLEXO Magazine**
- **Flexography Principles & Practices**
- **Press Pals**
- **Training CDs**

FTA STANDARDS/SPECIFICATIONS/PUBLICATIONS

- **Excellence in Flexography Awards**
- **Environmental and Safety Programs**

GCA STANDARDS/SPECIFICATIONS/PUBLICATIONS

- **T-ref Calibration Standard**—Densitometers
- **"Introduction to Densitometry: Users Guide to Print Production Measurement Using Densitometery"**
- **ANSI X12**

NAPIM STANDARDS/SPECIFICATIONS/PUBLICATIONS

- **NPIRI "Raw Materials Data Handbook, Volume 4 Pigments"**

NPES STANDARDS/SPECIFICATIONS/PUBLICATIONS

- **ISO/CD 12639**
- **ISO 12647-6** (Graphic Technology – Process Control for the Manufacture of Halftone Colour Separations, Proofs and Production Prints – Part 6: Flexographic Printing)
- **ISO 15416:2000**—(Information technology – Automatic identification and data capture technique – Print Quality Test Specification – Linear symbols)
- **ISO 15420:2000**—(Information technology – Automatic identification and data capture technique – Symbology Specification – EAN/UPC),
- **ISO 15930-1:2001**—(Graphic Technology – Prepress Digital Data Exchange – Use of PDF Part 1: Complete exchange using CMYK data PDF/X-1 and PDF/X-1a)
- **ISO 2846-5**—(Graphic Technology – Colour & Transparency of Printing Ink Sets for 4-Colour Printing Part 5: Flexographic Printing)
- **ISO 3034**—Caliper / Gauge / Thickness
- **ISO 3664: 1975**—(Photography - Illumination Conditions for Viewing Colour Transparencies and their Reproductions)
- **ISO 5-3: 1995**—(Photography - Density Measurements - Part 3: Spectral Conditions)
- **ISO 8791/3**—Smoothness - Corrugated & Paper
- **ISO 8791/4**—Smoothness - Paperboard